TRANSFORMING LANDSCAPES

MICHEL
DESVIGNE
PAYSAGISTE

Birkhäuser
Basel

Layout, cover design and typesetting
Brigitte Mestrot, Paris

Cover illustration
MDP Michel Desvigne Paysagiste

Project management
Martin Basdevant, Paris
Henriette Mueller-Stahl, Berlin

Translation from French into English
(except for contribution by Dorothée Imbert)
Garry White, Paris

Copy editing
Michael Wachholz, Berlin

Production
Heike Strempel, Berlin

Lithography
Les Artisans du Regard, Paris

Paper
130 g/m² Fly 05

Printing
optimal media GmbH, Röbel/Müritz

Library of Congress Control Number: 2019955005

Bibliographic information published by the German National Library
The German National Library lists this publication in the Deutsche Nationalbibliografie; detailed bibliographic data are available on the Internet at http://dnb.dnb.de.

ISBN 978-3-03821-982-8
e-ISBN (PDF) 978-3-0356-0997-4

French Print-ISBN 978-3-03821-983-5

P.O. Box 44, 4009 Basel, Switzerland
Part of Walter de Gruyter GmbH, Berlin/Boston

9 8 7 6 5 4 3 2 1
www.birkhauser.com

TRANSFORMING LANDSCAPES

MICHEL DESVIGNE PAYSAGISTE

Publication director Françoise Fromonot
Editorial coordinator Martin Basdevant

With contributions by
Françoise Fromonot,
Dorothée Imbert,
Gilles A. Tiberghien,
and two photo essays by
Patrick Faigenbaum

Birkhäuser
Basel

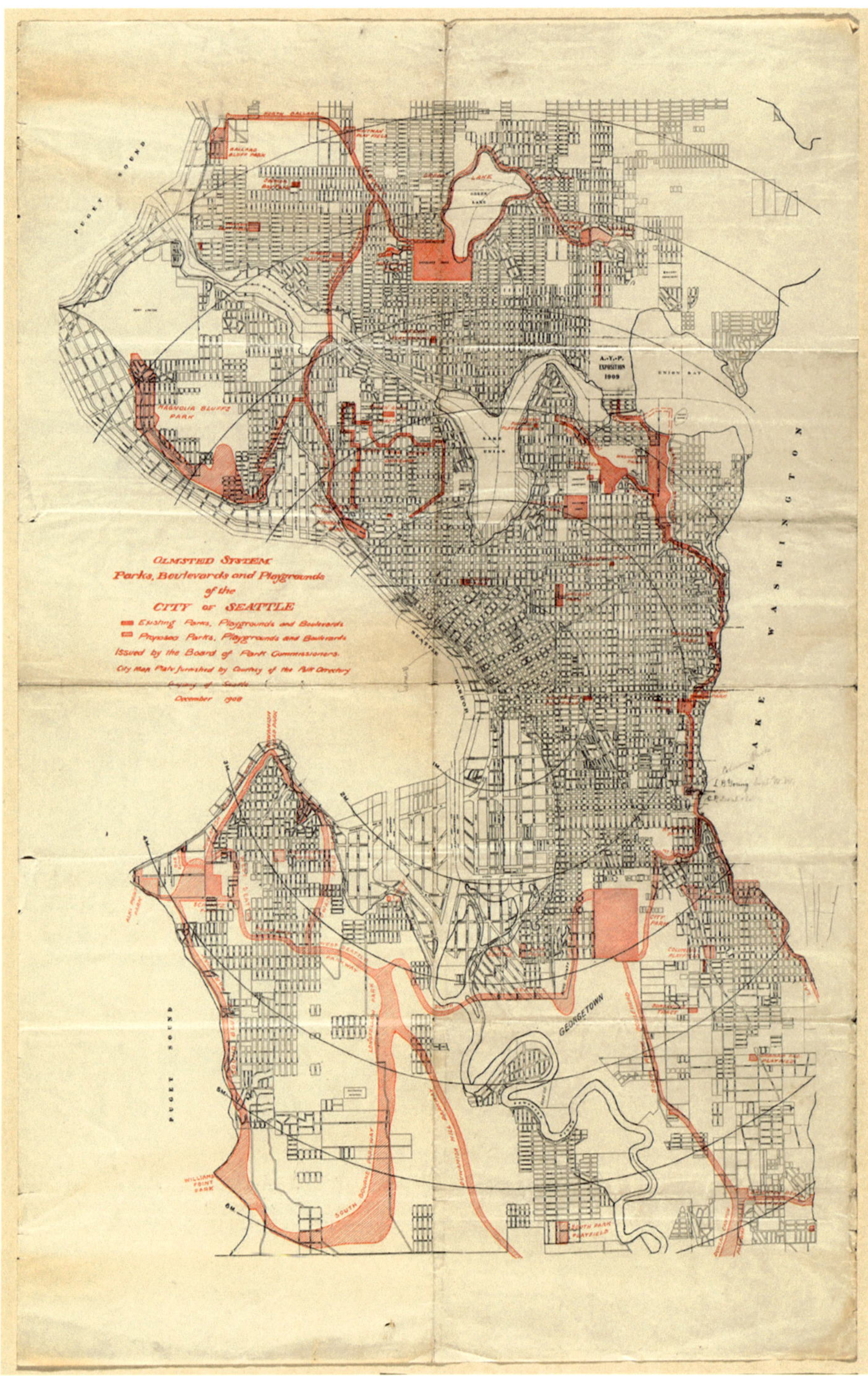

Olmsted brothers' plan for the Seattle park system, 1903.

FRANÇOISE FROMONOT
LANDSCAPE DESIGN AS URBAN DESIGN?

In a text written for the Grand Paris 2009 consultation process, in which he participated on Jean Nouvel's team, Michel Desvigne considers the "three major theoretical, formal and strategic models" that constitute "the contribution of landscape architects to urban planning".[1] The most ambitious and attractive of these, he believes, works from the natural geography of a territory to endow it with a landscape structure that will shape its urbanisation over time. This type of landscape strategy, initiated in the late nineteenth century, peaked in the park systems designed in the United States by the Olmsted firm, such as Boston's "emerald necklace" and the series of public spaces that continue to structure cities like Buffalo or Seattle to this day. A second type of model focuses, in almost the reverse approach, on designating specific areas where the nature supplanted by urban expansion is recomposed, for leisure or contemplation. This was the intention behind the creation of the parks – from the Buttes-Chaumont to Central Park – that still represent the quintessence of the modern large public garden set in the dense city. The third type, "antipodal [to] the preceding two", is more discreet – less ostentatious – as well as more discrete – less continuous in terms of its imprint – yet forms a whole all the same: the constellation of small planted areas that every metropolis contains, these sometimes tiny spaces that give a city its porosity and comfort of daily use. The abundance of such spaces is well illustrated by the numerous "pocket gardens" of Tokyo or New York, that "scattering" of little parks and gardens, as Michel Desvigne puts it, maintained because of their official status and providing a reminder of nature's presence in the city.

However, more than ever, landscape architects and urban planners are being called on to reform what is "already developed" rather than to create something new, under conditions (sites, commissions, institutions, objectives, electoral cycles, etc.) that are less and less conducive to the implementation of comprehensive, long-term strategies. Adopting one or the other of these models to drive a large-scale project, continues Michel Desvigne, leaves us open to disappointment or even failure. Focusing on the first, he argues, would require consistency and perseverance in the face of reality, other possibilities and the prevailing economic situation. The second model remains exceptional in his view, as it requires a willingness to intervene, an authority truly capable of carrying to fruition the invention of the park. This is the case with the recreational parks and outdoor activity centres created in the suburbs of greater Paris when the new towns were built, or, twenty years later, those of the mixed-development zones laid out in the former industrial areas of the capital. As for the third model, he points out that its reactivation or continuation require a prior inventory of existing spaces with an impressive level of diversity, one that invites the designer to take all these forms into account and look beyond pre-defined models: for this reason, this third model often remains ineffective.

Nonetheless, these types of action "need to intersect", adapt to conditions and places without abandoning the ambition of major transformations. And in fact, in his work, Michel Desvigne has always endeavoured, in a very personal way, to weave together these three conceptual horizons for this purpose, in combinations inspired by his reading of the situations he is asked to study. The ten proposals gathered in this book are all samples of this both speculative and pragmatic practice, characterised by the recurrence of its themes, the adaptability of its tools, the agility with which they are used and by an obsession: the establishment, through space and in time, of coherence – one of Michel Desvigne's key terms – in the territories in which he works.

1. Michel Desvigne, "Natural and artificial geography", Grand Paris 2009, interview by Jean-Paul Robert, 7 November 2008. This text can be consulted online on the MDP office website under the heading "Corpus".

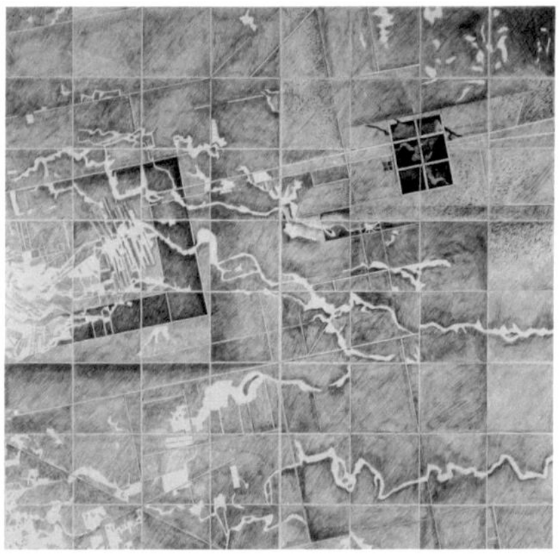

Michel Desvigne, drawing from the *Elementary Gardens* series, 1986–1987.

MDP, plans and sections showing how the planted infrastructure of the Greenwich Peninsula park, 1997–2000, is projected to evolve over time.

His work on the Saclay Plateau – one of the showcases of the Grand Paris scheme – is no doubt the project that most explicitly mobilises the three models. Here, Michel Desvigne has each model take charge of a geographical scale – large, intermediate and immediate – while counting on their interaction: through symbiosis (one project nourishing the other), nesting (one containing the other), and propagation (one extending the other). It took ten years for the "chain of parks" to start emerging into view on the land reserve located on the edge of the first two districts of the new campus. In its scope and material intimacy, the photographic essay by Patrick Faigenbaum opening this volume captures a moment of this transition from one state to another. The ditches and ponds, roadbeds and rubble, paths and valleys sometimes merge to such an extent that the current earthworks are no longer distinguishable from the agricultural land from which the work has moulded the contours of the new public space. A wetland is gradually becoming established between the masses of woodland accentuating the topography and the line of constructions in the distance. The road grid that runs alongside or through this very young park extends into the urbanised area, lined with shrubs that will flourish in the built grid – on a wide green, a square – before being disciplined anew further down as parkway or condensed into small gardens inside the urban blocks.

Another example: Euralens. In this case, there is a double historical heritage – the mining industry and the first attempts to rehabilitate the wastelands left in its wake – that Michel Desvigne engages with through his three types of strategy. The *cavaliers*, paths running along embankments formerly used as transport lines for mine materials, but which have now fallen into disuse, are seen as a potential network of links and walks that simply need to be revealed, reinforced and completed for them to become a system, linking to existing public parks and amenities and capable of integrating those that may be added later. As it deploys, the system works its way into the folds of the territory and extends to the housing estates, into their scattered gardens and along their paths; then its principle is extrapolated to the entire former mining basin. A similar analogy between industrial and natural systems – tributary, river, delta – also guides the Burgos project, likewise acting on several scales at once. In the manner of rosary beads, the new boulevard strings together small squares and plazas along its course, created from the random spatial *offcuts* left from plots that had been backed up against the former railway line. All so many iterations of the intricate negotiation that occurred between the three models, in relation to the three figures to which they refer (network, enclave, archipelago), the spatial properties associated with them (ramification, concentration, dispersal) and finally the conceptions of nature on which they are founded: amplification, recomposition, dissemination.

Cross-fertilisation between landscape logics also occurs through transfer or collage. Michel Desvigne's fascination with large territories finds its way into even his smallest projects through one of their most powerful archetypes, the forest. Ever since designing the rue de Meaux courtyard in Paris – a surface of barely 2,000 square metres, surrounded by housing blocks in a dense residential area – the woodland motif has been a preferred vector for the encounter between a certain sensation of geography and the pocket garden. The magic created from this intentional blurring of repertoires also works by extending nature into public urban space. In Tokyo, specimens of ancient trees cultivated in the mountains fleetingly introduce the atmosphere of a primary forest near the Otemachi tower.

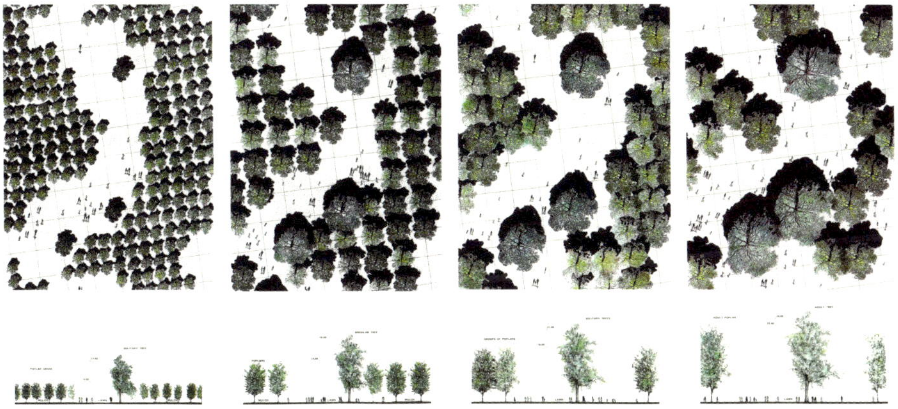

In the heart of the city, a walk can recreate, through artifice, elements of the great landscape from which the city broke free as it developed. Around the Old Port of Marseille, the carpet of white stone that stops right at the water artfully recomposes the juxtaposition of *calanque* limestone and the sea, typical of the coastal geography before its urbanisation. However, the reproduction of this geographical feature is effective only because it functions as the central component of a set of interlocked projects: the chain of parks that extends it – an idea added to the programme as part of the proposal submitted to the competition – and the micro-voids that aerate the city centre, shown on the plans as cracks, notches and crevices.

This way of seeing and conceiving simultaneously at different scales, by adding or combining intervention strategies, also makes it possible to reclaim, in an incremental manner, something of the "grandeur" associated with significant eras in the history of planning. Indeed, Michel Desvigne regularly expresses his regret that the ambitions and resources of the past are lacking in today's projects. The circulation we can observe in the office's work between different models is also explained by the coexistence at any time of various types of commission and the possible transfer of experiments from one to another. As shown by the timeline displayed in the following pages, which acts as a temporal summary of the projects it presents, commissions add to each other, resonate with each other or augment each other, sometimes over several decades. MDP typically manages dozens of projects at the same time, of all kinds and sizes, from prescribing trees and surfacing for an urban passageway to providing landscaping support on road networks, to designing the public spaces of a given urban development, to large-scale, long-term schemes. This broad range increases the office's chances of attracting projects that may extend those that were started in other circumstances but did not yield the expected results. Renzo Piano also likes to explain how his professional philosophy is never to let an idea die, but constantly to put it back to work, drawing from his dissatisfactions.

The size of MDP – employing a staff of around thirty as of 2019 – makes the office an exception among its French counterparts. This quantitative importance is certainly explained by its success, but also by Michel Desvigne's attitude towards commissions: accepting requests at a rate he himself describes as relentless. Whether design missions, consultancy jobs, project management assistance, participation in urban planning project teams, or even, for some years now, putting together teams as a lead consultant, he takes on large and small jobs, direct commissions as well as those awarded through the riskier route of competitions, "beautiful" and large-scale projects as well as those that initially seem too prescriptive or too restricted. In the latter case, the approach adopted is to try to express the "potential" of the projects – by reinterpreting the initial request, reformulating it, if not subverting it – going so far as to extrapolate the programme if necessary and even inventing it, in complicity with the client, which often represents a victory in itself. In Montpellier, it was a winning proposal for the treatment of the land bordering a motorway intersection that earned Desvigne & Dalnoky a host of contracts in new urban extensions. Over the course of thirty years, these interventions have had a durable impact, favoured by proactive municipal policies over several mandates to secure public land for this purpose. In Bordeaux, the drafting of a landscape charter for the City led to a project to redevelop the entire right bank of the Garonne and even beyond, driven by an uncommon political will.

MDP, plan identifying residual agricultural parcels on the outskirts of Issoudun, 2003.

MDP, diagrammatic plan for the new programmed "edges" lying between low-rise housing estates and agricultural areas, 2009–2011.

Through a knock-on effect, the critical volume of the agency and the projects it handles "increases its credibility and standing in the eyes of clients, design offices, architects and even insurance companies. The overabundance of work has ended up creating resources," states Michel Desvigne.[2] His knowledge of all these commissions is both intimate and from on high, in short mirroring his relationship with the territories they concern. The autonomy granted to project managers is balanced by the office's assertive stance and distinctive style, its elementary vocabulary and its recurrent palette of landscape art rudiments, combined with the fundamental ingredients of geography: further on in this volume Dorothée Imbert analyses the sources and effects of these "attitudes".

The office can therefore invest energy and time in missions that could not possibly be very profitable given the logistical resources it puts into them, not to mention the brain power that goes into studying various subjects, with little or no hope of a return, at least in the short term. A case in point is the transformation of areas that extend between the "edges" of urban sprawl and the croplands of intensive agriculture. This approach was first proposed for the outskirts of Issoudun in 2003, then articulated as a theory for the Greater Paris consultation process six years later,[3] and partially tested in Saclay; it continues to inform the office's prospective thinking, some elements of which are described here by Michel Desvigne ("New territories for public space"). Michel Corajoud, in his time, had made this space between city and countryside central to defining the landscape: "Today these two worlds exist in close but hostile proximity, knowing nothing of each other and each pushing away the other, yet this is precisely where the reconciliation projects I wish to see will be played out in the future", he wrote in 2003.[4] Fifteen years later, Michel Desvigne suggests going further, envisaging this in-between as a place in its own right, where public micro-infrastructures could be sited and programmed with their uses. In other words, by thickening, dilating and hybridising the borders and definitions of the two most problematic types of land use that the twentieth century has bequeathed to the twenty-first – extensive housing and extensive agriculture – he seeks to invent conditions in which a triple urban, agricultural and social ecology could thrive. With Bruno Latour's *Making Things Public*[5] in mind, we could view this landscape-based formulation of a new type of networked civic amenity as an alternative to the "mixed use" advocated by urban planners, this rather tired mantra that rarely leads to the expected mixtures. But how does one *represent* this space of encounters, that is to say – to follow the Latourian parallel – imagine its protagonists and give it a design?

While the office produces many study models to drive its research, for Michel Desvigne the plan remains the generator and preferred tool of representation, as it was for his great historical models. Laying everything out horizontally makes it possible to judge the "composition", a word that he often uses in an almost pictorial sense, but also in the more trivial sense of that which constitutes reality, and which can therefore be analysed and deconstructed to better serve as a basis for the project that will reassemble these elements, emphasising some while effacing others, through addition and subtraction. We recall his series of meditations on the virtues of the plan, written during his residency at the Villa Medici and published as *Jardins élémentaires* some years back. These patient transcriptions of large aerial views, drawn in pencil and produced by "editing" their complexity in the essential language of geography, became image-ideas by which to "give shape to nature and rebuild the landscape".[6] In the project, the

2. Interview with the author, 9 April 2019.
3. Michel Desvigne, "Épaissir les lisières", Grand Paris 2009, interview by Jean-Paul Robert, text reproduced in *Pour*, no. 205–206, February 2010, pp. 145–148. See https://www.cairn.info/revue-pour-2010-2-page-145.htm.
4. Michel Corajoud, "Autoportrait – Le paysage : une expérience pour construire la ville", in Ariella Masboungi (ed.), *Grand Prix de l'urbanisme 2003. Michel Corajoud et cinq grandes figures de l'urbanisme* (Paris: DGUHC, 2003).
5. Bruno Latour, "From Realpolitik to Dingpolitik, or How to Make Things Public", introduction to Bruno Latour, Peter Weibl, *Making Things Public: Atmospheres of Democracy*, catalogue of the eponymous ZKM exhibition in Karlsruhe (Cambridge, MA: MIT Press, 2005), pp. 14–43.
6. Michel Desvigne, Gilles Tiberghien, *Jardins élémentaires* (Rome: Carte Segrete, 1988).

plan therefore comes first and sections follow. The latter do not dwell on what lies in the thickness of the soil – geological strata, root systems – and rarely show their invisible engineering in detail: their primary purpose is to verify the vertical amplitude of above-ground volumes, in coherence with the plan. The vignettes drafted in plan for the Greenwich Peninsula project share the same scalar grid, gauging the growth of tree diameters over time and providing a basis for the presentation of the project; the section confirms the homothetic transformation of the plantings in the third dimension. To ensure that what will not truly take shape until the distant future makes sense as soon as it is put in place, the manner in which things are drawn counts, for the drawing must acknowledge – *display*? – its reference to figures that are already loaded with a shared meaning. Thus, a new alignment of trees will convey, by its very geometry, a promise and a meaning capable of transcending the reality of the young subjects from which it is composed.

Surely we would have to conclude that Michel Desvigne is an urban designer? In any case, the position he defends and practises seems quietly provocative with regard to the debates that have recently taken place in this field in France, placing him at a fertile distance from two of its main trends. One is the dominant trend of "compositional" urbanism, in which general design outlines and land divisions are drawn out on the ground, "top down", in keeping with the canons of the already formed city, and charted in master plans. The other, in contrast, has contributed to thinking on the transformation of cities in the last two decades by seeking ways of designing "bottom up", based on a painstaking preliminary analysis of the substrate and resources of the territories to be transformed. Inspired by thinking and design processes that come from landscaping, this urbanism of "revelation" managed for a time to infiltrate the institutional and professional world of the French urban project, so much so that it seemed capable of regenerating its productions.[7] But given the hazards and constraints of large-scale urban operations, Michel Desvigne is reluctant to rely on this method alone, as the delicate economy of the sites on which it is based becomes vulnerable if overly large programmes are imposed on them by clients. He can even be very critical of the participatory aspect of this approach, which risks reducing the designer's role to merely giving form to the eclectic demands "passed up" by residents and users, to the detriment of an overall project idea capable of transcending these demands. Designers must find ways of surpassing the dilemma between "formalism and social activism",[8] he argues, and bring back a term that, in the project equation, has become a little taboo, its *aesthetic*.

This "critique of pure revelation" suggests a type of landscape design that is ambitious in the present but fundamentally intended for the future: an objective landscape, in other words, one that is free from the most circumstantial affects of the era and oriented towards the construction of active processes with short, medium and especially long spans, guided by the hand of the designer. In the essay that concludes this book, Gilles A. Tiberghien returns to what this expression of an "idea in landscape" implies in terms of attention and determination but also effacement on the part of its designer. Thus, in his optimistic way, Michel Desvigne wishes to respond to the challenge that his historical models were able to bring to the fore and that contemporary urban planning seems to have too often abandoned to mere urbanisation. Speaking of the role of landscape architects,[9] he expresses this intention as a very simple imperative: "Imagine a city that gives daily happiness to its inhabitants and that future generations will still be able to love."

7. Concerning the operational and theoretical categories of urban planning at the beginning of the twenty-first century and their historical affiliations, see Françoise Fromonot, "Manières de classer l'urbanisme", *criticat,* no. 8, September 2011, p. 40–61.
8. Michel Desvigne, "Le rôle des paysagistes : des progrès considérables et fragiles", *Urbanisme*, special issue no. 56, June 2016, interview by Frédérique de Gravelaine.
9. Ibid.

TIMELINE OF THE TEN PROJECTS

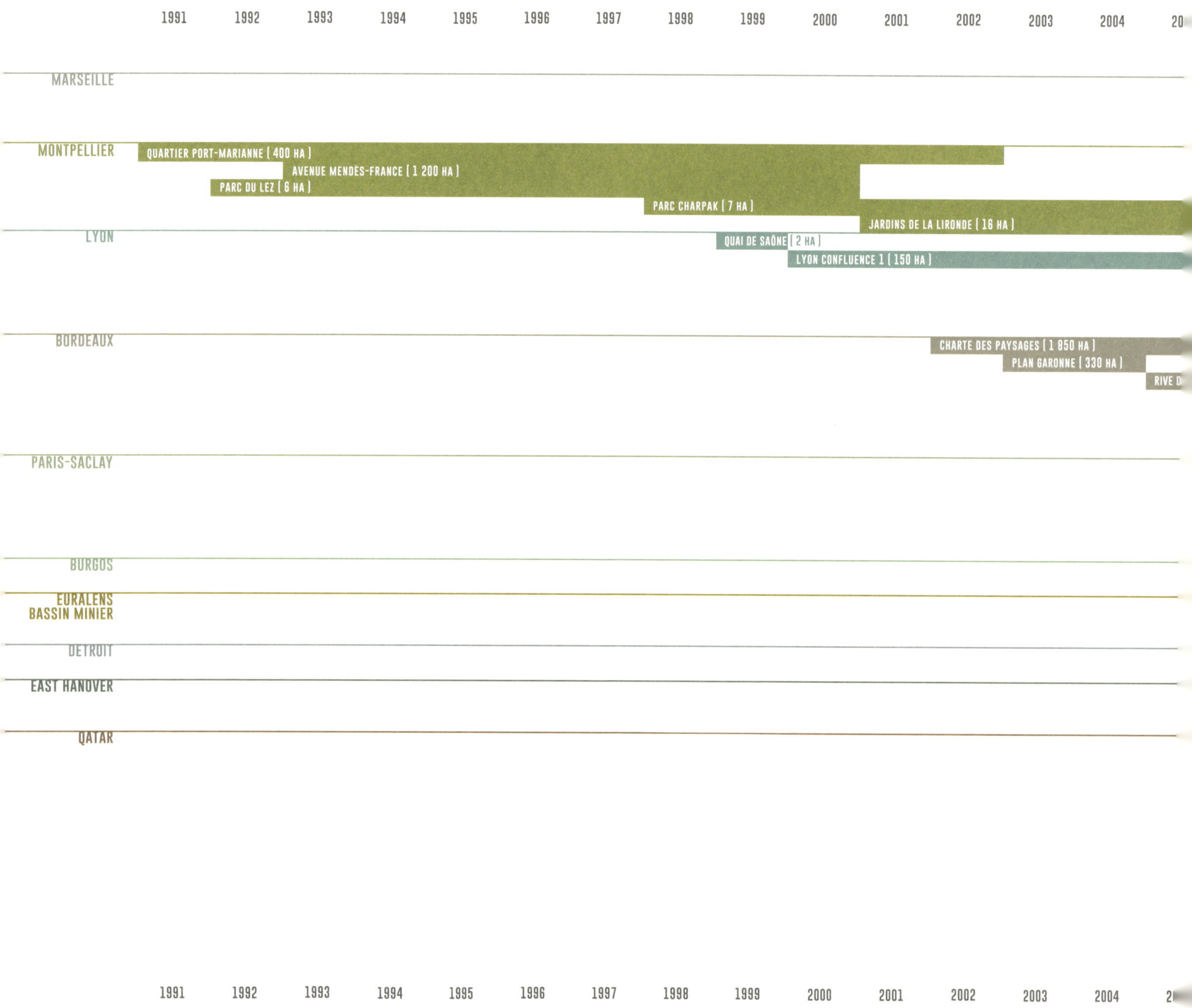

The synoptic links between the ten projects presented here highlight the office's early and subsequently intensified participation in major territorial projects.

Each of these projects was built up in stages over time with commissions following one after the other, overlapping or sometimes interrupting each other.

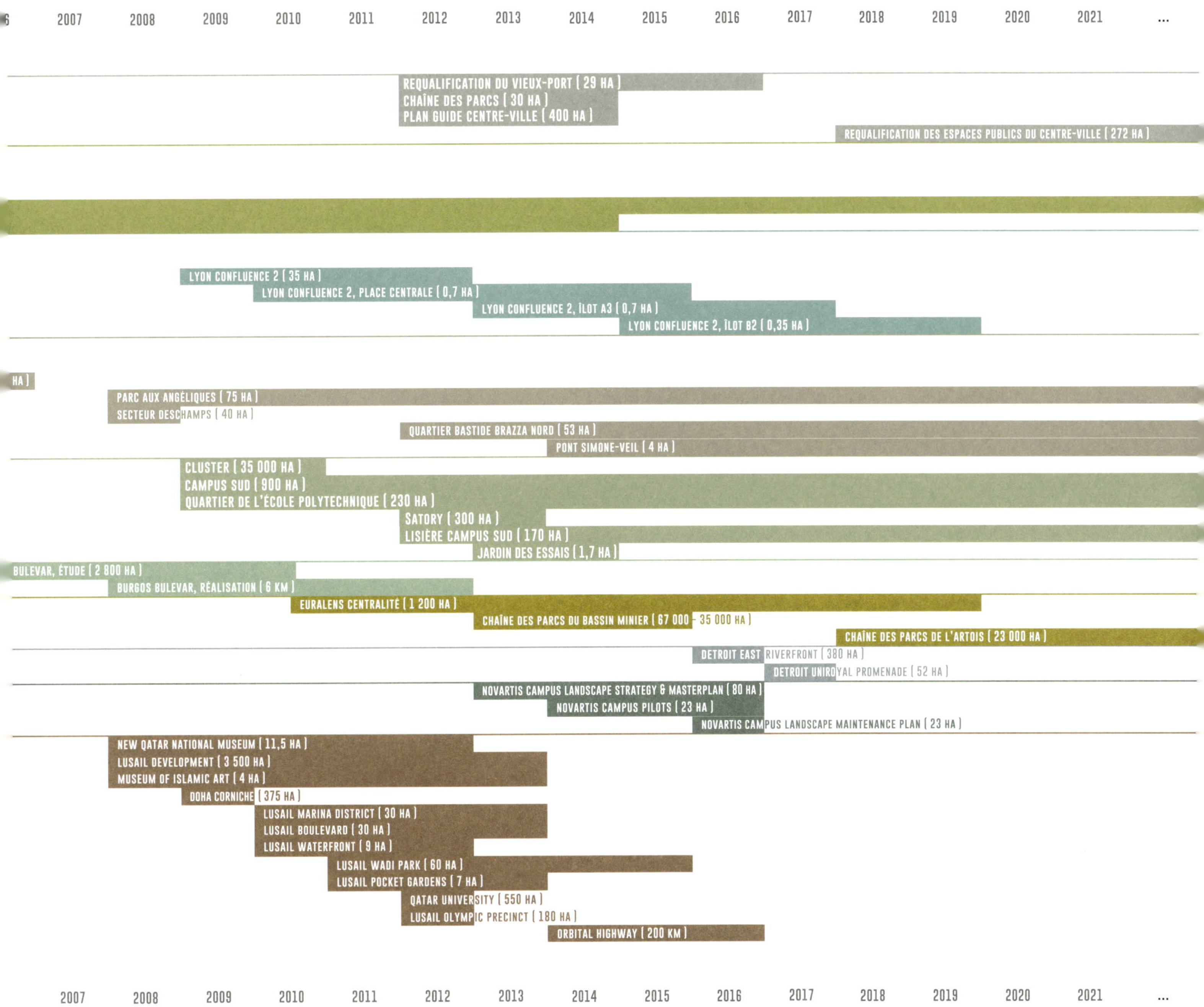

2007 2008 2009 2010 2011 2012 2013 2014 2015 2016 2017 2018 2019 2020 2021 …
REQUALIFICATION DU VIEUX-PORT [29 HA]
CHAÎNE DES PARCS [30 HA]
PLAN GUIDE CENTRE-VILLE [400 HA]
REQUALIFICATION DES ESPACES PUBLICS DU CENTRE-VILLE [272 HA]
LYON CONFLUENCE 2 [35 HA]
LYON CONFLUENCE 2, PLACE CENTRALE [0,7 HA]
LYON CONFLUENCE 2, ÎLOT A3 [0,7 HA]
LYON CONFLUENCE 2, ÎLOT B2 [0,35 HA]
PARC AUX ANGÉLIQUES [75 HA]
SECTEUR DESCHAMPS [40 HA]
QUARTIER BASTIDE BRAZZA NORD [53 HA]
PONT SIMONE-VEIL [4 HA]
CLUSTER [35 000 HA]
CAMPUS SUD [900 HA]
QUARTIER DE L'ÉCOLE POLYTECHNIQUE [230 HA]
SATORY [300 HA]
LISIÈRE CAMPUS SUD [170 HA]
JARDIN DES ESSAIS [1,7 HA]
BULEVAR, ÉTUDE [2 800 HA]
BURGOS BULEVAR, RÉALISATION [6 KM]
EURALENS CENTRALITÉ [1 200 HA]
CHAÎNE DES PARCS DU BASSIN MINIER [67 000 - 35 000 HA]
CHAÎNE DES PARCS DE L'ARTOIS [23 000 HA]
DETROIT EAST RIVERFRONT [380 HA]
DETROIT UNIROYAL PROMENADE [52 HA]
NOVARTIS CAMPUS LANDSCAPE STRATEGY & MASTERPLAN [80 HA]
NOVARTIS CAMPUS PILOTS [23 HA]
NOVARTIS CAMPUS LANDSCAPE MAINTENANCE PLAN [23 HA]
NEW QATAR NATIONAL MUSEUM [11,5 HA]
LUSAIL DEVELOPMENT [3 500 HA]
MUSEUM OF ISLAMIC ART [4 HA]
DOHA CORNICHE [375 HA]
LUSAIL MARINA DISTRICT [30 HA]
LUSAIL BOULEVARD [30 HA]
LUSAIL WATERFRONT [9 HA]
LUSAIL WADI PARK [60 HA]
LUSAIL POCKET GARDENS [7 HA]
QATAR UNIVERSITY [550 HA]
LUSAIL OLYMPIC PRECINCT [180 HA]
ORBITAL HIGHWAY [200 KM]
2007 2008 2009 2010 2011 2012 2013 2014 2015 2016 2017 2018 2019 2020 2021 …

OLD PORT AND PUBLIC SPACES IN THE CITY CENTRE MARSEILLE, FRANCE, 2012–

Here, the nature of the commission was important. It was almost part of the project, as was the management structure, based on a partnership between the City and the urban authority for the greater Marseille area at that time, Marseille Provence Métropole. The competition we won in 2012, as lead consultant for a team including Foster + Partners, concerned a twofold mission: the "semi-pedestrianisation" of the quays of the Old Port and the establishment of a framework plan, that is to say a strategic proposal open to adjustment over time, for the public spaces of the centre, corresponding to approximately 400 hectares. We added a specific proposal for the Faro district, which extends south of the port to the seafront: by reorganising and linking existing green spaces, it was possible to envisage a richly planted "chain of parks" to complement the remodelling of the port, whose refurbished ground was uniformly mineral. The transformation of the quayside of the Old Port in the first phase of the project was therefore recast as the centrepiece of a vast study more broadly encompassing the redevelopment of public spaces in historic Marseille.

Old Port

In their pre-existing state, the quays of the Old Port were 75 per cent dedicated to car traffic. The remaining 25 per cent were occupied by huge grassy roundabouts of little use and, along the waterfront, by work spaces related to nautical activities (the port has mooring for 1,000 boats) enclosed behind barriers. With barely a third of their perimeter accessible to the public, the quays were literally privatised: people had become accustomed to walking along these barriers, on the edge of busy roads. As the politicians wanted to keep cars on the quays until the bypass was completed, we had to reconcile the different modes of traffic rather than create a large pedestrian space.

The project consisted in reversing the inherited proportions by attributing three quarters of the surface area to pedestrians and one quarter to cars, and in making the entire perimeter of the quays accessible to the public.

The reorganisation of the road network also included implementing dedicated-lane public transport running in both directions. Some of our competitors pushed the latter back from the quayside, to other streets. The proper functioning of a large public space such as this one suggested instead that these dedicated lanes should be integrated into the quay, which was a constraint because a considerable number of buses pass this way. We emphasised the idea that everyone should be able to come to the port directly. The road network will evolve, and in particular on the Quai de la Fraternité (formerly Quai des Belges), at the back of the port, where car traffic will eventually be phased out. The proportion of the quay devoted to traffic remains in a reasonable balance: of the ten car lanes that existed, two remain, plus the two bus lanes.

The overall space is treated like a vast stone plateau, simple and homogenous. Proposing vegetation here would have made no sense historically. It would almost have been a desecration! Or a trivialisation at least.

The architectural interventions designed by Foster + Partners stand out from this ground plane, allowing for it to be read more easily and used more freely. Nautical activities were transferred to platforms elevated on stilts above the water, without reducing the width of the central channel. These activities used to pollute the Old Port terribly. On the

The Old Port appears as if embedded in the mineral density of Marseille Centre. Around its perimeter one can make out the asphalt strip of the roadway and the quays that surrounded it before redevelopment. In the foreground, to the right, beside the sea, the Faro district, dominated by the palace of the same name overlooking a cove; on the left, on the northern side of the Old Port, the Fort Saint-Jean and the various post-war redevelopments by Fernand Pouillon.

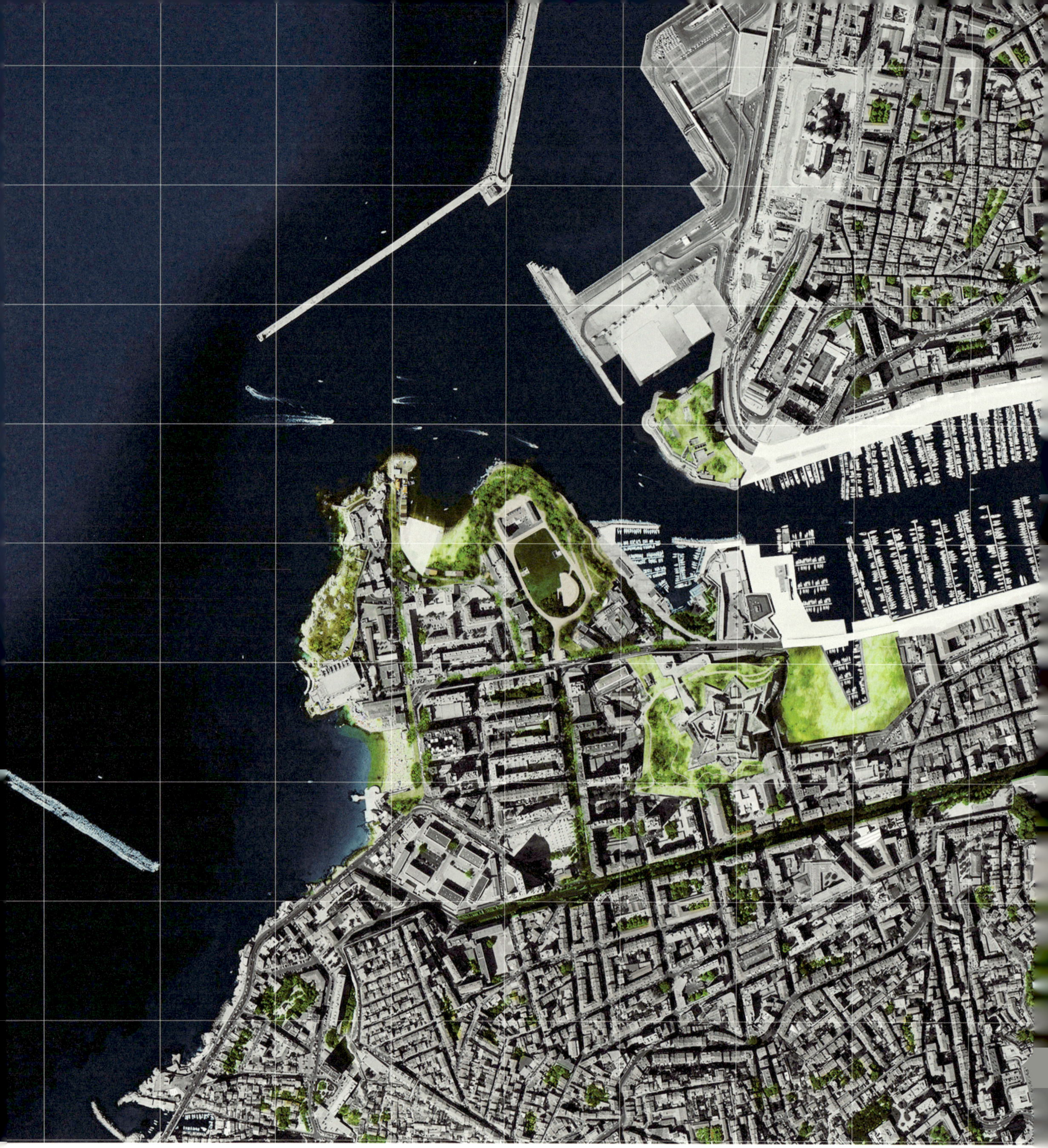

The framework plan shows the complementarity of the three public-space projects. In the centre, the reappropriation of the quays of the Old Port and the redevelopment of the ground plane with a single material restore unity

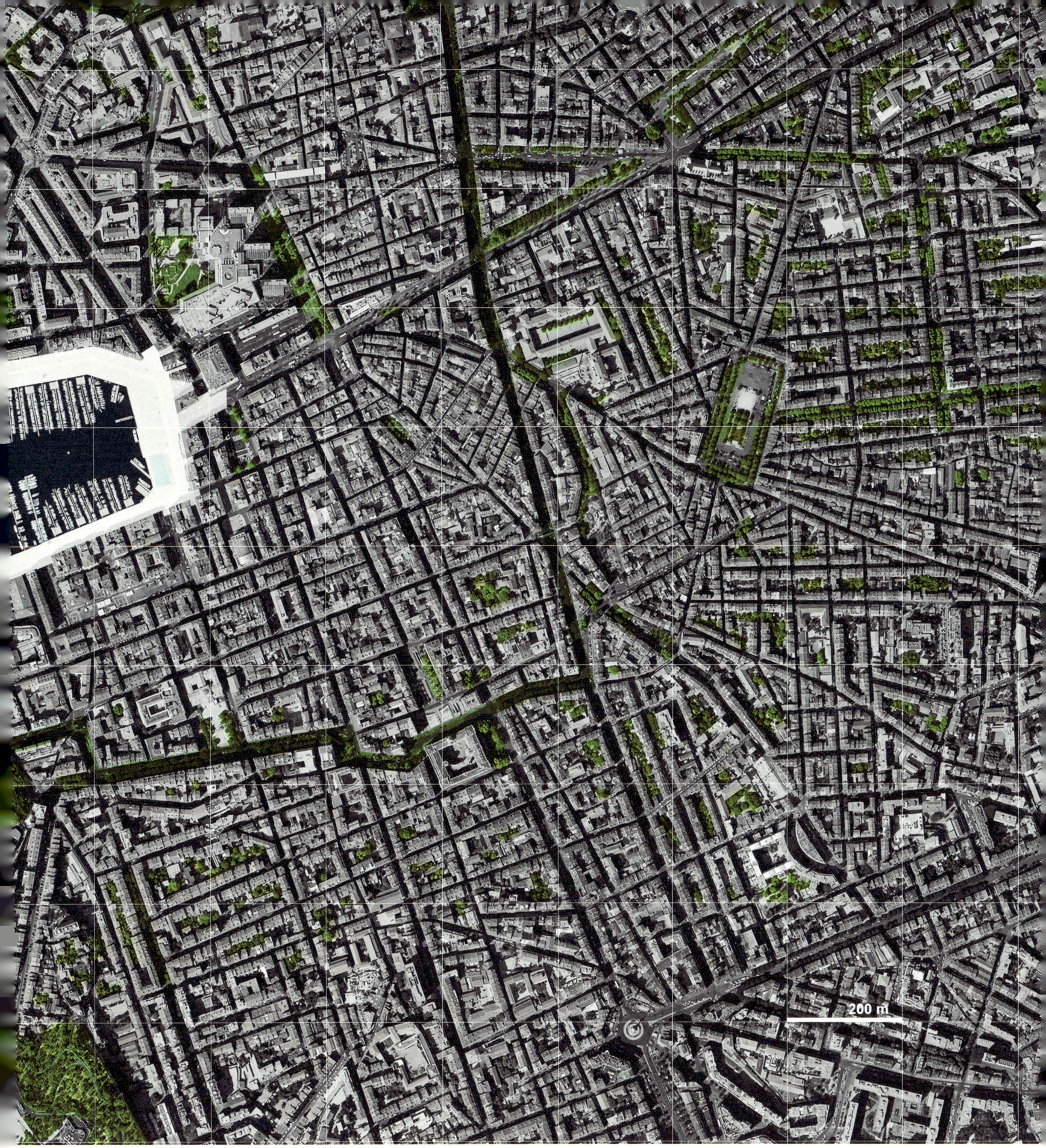

to the promenade around it. To the southwest, in the extension of the quays, the green spaces of the Faro area (existing), together with those of the Fort Saint-Nicolas glacis and the yachting club (to be created), form a potential chain of parks: a vegetal counterpoint to the minerality of the Old Port promenade.
Elsewhere in the city centre, through the methodical identification of streets, plazas and squares to be improved, interventions on these public spaces – typical and specific at the same time – can be envisaged. Some projects were relaunched in 2018: in the east, extending from the Old Port, the renovation of the major axis of La Canebière; in the north, across the hill, that of the very old Rue Caisserie, whose winding route separates the sectors reconstructed after the Second World War from the old district of Le Panier.

platforms, the wooden huts contain the equipment necessary for maintenance work, supplemented by small cranes to lift the boats and clean their hulls. Their use is private. Sailors meet at the club, do a bit of work, sit around for an early evening drink; the boats don't go out much. Apart from the picturesque aspect of this spectacle, one of the attractions of the promenade is the working atmosphere that prevails on the port, which we wished to preserve.

On the Quai de la Fraternité, the Canopy creates a very special moment in the public space. Foster had come up with two hypotheses: one was massive, a block of stone supported by arches – a reference to the architecture of Fernand Pouillon; the other – the project ultimately chosen by the politicians – was light and more readily brought to mind an Anish Kapoor-like effect: a horizontal metal blade with an edge only a few millimetres thick, raised to a height of 6 metres by eight pillars resting on a buried framework, making for a genuine technical feat. Like a mirror, its polished stainless steel underside reflects the movements of the crowd on the light granite ground, and the sea.

During the competition, our team was the only one to propose a void. You generally lose when you propose this type of solution as people are wary of a void. In this case, it won the competition for us because it didn't impinge on the vitality of Marseille. When the site was opened to the public, it was an immediate success. The natural geography of the city is gravitational: all the districts converge towards the Old Port, where social life, sailing clubs and cafés still exist. Far from being an unplanned area of 20 hectares, the quays take into account a whole set of fixed uses: the fish market, the flower market, the ferry terminal, the surrounding cafés and restaurants with their needs, etc. The City conducted a formal and informal consultation, negotiated fees, and organised a comprehensive support process for the project with the collective interest in mind. This work – fifteen years of reflection, eight months of work at a cost of €100 million (in 2019) – therefore combines the territorial dimension with an attention to materials, their meaning and the enjoyment of use. The European Prize for Public Space was awarded in 2014 was also in acknowledgement of these qualities.

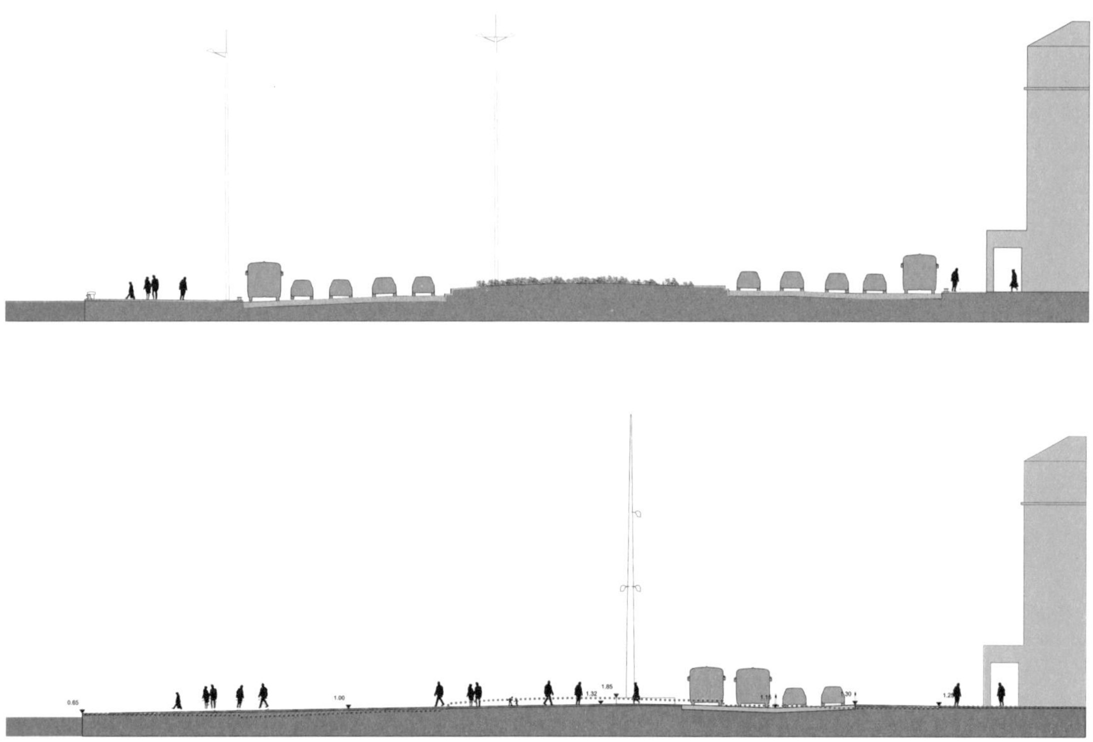

This page: before-and-after cross-sections on the Quai de la Fraternité (formerly the Quai des Belges).
Opposite page, top: at the back of the Port where it meets La Canebière, the quay is reserved for pedestrians and non-motorised transport. Treated as an esplanade and capable of hosting major urban events, the scheme is based on the redesign of car and public transit lanes.
Bottom: the uniform minerality of the quay continues along the entire north side (Quai du Port), running past the neoclassical city hall and along the light-coloured façades in Gard limestone of Fernand Pouillon and André Devin's 1950s apartment blocks. On the pontoons, facilities for the upkeep and repair of boats have been renovated and rationalised (architect: Foster + Partners).

BUS BUS

MA 224754

Comparisons between the pre-existing state (2010) and the renovation (2013).
Opposite page: on the quay, once divided by barriers, a pedestrian walkway extends as far as the water, highlighted by the preserved stone quayside. In the middle, one can make out a wild fig tree saved during the work.
This page, top: Quai de la Fraternité, car traffic once dominated, circulating around two median strips planted with flowers. It has been replaced by differentiated traffic, separated by the bus bays.
Middle: the open esplanade on the Quai de la Fraternité provides visual continuity to the mineral surface of the pedestrian area and the body of water framed by the Old Port.
Bottom: the same principle applies on the Quai de la Rive Neuve, where small boat maintenance workshops and their cranes have replaced the anarchic constructions built over time.

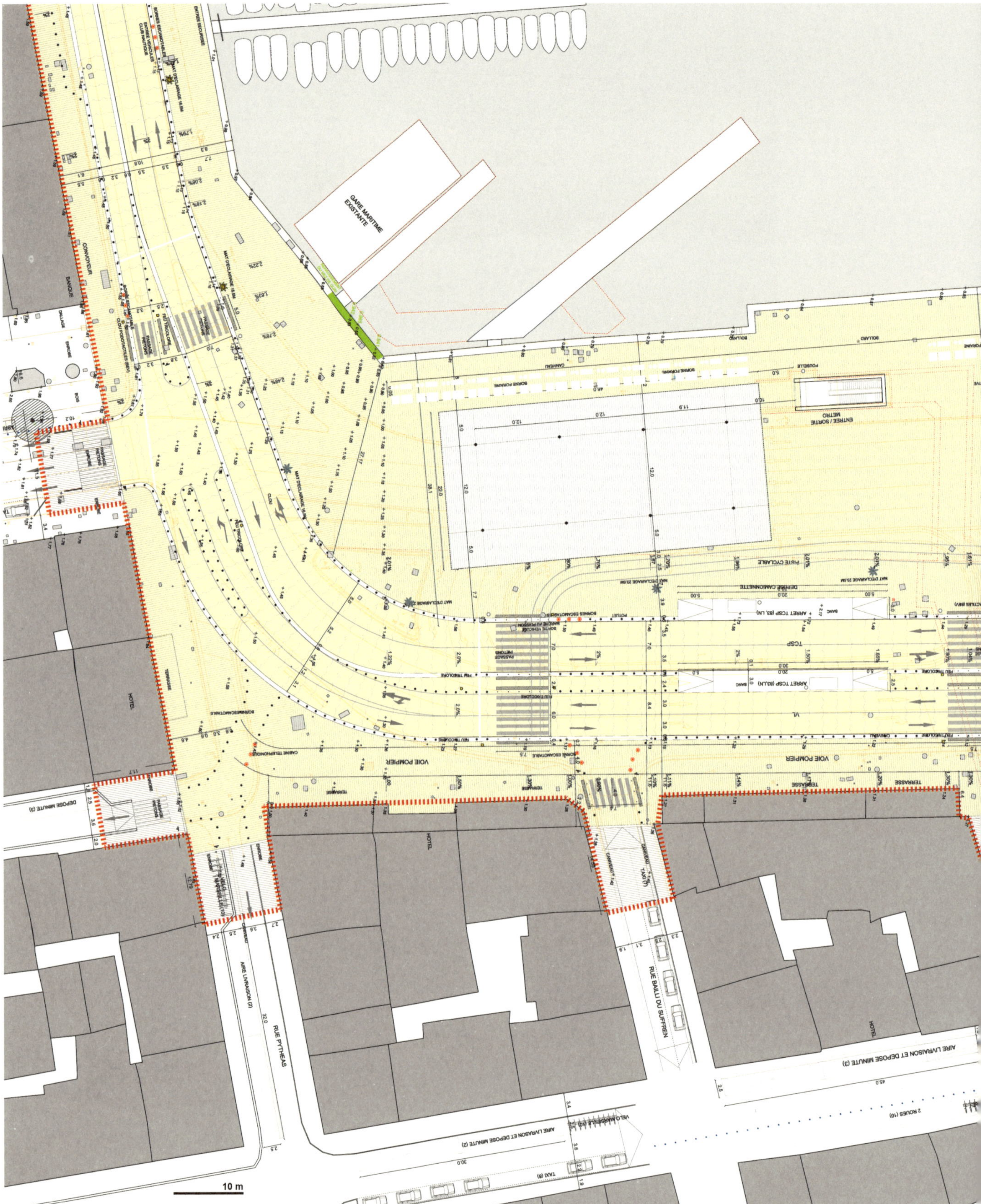

Implementation plan for the development of the Quai de la Fraternité. The outline of the former roadway can be made out in bistre. To the left, the Canopy and the sites intended for micro-activities (market, temporary fish stalls). The red line indicates the boundary of the project footprint. Using a single material, a light

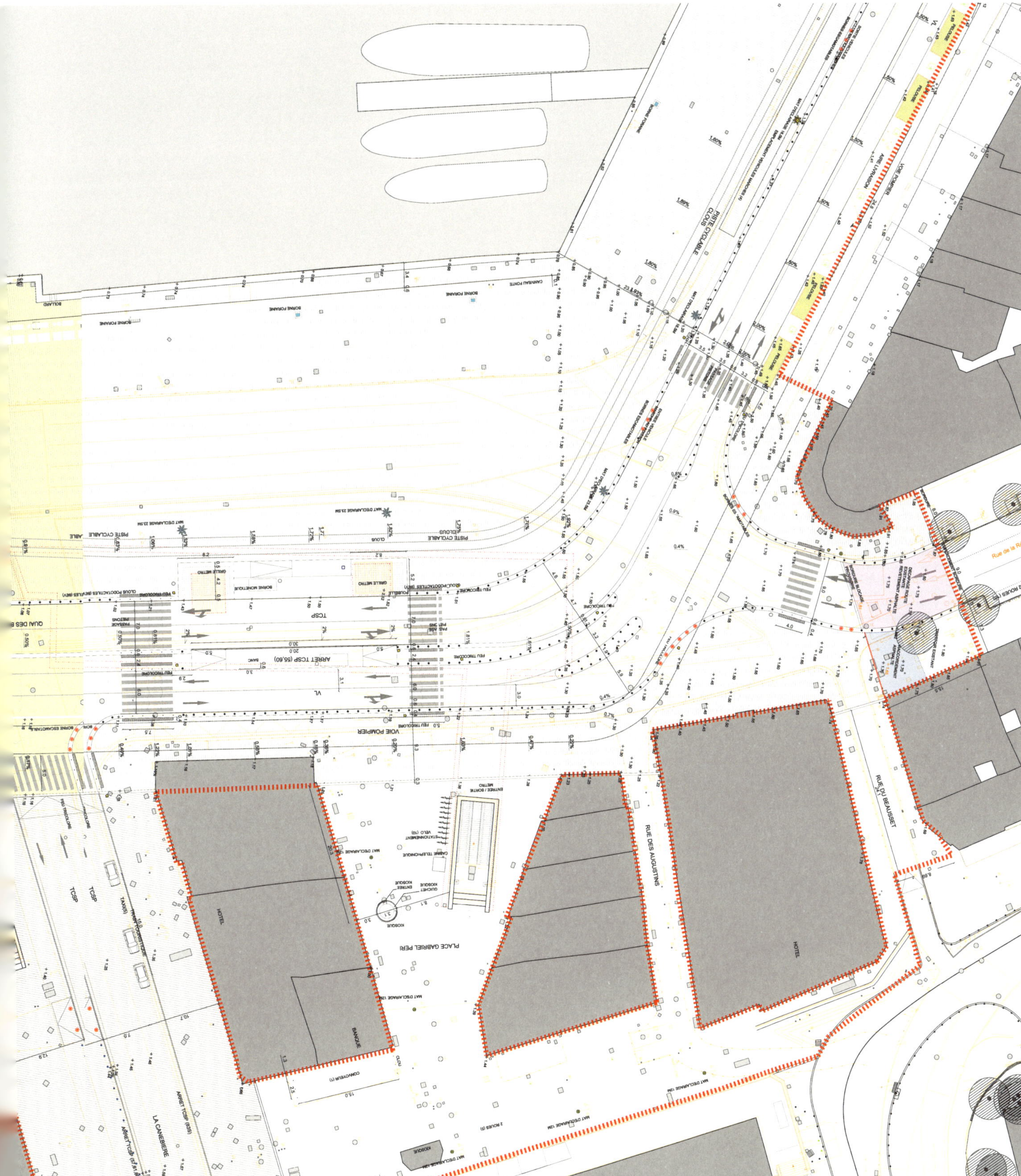

Spanish granite, the design of the ground plane alternates different cuts, finishes and layout methods depending on the type of circulation: rough paving slabs for pedestrian surfaces and setts laid in bogen patterns on vehicular roads. The boundary between the different zones is indicated by the lips of the underground gutters and the alignment of small cylindrical traffic bollards. Some are retractable to allow vehicle access to the sailing clubs. The wide pavements can accommodate café terraces at the foot of the buildings.

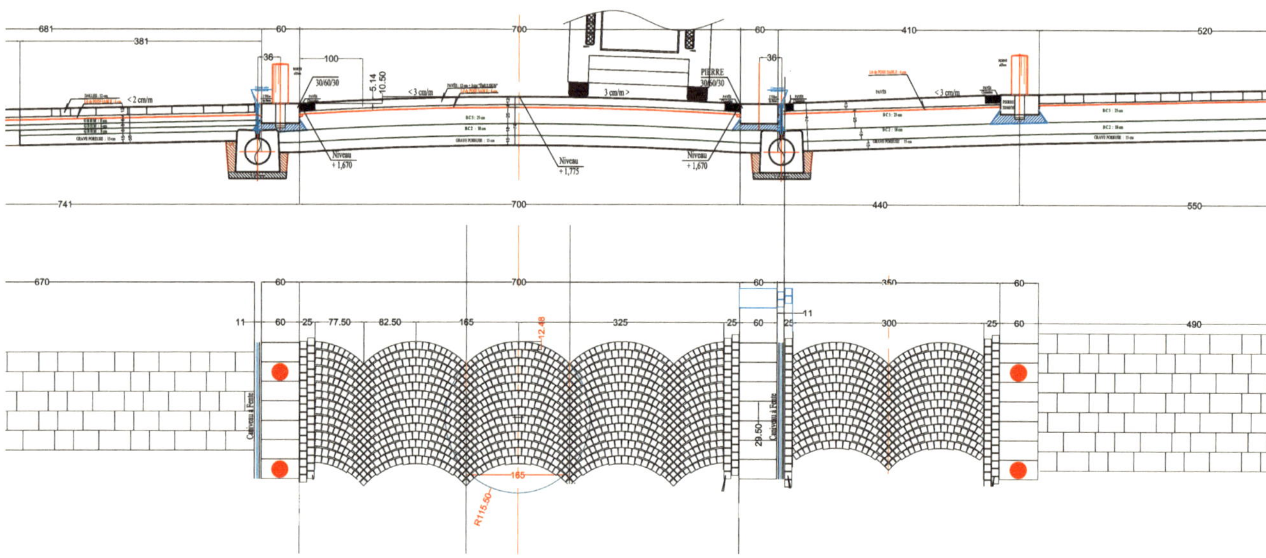
681
381
60
700
410
520
38
100
PIERRE
30/60/30
3 cm/m >
< 3 cm/m
< 2 cm/m
Niveau
+ 1,670
+ 1,775
741
440
550
670
350
11
60
25
77.50
82.50
165
325
300
490
29.50
R115.50

Opposite page: implementation plan and cross section. The levelling of the different types of surfaces channels runoff water into large underground drainage ducts.

This page: the Cadalso de los Vidrios quarry, near Madrid, provided the white granite used for the entire operation. The first extraction (35,000 m²) produced 250,000 12 cm slabs, 1,000,000 8/12 paving stones, 1,500 m of 30 x 60 cm borders, and 700 m of special 300 x 50 x 40 cm borders for bus bays.

The slabs and paving stones are laid on sand and their joints sealed with emulsion to facilitate extraction in the event of work on underground systems.

(1)

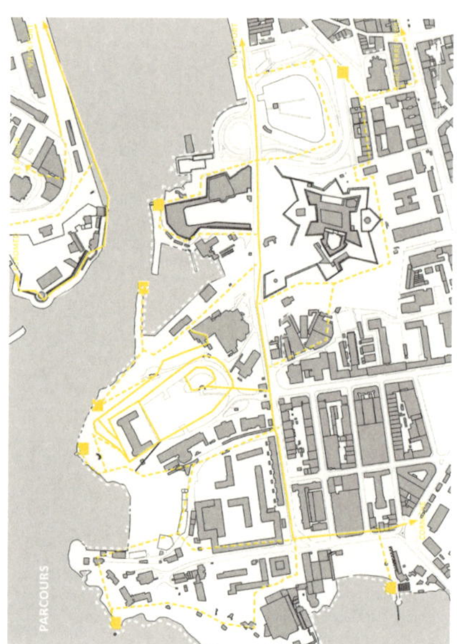

(2)

(3)

Chain of parks

From the outset, there was a striking equivalence in the surface areas of the Old Port and the system of planted public spaces that it was possible to organise around it, based on existing sites. The attraction of the project lay entirely in this couple formed by the minerality of the Old Port and this potential succession of green spaces. They presented similar dimensions, were similarly significant, and would clearly be complementary in redefining the city centre seafront in Marseille. Creating this chain of parks meant, on the one hand, grouping together places that had a public status but belonged primarily to the army - forts - and, on the other, improving the treatment of certain private plots: a step-by-step transformation in order to gradually set out a sequence of green spaces running from the Fort Saint-Jean to the Catalans beach, linked by continuous walks from the city and the sea.

On the Faro cove, for example, the retaining walls of the existing buildings cut directly into the hillside and block off any access to the water. The restoration of the embankments on the site of the former warehouses makes it possible to restore a continuous path between the Faro Palace and the university, passing through the cove where nautical activities are preserved. The large complex higher up could finally enjoy access to the sea. At the foot of Fort Saint-Nicolas, a port occupies the centre of the interchange that leads to the entrance of the Old Port tunnel. With the Foster agency, we imagined covering this road infrastructure with a green glacis, a vast sloping meadow that would house car parks and give access to the chain of parks.

Some places already exist and need to be re-landscaped, others have to be created. Between lawns, scrub and thickets, new pedestrian paths will be put in place to run through the entire chain. The parks are animated and equipped with amenities (congress centre, hotels, museums, nautical village etc.); for the added public spaces a recreational and cultural programme will be developed.

Opposite page: the linking of existing or newly created green spaces through the chain of parks gives the city centre a walking and leisure area equivalent to the surface area of the Old Port. Currently, waterside paths are interrupted by various obstacles due to their interference with property boundaries, infrastructure and topography.
The mapping of land use (1) and pathways (2) shows the potential extent of the "park" that could be created (3).

This page: projected view of the new seafront, between Fort Saint-Jean, on the left, and the Faro Palace, on the right, flanking the mouth of the Old Port.

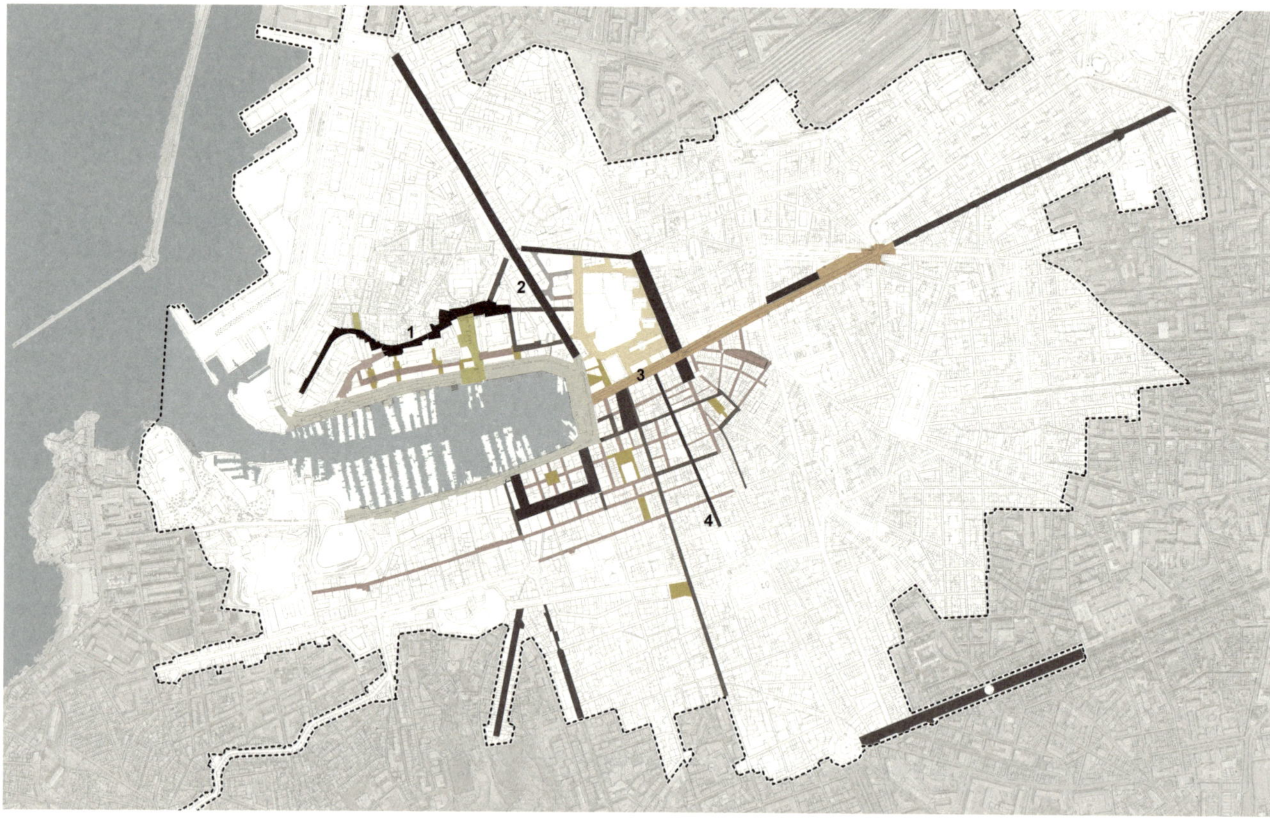

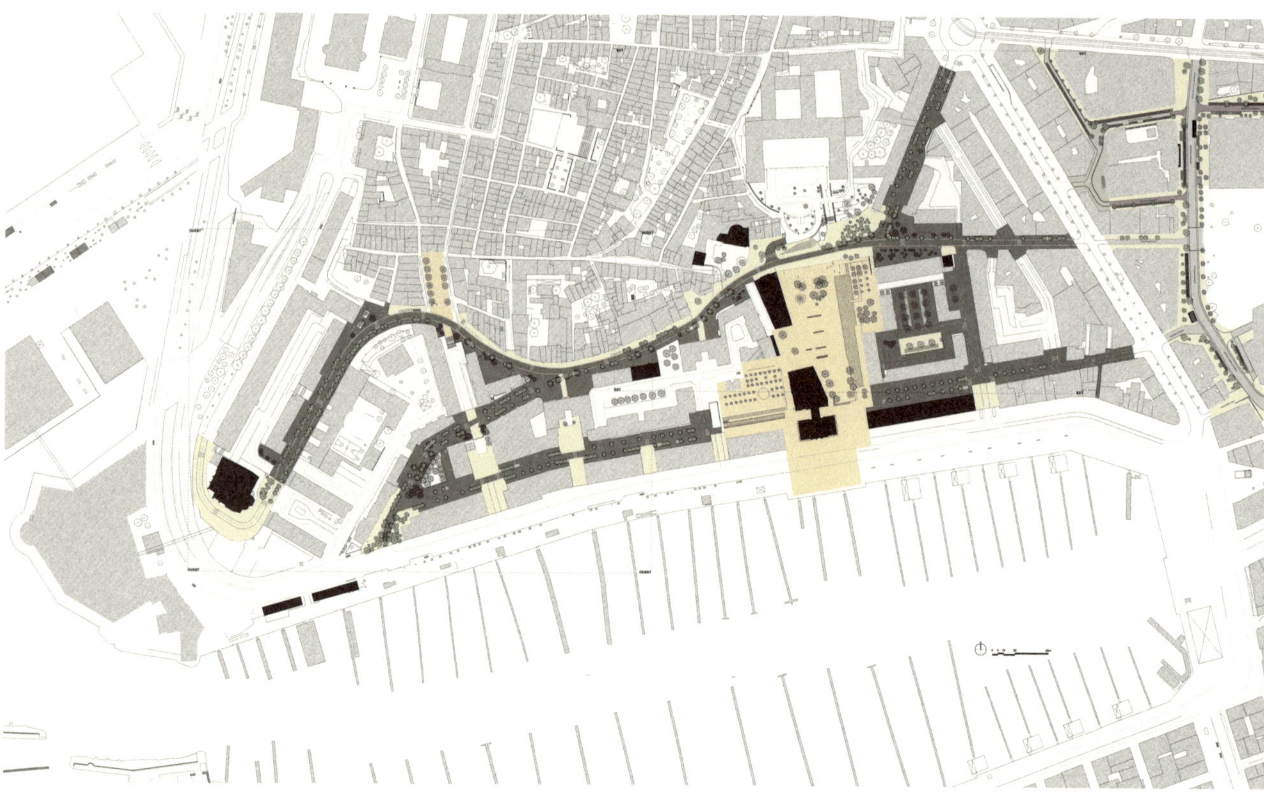

This page: following the framework plan, some significant public spaces in the centre have been redesigned or are under construction: to the north, Rue Caisserie (1) and Rue de la République (2); to the east, La Canebière (3); to the south, Rue Paradis (4).
Bottom: detail of the north side of the port. In the Panier district, due to its history, the route followed by the Rue Caisserie presents countless "accidents" that originate from its history, spaces earmarked for landscape interventions.
Opposite page: two approaches (roads and plantings) to the transformation of this ancient route: beginning of the street, in the perspective of the Grand-Rue (left) and, lower down, near the Roman Docks Museum (right).

City-centre public spaces

The samples of public spaces that feature in the framework plan were selected and processed according to a method initiated in 2001 for a project in Monaco and then improved in Bordeaux. The selection of these samples constituted a very important phase in Marseille. The most frequent typologies were identified, i.e. plazas, gardens, streets, alleys, avenues – ultimately, in any city, their number is limited – as well as cases that serve as models and where it is relatively easy to act. We divided them into common and exceptional spaces, the latter resulting from particular physical situations or accidents – linked to historical transformations, for example – that have created atypical urban connections.

During the process of identifying relevant sites, working meetings were held with local stakeholders. They helped us to understand the sites, define programmes and guide transformative solutions. Establishing this typology was a prelude to the production of a book laying down the rules, and the significant number of samples recorded in the book provided the basis for acting on all public spaces in Marseille in their variety. In a way, this work is equivalent to using significant special cases to draw the portrait of a city centre.

The framework plan proposes strategies for creating unity in this process of redefinition, through this patchwork of small transformations: it is a classic urban technique that seeks to generate the experience of a whole through an assembly of case studies.

The sixteen projects we listed therefore did not result in a regulatory charter; rather, they established a series of case studies based upon which specifications were drafted for tenders to fellow agencies for the production of a number of prototypes.

At the outset, most elected officials were primarily interested in the development of the quays on the Old Port. However, we convinced them of the importance of transforming the fabric of the centre's public spaces on the basis of our study. In 2018, Marseille Métropole decided to undertake significant work on these spaces, and has secured the funding to do so. Following our framework plan, its services carried out the transformation of Rue Paradis themselves. The experiment highlighted the historic centre's potential to evolve and the knock-on effects this could have within the urban fabric.

A consultation was therefore launched on the basis of the framework plan, and we won a project management contract to redesign some of the public spaces in the city centre.

The situations we inherited are varied. Some public spaces are old, others are marked by recent work; some are uniform, others more vaguely defined, etc. The Canebière was transformed about fifteen years ago, as was the Haussmannian Rue de la République. To the contemporary eye, the materials used at the time to create the ground plane appear dated and generic, typical of the time when the spaces were designed. The surfaces could have been more specific or more distinct, and they are often badly matched to the surrounding buildings. To give the whole a consistency, everything would have to be demolished, which is not an option. First, we had to take stock and accept compromises. To ensure that the "pioneering" projects – the first ones to be implemented – do not accentuate the existing patchwork of surfaces, we revised the framework plan to identify consistencies. This was a logical evolution of this document, which lacked a synthetic cartographic vision, as the question had not arisen in these terms at the time. We now had to redefine not only the materials, but also the thresholds from one space to another: the connections as well as the seams between artificial grounds often left something to be desired, both functionally and visually. Transitions, or their absence, needed to be made very obvious.

Behind the Old Port, in the lower part of the Panier district, for example, Rue Caisserie – a former Roman street – follows an uneven topography between large reconstructed sections, from Haussmann to Pouillon. It is a dividing line at the same time as a true ancient vestige; when you walk along it, you can understand the age of the path it follows: people have been using it for 2,000 years. It is punctuated by a multitude of urban "leftovers", interstices, depressions and gaps. These are the spaces we will plant with tall trees, favouring the use of a binder to "pretty" paving for the surfacing. Rather than disguise this road as a heritage street, the aim is to restore the legible presence of its history.

THE LIVING GROUND

In a way, there isn't much to see at the Old Port, and that was exactly our intention: that it be a "designed nothing". The quay gives the impression of being a continuous mineral ground, extending from the threshold of the surrounding buildings to the water, free of ornamentation or interruption by "micro-plazas": it is a quay. Nonetheless, variations occur along its surface. The Architectes des Bâtiments de France pointed out that drawing a single plan from the foot of a façade to the quay was an aberration; it had never been done before in municipal construction. So first we designed a pavement, then a bus bay, then a traffic lane, then the quayside, where pedestrians circulate.

The unity of the whole would come from the material. Historically, the quays of the Old Port were paved with a mixture of stone types, including the famous Cassis limestone used for the Suez Canal. However, the quarry had been exploited to a degree where sufficient quantities of stone were no longer available to cover the required surface fully. We therefore chose a Spanish granite, which offered the same quality of whiteness as the stone from the *calanques,* and satisfactory mechanical properties, as well as a good price and transport conditions. It is applied in two forms – paving stones for the traffic lanes, slabs for pedestrian zones – but on the whole maintains a monolithic aspect that seems fitting in response to Fernand Pouillon's architecture.

The planning of public space falls within the remit of civil engineering. A fussy design such as that of a bank lobby would not be to scale. Yet, since the 1980s, the management of public space – in Barcelona, Lyon and elsewhere – has all too often been placed in the hands of architects, who have reproduced externally, in the city, what they were doing inside their buildings. The bonding of the stonework was too precise and too rigid, making it unfit to withstand the stresses typically endured by an urban ground, subjected to intense use but, more importantly still, prone to expansion because of temperature variations. As a result, the stones cracked and the pavement broke up.

The engineers of the City of Paris have known since Alphand that the slabs or flagstones of the capital's pavements are laid on flexible foundations; they float on sand between joints simply sealed with bitumen or thin mortar. One of the most beautiful references we used was Milan, a centuries-old urban ground composed of magnificent blocks of alpine granite bedded on sand. To carry out road works, the blocks are lifted using small machines and put back in place by refilling the sand bed. This modular surface can be opened and closed in the case of intervention; it can move or even break: damaged parts are replaced. It's a living ground. Similarly, in Paris, it used to be very easy to remove paving stones and put them back again to gain access to the systems below. Today, trenches are cut into the pavements and are then patched over with asphalt or concrete. This lack of respect for soil depth, whether on mineral or planted grounds, and this ignorance of stratification and its benefits over time are responsible for the desolation that afflicts some contemporary public spaces. For the engineering of the surface level to be successful, it must effectively maintain an awareness of the sedimentary layers that comprise it and which form a kind of geology.

In the Old Port, the joints may appear coarse. This is deliberate, for reasons of economy, but above all so that the stones can easily be removed. For the road system to work, the paving stones are arranged in bogen patterns in both directions, in plan and in section: their surface resists pressure in all directions. The ground is slightly concave, wedged between huge borders. Groundwater is collected by large, 50 centimetre high steel gutters. These gutters lie on concrete drains cast on an inflatable box-out inserted at the bottom of the trench. At the bus stops, the flagstones are 2.50 metres long, 60 centimetres wide and equally thick. With use, this stone will become dirty and a patina will form, resulting in a uniform, neutral surface, much like concrete – a material that would already be ruined had we had chosen it. The ground becomes a fully fledged piece of heritage: magnificent, durable and of palpable thickness.

Mastering the foundation means respecting the ground and taking it into consideration. And proper consideration of subsoils means not only looking at their stability, but also at how they coexist with plants. To plant trees in the city, soil is needed, in volumes proportional to the expected longevity of the plantings. The large pits into which these fertile soils are deposited lose their shape as they subside. What is the best way to coordinate them on the surface with the paving stones? When placed excessively close to plantings, the paving is subjected to movements it can't cope with. Traditional techniques have solved the problem in various ways: by adding sand – less compressible than soil – to the planting mix, as the Dutch do, or by delaying the laying of paving stones around trees until their substratum is compacted. But that can take years. Nor is it possible to trample the soil: the gas exchanges between the roots and the air are crucial for plant health. Hence the invention of tree grates, laid flush with the ground, which can be walked on and whose concentric circles could formerly be adapted as the trunks expanded. Neglecting or forgetting these concerns and techniques has caused many plantings to fail, a fact that became apparent at the end of the twentieth century.

Today, we are trying to imagine porous soils of a different kind. In Luxembourg, we superimposed a pine and beech forest on the square in front of the new Museum of Modern Art, a space we viewed as poor and austere. Six hundred trees were planted on grass-joint paving, which, more than just a surface, presents itself as a landscape. However, conditions, means and techniques are required for such a result to be achieved. It is not enough to draw blades of grass between paving stones. A landscape is not formed by pasting images, nor is it merely an amenity; it is a complex, rich thing – an aesthetic pleasure too.

As I often point out, the twentieth century failed to build fitting public spaces for its cities. But it's not true: a great number of very large car parks were built everywhere. What is to be done with them? One hopes they will evolve, but it will take a lot of money. Who will pay? A transformation is required. But what's the best way to go about it? Their ground was completely sealed up, covered with asphalt: it is dead. In Bordeaux, where our "landscape charter" prescribed wooded car parks, we began transforming one such car park to serve as the southern entrance to the Parc floral. Deep parallel trenches were dug, 2 metres wide every 10 metres, corresponding to 20 per cent of the surface area: we could only treat a limited portion of the ground, otherwise parking space would have been reduced too much. These trenches were filled with a mixture of volcanic soil and topsoil – the Cornell mix, which is draining and fertile – in order to grow shelterbelt trees. Also in Bordeaux, we adopted the same approach around the new stadium, with Herzog & de Meuron, and at both ends of the future Simone Veil Bridge plaza, with OMA. And we will soon be using it in Mérignac, near Bordeaux airport, where a suburban area including a huge shopping centre car park will gradually be converted into a residential zone.

It is also possible to anticipate the future reuse of car park land from the initial construction phase. This is what we set out to do with Christine Dalnoky in the early 1990s for the Thomson factory in Guyancourt, designed by Renzo Piano. The site was divided into plots by drainage ditches that flowed into a holding basin dug for this purpose, then these plots were planted with rows of willows. Before being covered in asphalt to provide parking for 1,000 cars, their soil was stabilised with lime in anticipation of the possible future conversion of the site. The lifespan of an industrial plant – thirty years or so – corresponds to the time plants need to mature fully: today, the factory is leaving and the site will be urbanised. Thus, the practice of identifying and accumulating small consistencies helps establish an overall logic, in space and in time.

PORT-MARIANNE
MONTPELLIER, FRANCE, 1991–

In 1991, in collaboration with Christine Dalnoky, we won a competition for the development of the approach road to Montpellier, on a site extending for 3 kilometres between the motorway and the river Lez. The pretext for the competition was the broadening of the road from two to four lanes and our brief was to design the landscape alongside it. At the time, the areas lining the road had not yet been constructed and only a very narrow strip of land was left over after roads and interchanges had been built. Traveling 3 kilometres at 60 kilometres per hour takes only three minutes. It was therefore necessary to design a unified, striking landscape – a condensed version of the landscapes found in the region – and place it in the residual scraps of land on either side of the road. We imagined a scenographic device of planted curtains that, viewed from the road as well as from the surrounding area, would multiply horizon lines and amplify the impression of depth. These "backdrops" created the illusion of a forest – a thick landscape made of lines – and framed views for future buildings. They created a showcase for Montpellier.

We then convinced the mayor, Georges Frèche, that a landscape project would enable him to control the ongoing extensions of his city. The next competition was for a 3 x 2 kilometre urban sector to the east of the city, for which Ricardo Bofill had already drawn up a vast development plan. It encompassed the Antigone district and the Regional Council Headquarters, including major roads, whose routes had to be taken into account and put to use in some way. We had identified two recurring features in the agricultural landscape around Montpellier: the high hedges planted east-west to protect crops from the north wind, and, running roughly perpendicular to the hedges, natural geographic elements such as small valleys and rivers flowing to the sea, bordered by groves and characterised by a specific flora. The first category involved precise geometries and a limited number of plant species, the second a palette of riparian plants found along watercourses. The agricultural land earmarked for the construction of what would become the Port-Marianne district still bore the traces of this organisation of the rural landscape. This specific vocabulary could be preserved and amplified, turning Bofill's diagrams into neo-horticultural structures.

We proposed a master plan that transposed these principles to the inherited plan. Nine thousand large deciduous trees – avenues of plane trees, lime trees and hackberry trees – were planted, materialising east-west urban lines, while the north-south routes were dotted with pine groves. By chance, the City services have quite consistently called on us, right to up to the present, to continue implementing this landscape, one piece at a time, in different neighbourhoods defined by this framework. Since 1998, we have been commissioned with six or seven consecutive projects on the Charpak Park site, which has gradually been built up in coherent strata from its starting condition – a detention basin to prevent flooding of the city's two rivers. To the west, near the Lez, we gradually established a park associated with a district developed by the urban planner Adrien Fainsilber, and another further north for the Lironde garden district, a project designed by Christian de Portzamparc. As a result, landscape provides a structure to the very rapid urbanisation of this sector: fifty years ago, the Port-Marianne district did not exist.

In Charpak Park, a stormwater reservoir is planted with rows of poplars running east-west (top) while the banks of the river Lironde, running north-south, incorporate a series of groves linked to the wetland (bottom).

These systems use two typical modes of organisation of the Mediterranean landscape. They establish the basic framework guiding the development of the entire Port-Marianne area. These photographs date from 2018.

The framework plan, annexed to the city's land use plan, has served since 1992 as a reference document for all public space projects in Port-Marianne. It superimposes a simulation of the double planting system on the satellite image of the territory. This system accompanies, extends or absorbs the different types of routes anticipated in the district's urban plan.

Identification of operations undertaken over successive commissions:
1 – The dual carriageway and its pine plantings, which connect the access roundabout to the motorway (to the east) and the Antigone district. Planned in the late 1970s by Ricardo Bofill, its major axis runs perpendicular to the Lez (to the west).
2 – Charpak Park, designed over the course of successive interventions around a large stormwater basin, between mixed development zones entrusted to Architecture Studio.
3 – The Lez Park, which links the banks of this river to a new district designed by Adrien Fainsilber.
4 – The Lironde Gardens, created as a counterpart to the inhabited archipelago designed by the De Portzamparc agency.

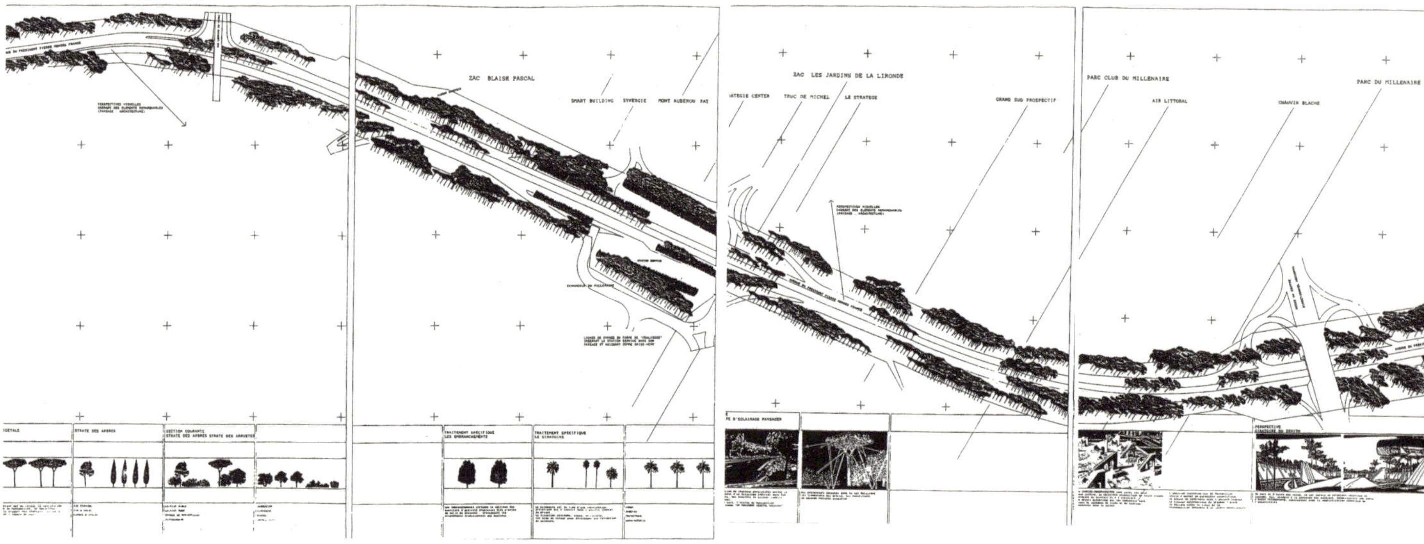
ZAC BLAISE PASCAL
ZAC LES JARDINS DE LA LIRONDE
PARC CLUB DU MILLENAIRE
PARC DU MILLENAIRE II

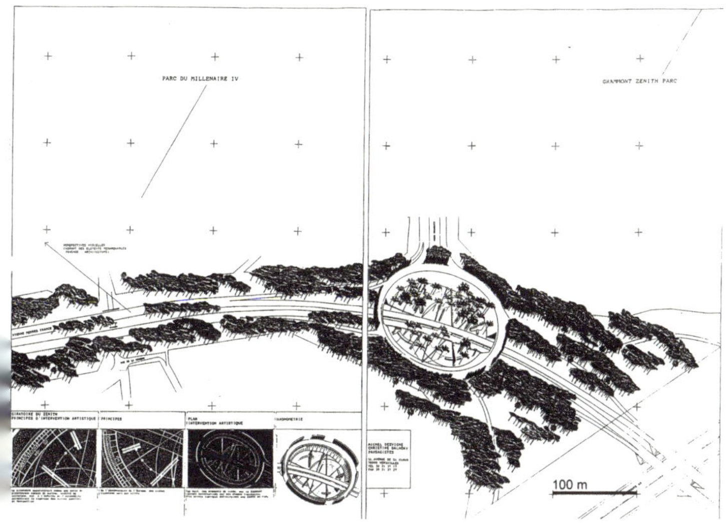

Avenue Mendès-France

We designed this dual carriageway as a parkway rather than an urban boulevard. Having lived in Rome where the southern entrance of the EUR was planted with wispy pines in the course of upgrading the project, we imagined a similar effect for Montpellier: a huge forest of umbrella and Aleppo pines. The Compagnie Nationale du Rhône owned a nursery that it wanted to sell. The Mayor Georges Frèche bought 14,000 of its umbrella pines, most of which were very small, about 1.50 metres tall. They were planted very tightly to give an immediate presence to the landscape, in the manner of forestry operations. Some died, others were mown down by cars – the mayor had accepted the lack of side protection. Twenty-five years later, the presence of the young pine forest is beginning to become visible in the landscape; when it is 120 years old, it will have really taken form.

Plan submitted to the 1991 competition. The new access road to the eastern districts of Montpellier was designed by widening the route as much as possible to plant rows of trees on the median strip. The planting scheme plays with the constraints of road design to create a landscape on the scale of the territory through which the road passes.
In the heterogeneous context of this city entrance, the strips of the young pine forest unify the vision from the road without blocking it. They overlap and shift in perspective as you drive past, to present a moving landscape.
The photographs taken in the late 1990s and 2013 (bottom left) show the evolution of the density and effect of the planted masses over time.

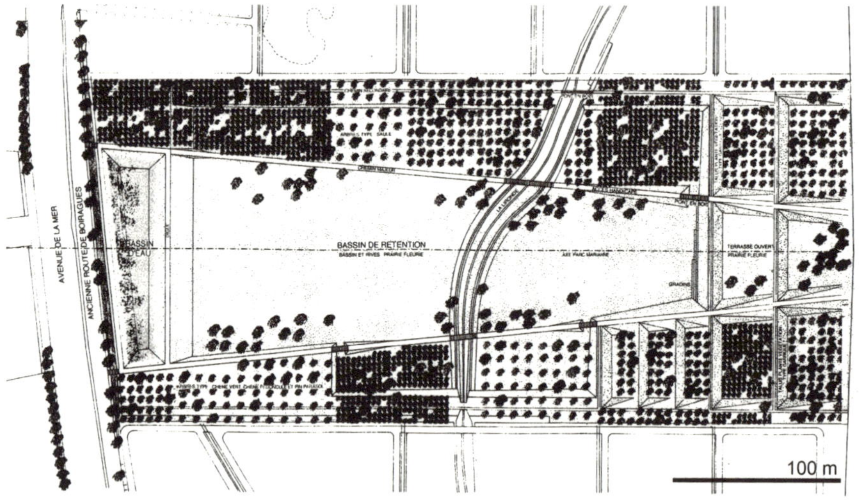
AVENUE DE LA MER
BASSIN DE RETENTION
100 m

Charpak Park (1998–2013)

Following flooding in the area, the zone Bofill had set aside for the park had become a stormwater reservoir connecting to the Lironde and Lez. We were initially asked to make it the starting point of the park: a large central void, hemmed in by embankments, with vegetation present on either side earmarked for alcove gardens, and isolated trees dotted along the river. In 2000, we broke with the formal plan by introducing sequences of forestation. To avoid a bare plot, we planted a meadow where people came to pick armfuls of flowers. In 2008, a new step was taken: the reservoir existed, the meadows had settled in, a few trees had been planted and Architecture Studio built the mixed development zones all around. How were we to give this lateral afforestation an acceptable reality since it would take decades before it acquired a presence, in the harsh physical conditions on the fringe of the site? Returning to the language of 1991, we added rows of poplars, along the axis of the road while distorting them to play with views and form backdrops. Thereafter we implemented an irrigated lawn, and gradually laid out paths. The time will come when there will be a need to think about furniture and objects.

In the end, what is significant about this park? A spatial organisation, largely dictated by hydraulic requirements – the shape of the basin, the presence of the river – but also by our own charter, on a larger scale: the species to be planted, the geometric vision linked to the development of the east of Montpellier. This artificial countryside is the raw material of a park in the making; the rest evolves in keeping with the constructed reality. The process transfers to the public space the empirical logic a person would apply to their own garden: plant first, then adjust over the years according to what has grown or not.

Bordered to the west by the Lez and crossed by the Lironde, the flood reservoir is an enclosed basin covering a surface of 5 hectares (for a total of 7.5 hectares of park), bordered by two large embankments. The tops of the embankments are planted according to a forest grid of varying density. The landscape changes with the seasons (prairie or wetland), as the walk progresses (revealing unobstructed views of a kind of countryside, views from the top of riverside constructions, perspectives of the straight paths), and the effects of the pine forest vary according to the density of the planting.

Lez Park

Our linear plantations follow Fainsilber's east-west grid in one direction, extending it to bring great transparency to the paths and buildings he had imagined. In the other direction, for a long stretch, with varying spacing, the tree planting follows a "comb" pattern, organised in groves composed of many species. The desired kinetic effect will be stronger when these very young trees have grown. We initially surrounded them with fences so that people would not rip them up, and they almost spontaneously turned into a park, without the landscaping work that could have accompanied their growth. The structure of this park gives it a particular legibility, local people have appropriated it, and it has grown well. It extends into the district through a few simple squares, mineral surfaces planted with loose pines.

Lironde Gardens (2007-2014)

This garden neighbourhood is designed by the De Portzamparc agency as an archipelago of inhabited "islands", themselves composed of several buildings of different heights. They form open islands of varied plans, scattered in a landscape that combines a public park with private gardens and that, by its very principle, associates rural components already present on the site such as vines and olive trees. Groves, planted embankments and uncut hedges mask the garden fences. The car parks are densely planted following an orthogonal grid. To the north, the complex connects to the Avenue Mendès-France, whose rows of pines extend the park's tree-filled landscape.

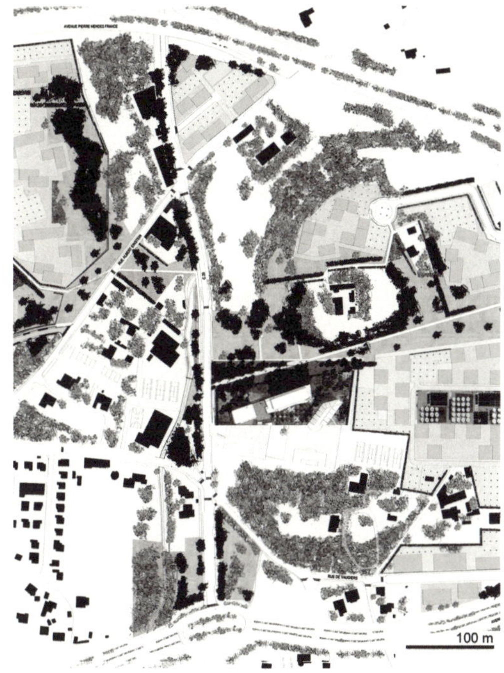

Opposite page: in the Lez Park, clumps of pine and holm oak are spread over grassy areas delimited by a grid of paths on stabilised ground. Running east-west, the hard-surfaced paths, perpendicular to the Lez, link up, through the park, with the internal circulation of the housing development on the banks of the river.

This page: in the Lironde Gardens, garrigue and a succession of flowering meadows unify the walks, materialised by solid paths. The strong presence of the planted masses forms a continuous blanket from which the built blocks emerge.

TIME AND COHERENCE

The time of plant matter, the time of the design process: all our projects play on these two fundamentals. Bordeaux, Lyon Confluence and Montpellier are constantly at the project stage. The goal is not to verify that these operations have been completed or that they comply with an initial drawing, but to accompany them. For the Charpak Park in Montpellier, we produced an image projecting as far as possible into the future and, with each new stratum, we repeatedly reassess what was done previously while re-evaluating the original project. These successive layers of the project correspond to a series of missions spread out over time.

It all starts with earthworks, which have an irreversible quality because they determine water flows. Once the trees are planted, the levels cannot be changed. There are therefore physical invariables: the ground and its gradient, water – its flow and storage are inescapable – and some plantings. Everything else is subject to constant variation: land use, paths, subsequent plant layers and, of course, all the objects that can be inserted into these defined structures. Consequently, certain layout drawings, at least topographical ones, are necessary from the outset to establish permanence. In Saclay, we dug huge basins, large furrows and flood expansion zones to prepare for the urbanisation phase and anticipate the future management of water on the site: this is a prerequisite in the hierarchy of operations, and as such it is determining, long-lasting and binding for the future. Deploying utility networks implies significant planning of the site. In our work on public spaces, roads and various utilities – the subsurface level therefore – have much greater influence than vegetation.

I like to contrast the site preparation methods practised by engineers and urban planners with those I observe in some twentieth-century landscape architects such as Olmsted or Forestier. In the former case, a sort of "Roman road" can be identified, flanked by a gutter and along whose edges the façades will line up. In park systems, on the other hand, the necessities of site preparation – water management, roads, earth movement – create a landscape. To achieve this result, you need a spatial vision, a balance of proportions and a sense of composition. However, not everything is determined. The project is not consigned to a layout plan for eternity. It depends on a certain number of founding actions that have a long-term impact. In Bordeaux, our park has value only in relation to the continuous urban changes on the right bank: we cannot isolate it from its context and consider its plan as a design or a style. Its graphic organisation as a series of lines is derived from the water and parcels management system, which we intend to extend into the new districts, like a matrix. This is a way of thinking and executing that takes into account the long time frame of the city's overall transformation.

These continuities taking place on a vast scale can accommodate a remarkable degree of flexibility. In large sites such as Saclay, we are both designers and project managers for some public spaces, and simply specifiers for others. The "frameworks" of our project and the statement of their founding principles should be sufficient for others to implement them in the same spirit. However, this is not the case. An enormous amount of spatial, visual and architectural expertise is involved in mastering the initial canvas and its components. The system of coherence we believe we have established is not just about principles. It stems from a whole series of reactions to smaller things: such and such a well-placed hedge, etc. These permanent reformulations require creativity, at the risk of history becoming trite or forgotten. This requires a certain intelligence in the execution, but above all it depends on how the missions are defined with our clients. We must help invent the commission in such a way as to remain present on the projects over several decades, even precariously, so that we can assist in the interpretation of our principles and act as their guarantor. Successful operations are the ones in which the clients understand the need to foster a narrative.

Conversely, we can also ask ourselves: should we avail ourselves of the means to make what has been composed with geography exist from the beginning, in order to make these projects more rapidly acceptable? What is the critical threshold in their development that makes them useful? When do they become legible? In Lens, our strips of woodland were designed to produce a very short-term result and to define boundaries and a contour right from the start. It will be fascinating to observe the successive stages of their evolution. From the outset, some of the plantings have had a presence, and from these clusters majestic trees will gradually emerge – if they are willing to survive. One day, they'll be 100 years old! When you plant a young forest, it looks like a surface, a carpet, a forest plan. Then it rises, table-like, growing into masses that are gradually sculpted. In Burgos, the trees that were planted are definitive. It was the unplanted forest masses that were supposed to derive from this logic of successive states. That they were not planted constitutes a kind of drama: they could have produced this immediately perceptible effect, which is missing.

As all these things happen slowly, our capacity for self-renewal sometimes runs dry. The tendency to self-reference, the formal vibration that becomes ingrained in our drawings and repeats itself to the point of resembling a style can alter the meaning of the project. In Bordeaux, elaborating the park's programme was not part of the initial commission. Thinking about the programme earlier would have been ineffective since the needs had not been identified nor formulated at the time. Suddenly, thinking about the programme made sense and helped us to renew our approach. We were inundated by requests to insert very diverse activities into the public spaces that had already been created. To resist this trend towards filling and proliferation, we had to reflect on the distribution of these programmes: where should they be placed and where should indetermination be preserved? We had to reconsider some proportions, re-examine the space, and even admit that there was a certain mannerism to our drawings and their repetition of lines. We simplified them. This programmatic phase forced us to take a step back from our design, and to find a grain that felt right.

Projects are also enriched through the feedback provided by the people who manage them and the people who use them. In Bordeaux, the city's technical services were concerned about the density of our plantings and the proximity of the trees. For the people in charge of the site and its long life to understand the project, it must be acceptable to them. We are also aware of how this park is used and seen by the public, of what it represents to local residents. Against all odds, they have appropriated our clearings, perhaps because they are very simple, almost rustic, already familiar. If the site were misunderstood or maltreated, the project would have to be modified.

Yes, what I do is an artifice, and it must be an explicit one. Yet I know that time will pass and that for many more or less random reasons, the initial object will mutate, and that a form of nature will appear. Jacques Simon initiated this practice, and we are his heirs through Michel Corajoud. We try to do this with a certain radicality, remaining faithful to the legibility of the processes that produce this nature. I refer to it as "intermediate" because it is still freeing itself from the visible artifice by which it was initiated. Thinning is a gardener's act, motivated by technical and aesthetic concerns. In Bordeaux, we selected certain trees, and other species later contaminated the initial plantings. It all evolves, life takes over. In Saclay, we are planting parcels of woodland on regular furrows, with very young trees that are 25 centimetres high; like foresters, we protect them with proper tree grids of a good size to provide an enclosure, which gives the site a legible order. We planted some borders straight away so that the trees' growth would irreversibly prevent urbanisation. Planting quickly also makes it possible to anticipate the future preservation of the landscape.

This obviously presupposes a form of continuity, and even permanence in the management of the project. Fortunately, in public commissions, elected officials sometimes respect the decisions of their predecessors. The time of political and economic cycles more strongly determines the fate of our projects than that of the cycles of nature. It is these cycles that safeguard or disrupt the coherence we seek to instil in the long term. This is often the case in the administration of major public projects, and of some elected officials. In Montpellier, the mayor's memory of what we have proposed and done there spans several decades of the city's history; the municipal departments have remained faithful to our project and regularly consult us to revive, renew and pursue it. It has become a common vision, nurtured by responses to the new questions that arise over time.

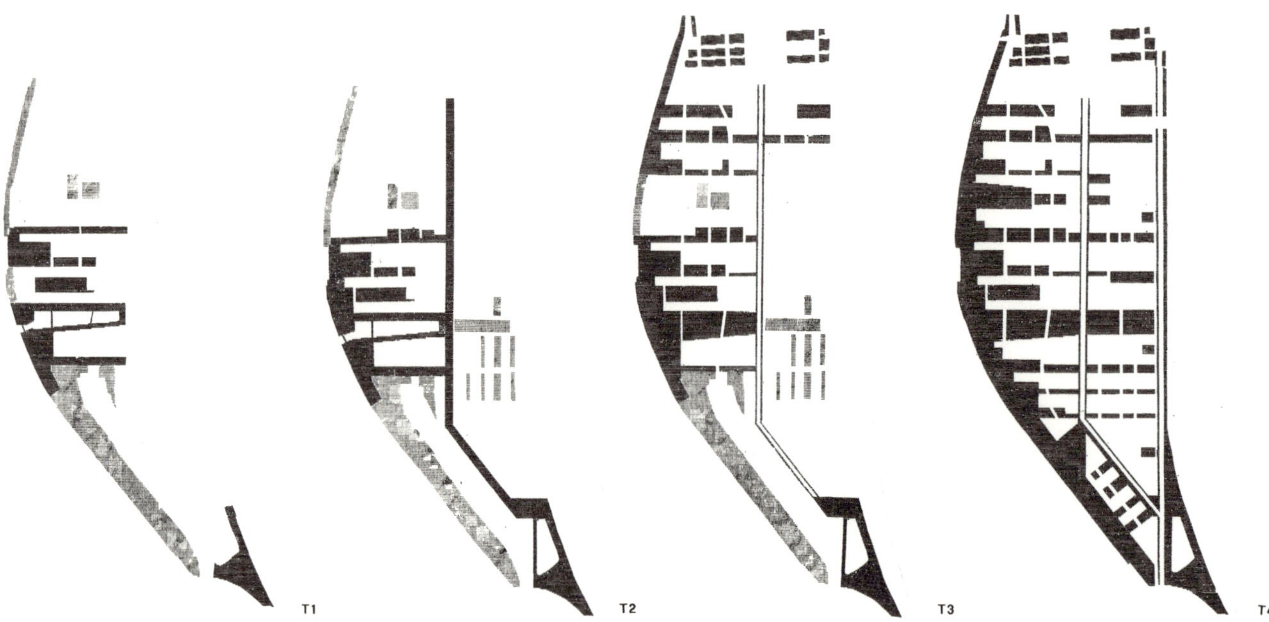
T1
T2
T3
T4

LYON CONFLUENCE
LYON, FRANCE, 1999–

In this case again, the project can be partly explained through the succession of commissions and the nature of the missions they involved. Managing them over time required some juggling, as did their stratification and occasional ambiguities. The first commission, to mark the new millennium, was to organise a walk along the Saône. The embankment was in a state of abandonment, with a bad reputation – it was a hotspot for prostitution and drug dealing – and most of the adjacent industrial buildings had already been demolished. The aim was to make it accessible as far as the tip of the peninsula, while designing a preliminary scheme for the future transformation of the site. The brief was limited and precise: to develop 2.5 kilometres of temporary walkways in this part of Lyon.
We then teamed up with urban designer François Grether for a competition encompassing the entire peninsula. This highly desirable piece of natural geography in the centre of Lyon has always inspired projects, including one by Tony Garnier in his time. Oriol Bohigas and the Lyon-based architect Thierry Melot had just made a proposal for the redevelopment of the whole site. They had clearly divided it into two zones: one part dense neighbourhood and one part park, at the tip end. But the converging railway lines, the busy motorway and a few industrial activities still in operation – including a wholesale market – made this proposal unrealistic: it would have meant waiting until everything had moved out before starting to redevelop the site. The new competition, which we won, therefore called for this composition to be revised to make the project operational, independently of the pilot project for the Saône river walkway.
Ten years later, we were awarded a new commission, this time with Herzog & de Meuron as master planners, to urbanise a specific area anticipated by previous plans. This area corresponded to the very large sector known as the *marché-gare* (wholesale market), and extended as far as the motorway on the Quai du Rhône. I remained the landscape architect for this sector. The idea of the park was revived, this time in a district of different density. The master plan included the renovation of a number of existing buildings. The inhabited park continued towards the tip, running beyond the limit of the urban grid, between the railway lines, which in the end were integrated, and the motorway (decommissioned in 2016).

Confluence 1

Originally, the intention of the then mayor, Raymond Barre, was to create such attractive city-centre living and working conditions on the peninsula that young households would forget about moving to suburban housing estates. Our first significant decision, with Grether, was to abolish Bohigas' partitioning of the site into zones, in favour of what we labelled a "ramified park", which could expand as land was gradually freed, and establish intimate, new relationships between public spaces and the future built environment. We proposed to progressively establish strands or "filaments" of vegetation running towards the interior of the peninsula, perpendicular to the Saône quay. Some of these would even be temporary, to give public surfaces status. Ultimately, the whole "ramified park" system would connect each of the plots defined by these planted paths to a garden or a passageway leading to the Saône park, the centrepiece of the plan.
These principles then had to be translated into urban and landscaping rules for the architects and landscape architects who would be implementing them. We revised the proposal

Top: aerial view of the peninsula at the beginning of the redevelopment. At the confluence of the Saône (to the west) and the Rhône (to the east), this still-industrial territory is criss-crossed by active railway lines. The tip is truncated by the *Autoroute du Soleil* (A7), the motorway linking Lyon to Marseille, which runs along the quay to the north, on the Rhône side. To the north of the park, one can make out the regular grid of the abandoned wholesale market, at the end of the harbour basin being dug on the Saône side.
Bottom: schematic diagrams illustrating how the "ramified park" would take form over time. As the plots free up, the planted strip along the Saône embankment penetrates inwards and blends with the built spaces.

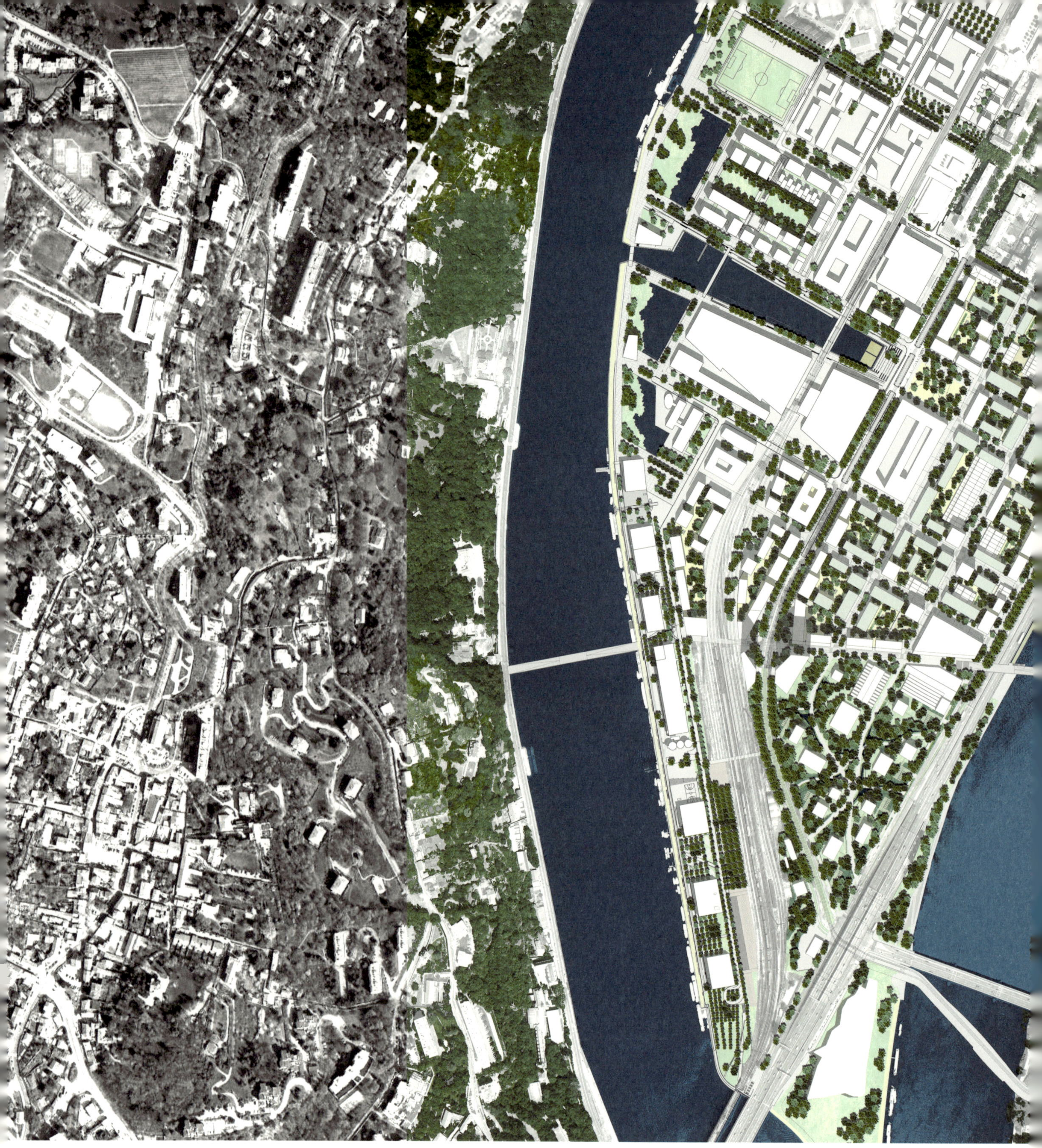

Cumulative massing plan of developments on the peninsula. Transformed into an urban boulevard equipped with a tramway, the Cours Charlemagne runs from Perrache train station and connects the two successive sectors undergoing development: to the west, Confluence 1 (master plan: François Grether); to the east, Confluence 2 (master plan: Herzog & de Meuron). The project site extends to the park on the tip of the peninsula.
On the Saône side, the choice of an urban plan centred on large

objects ("Le Monolithe" housing complex, shopping and leisure centre, Regional Council building, etc.) rendered MDP's proposal for an incremental "ramified park" obsolete. Along the riverbank promenade, aquatic gardens (landscape architects: Georges and Julien Descombes) extend laterally to the foot of the large urban blocks, on either side of the harbour basin, structuring the public spaces.

In contrast, on the Rhône side, the second phase develops an urbanism of small open blocks, which combine buildings of varying heights and fragments of the former wholesale market. At the junction with the harbour basin, this district is linked to the Cours Charlemagne by the "central square". The landscape project proposes varying degrees of tree cover, with tree plantings colonising all public spaces in various densities: squares, streets, passages, accessible courtyards and so on. In the south, the buildings are scattered throughout the heavily planted landscape of an "inhabited park".

to make it operational over time, in step with the gradual release of the plots. This six-year mission was initially renewed for a further ten years. The client allowed us to design the project to an extent that went well beyond the usual brief of a project management assistant. The choice of contractors was discussed at length. Georges and Julien Descombes were selected for the public spaces of the first phase. They sought to closely interpret our intention, and even enriched it. Further south, on the strip between the railways and the Saône, Peter Latz implemented our prescriptions more romantically. However, the initial project was only partially realised, as it was undermined by the programme imposed by the City – digging a harbour basin at great cost, construction of a major shopping and leisure centre, etc. – as well as the consulting process to allocate the very large blocks to developers. The result looks less like a hand with extended fingers than a series of green patches left in front of the urban blocks.

This page: general and detailed plans of the landscape principles developed for the banks of the Saône. The waterfront promenade runs alongside a series of "aquatic gardens", flanked on one side by the large wet zones of the gardens and on the other by the river. These ecosystems are separated from the bases of the buildings by paved pathways. To the north of the harbour basin, the gardens continue into the courtyards of the housing blocks, vestiges of the ramified park idea in which vegetation and buildings were closely associated. Opposite page: some views of the developments carried out according to these principles by the Geneva-based landscape architects Georges and Julien Descombes. The harbour basin occupies the centre of the large, mineral Place Nautique, spanned by a footbridge. On the banks of the Saône, the stabilised walkway reserved for non-motorised transport is treated more naturalistically. It is separated from the road by strips of flowering grasses, or by benches. The riverbank atmosphere is accentuated by the presence of bargemen; the quay is extended by small pontoons. In the "Saône Park", the ponds planted with reeds evoke the former landscape of the riverbanks; they are connected to the quays by stretches of meadow or by hard-surfaced squares, bordered by screens of trees.

Three variations of the landscaping principles of Confluence 2: top, a bird's-eye view of the central square (Esplanade François-Mitterrand); bottom left, a model of the plantings for the setbacks planned by Herzog & de Meuron in the street layout; right, a model of the planting principle in the courtyard gardens of the A2 block. Opposite: detailed plan of the blocks (A1, A2, A3) to the north and east of the central square. The landscape strategy is based on the continuity of the design (tree strata) between the public space (the plaza, the streets) and the cores of collective blocks allowing for public passage (in grey). The red arrows indicate entry points into closed courtyards.

Confluence 2

In the *marché-gare* district, Herzog & de Meuron opted for a "composition" in very dense open blocks. Their rule of thumb was to keep the street structure, along which they organised the buildings, modulating the volume and height of the latter in relation to hours of sunshine, views and a number of preserved buildings (about 30 per cent). For us, this "random systematism" was mirrored by a similar landscaping strategy: an abundance of vegetation, inside and outside the blocks, and three types of ground depending on the situation (courtyards, thresholds, streets).

The pathways are not strictly aligned, but punctuated by recesses and widenings that form mini-plazas precisely designed by Herzog & de Meuron: this is where we planted. Through the private spaces of the block interiors, we provided public passages wherever they were acceptable. These spaces form "courtyard gardens" with stabilised soil that lends itself to all kinds of uses. The large trees and the shrubbery at their feet occupy little surface area, but when seen in perspective, the "patches" they form suffice to give the impression of a garden. The streets are covered with sanded asphalt and the thresholds are made of *gorrhe*, the traditional decomposed granite of Lyon's public spaces. We applied the same principles when landscaping the central square, which extends the harbour basin at the entrance to the new district. It is one of the major urban spaces: its dimensions are comparable to those of the Place des Terreaux in the city centre.

At the tip, the "Champ" (Field) is structured by a network of paths bordered by hedges, which absorb the boundary with the plots and hide the car parks: the aim was to give the impression of a habitat scattered throughout a large park. A network of ditches inspired by the ancient meanders of the confluence provides flood protection and defines the limits between public and private spaces.

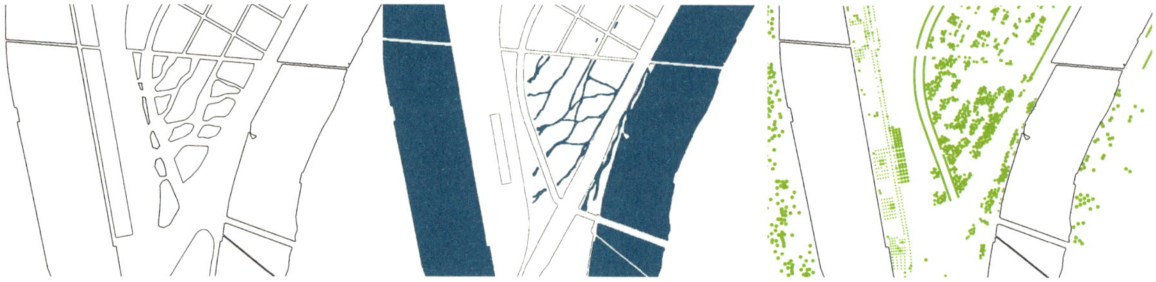

PARCELLES NOUES ARBRES

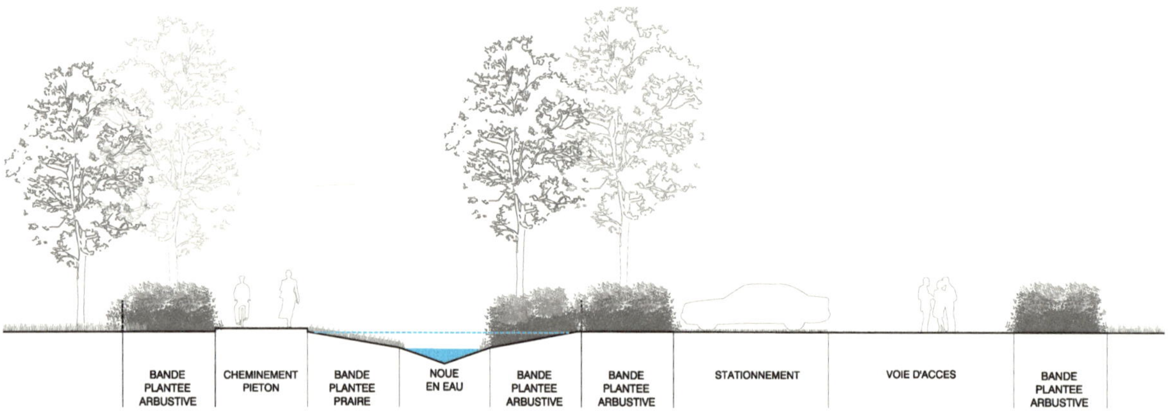

In the park on the tip (the "Champ"), the drainage ditch layout, the path network and the planting distribution are inspired by the old geography of this end of the peninsula, before stabilisation. In cross-section, the combination of these elements defines a system that combines wet swales with two types of traffic: pedestrian paths and access paths to urban blocks. At the edge of the parcels, a low band of shrub screens the car parks from the non-motorised pathways.

Opposite: general plan of the inhabited park. The network tightens as the site narrows towards the tip, in sync with the reduction in plot sizes and building footprints.

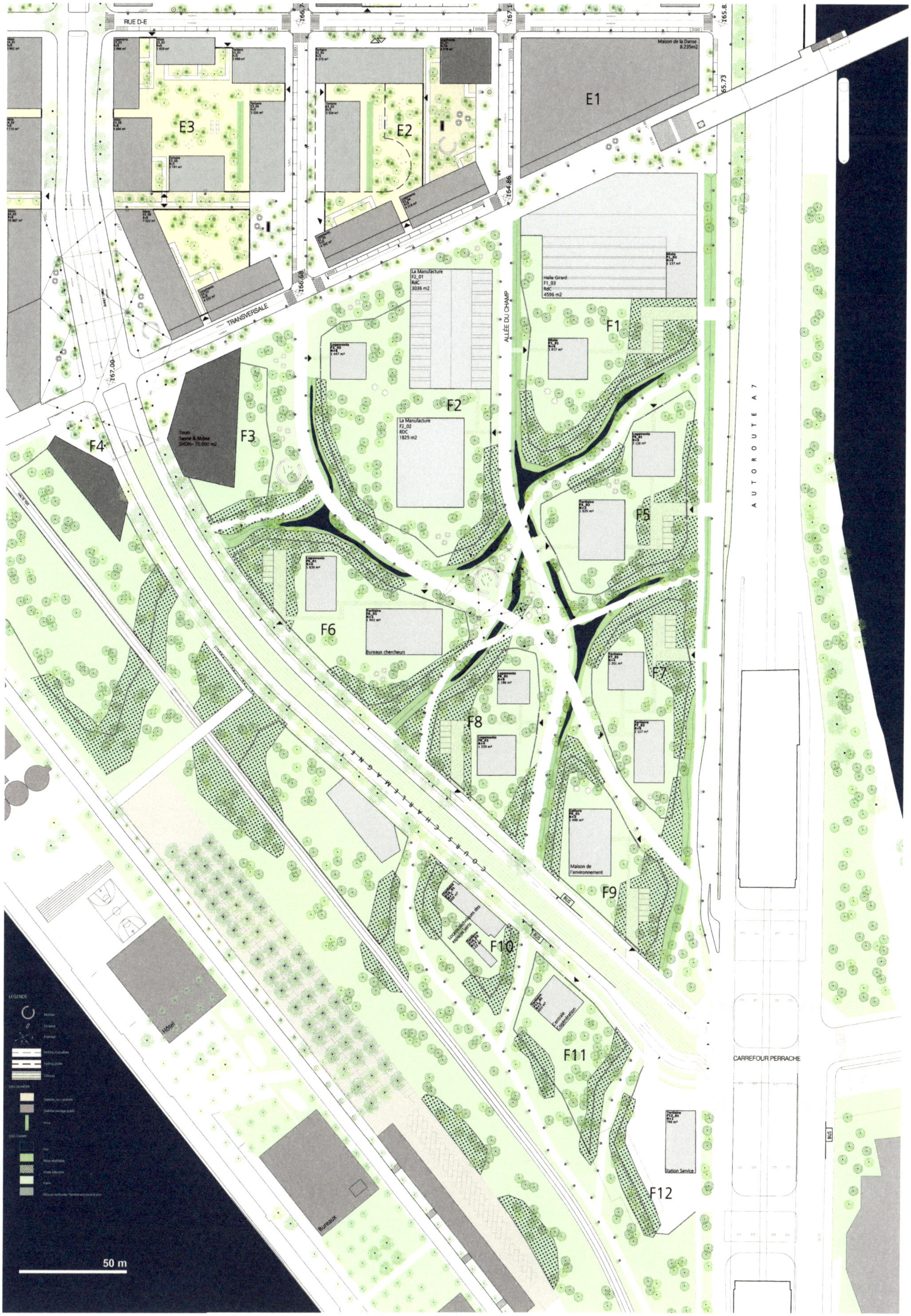
RUE D-E
Maison de la Danse
8.235m2
E1
E2
E3
TRANSVERSALE
La Manufacture
F2_01
RdC
3036 m2
Halle Girard
F1_03
RdC
4596 m2
ALLÉE DU CHAMP
F1
F2
La Manufacture
F2_02
RDC
1825 m2
Tour
Saone & Rhône
SHON= 70.000 m2
F3
F4
F5
F6
Bureaux chercheurs
F7
F8
F9
Maison de l'environnement
F10
F11
F12
Station Service
AUTOROUTE A7
COURS CHARLEMAGNE
CARREFOUR PERRACHE
BUS
Hôtel
Bureaux
LEGENDE
50 m

BORDEAUX RIVE DROITE
BORDEAUX, FRANCE, 2002–

Our involvement in the construction of public space on the right bank of the river Garonne has been a long-term process, spread over a series of commissions. It began in 2002 with the landscaping charter we drafted at the request of the City of Bordeaux. Drawing on enough case studies to make it sufficiently exhaustive, the method was experimental in the true sense of the term: it was based on intuitions developed in a number of real projects, in dialogue with the City's services. It gave rise to a set of guidelines that, ever since, have been followed by all planning stakeholders in Bordeaux. Shortly thereafter, in 2003, the City was due to review its local urbanisation plan (Plan local d'urbanisme, PLU). Making use of our experiment and in particular one of the ideas that emerged from it – the creation of a park in the city centre – the City asked us to conduct a case study on the waterfront of the right bank of the Garonne. In 2005, we were awarded a landscaping commission for this area alongside the urban planner and architect Bruno Fortier. This was followed in 2006 by a consultancy mission to study the progressive implementation of a landscaped park. In 2008, when one section of this park entered construction, we were appointed assistants to the client – the City – which was also the project manager. The planning of the Deschamps sector, further south, was subsequently entrusted to Christian de Portzamparc, with our team kept on as landscape architects. We provided project management assistance for certain sectors of the Angéliques Park, then won a competition that extended this mission to other operational sectors – Queyries, Brazza – both to manage the phases already implemented by the City's services and to oversee new phases of construction work.

On the right bank, the City reclassified constructible land and purchased other plots, guided by the conviction that a very large urban-scale park should be built along the river – on a 6 kilometre long site. We had imagined a whole series of ramifications extending inland to structure the new districts. This park is not just a green band: it also incorporates massive strips of industrial land. Dominique Perrault, who was consulted before us about part of this territory, had proposed exactly the same urban development strategy as for the Bastide district. At first, I contrasted, somewhat assertively, the geographical vision – a large body of vegetation on the scale of the river – with a more historicising vision of a project built on the traces of the site's industrial heritage. I considered that the latter was of little importance compared with the strength of the natural geography of the river, which it was essential to take into account at its scale.

At the time, Alain Juppé was a frequent visitor to North America; he was familiar with the park systems that each major American city had built along its river in the nineteenth century. The parallel with our strategy was obvious. In Bordeaux, a deep green façade would both mirror and act as counterpoint to the famous mineral façade that had been steadily extending along the Garonne's left bank since the eighteenth century. Since it was not possible to compete with this historical coherence, since we are condemned to eclecticism in architecture, vegetation could give the right bank a homogeneity equivalent to that of the dense city. Alain Juppé used the term "green airbag". The deepening of the river channel had caused alluvium to settle on the convex part of the bank; it is in this environment that vegetation tends to develop most naturally. It was therefore not absurd to propose that the city adopt these two contrasting faces. This resulted in a modification of the local urbanisation plan, which delisted some 50 hectares and made them unbuildable so that the land could become a park. It was a great victory to have convinced the mayor, against the advice of all his planners and advisors, to give up these constructible sites along the river when everything was already designed.

Bordeaux at the beginning of the twenty-first century: the right bank, between the river Garonne and the railway line, which, to the east, delimits the industrial and port sector; the Bastide district has been in decline since the 1970s. Industrial buildings were constructed on former rural plots: the large plots cut into strips perpendicular to the river still contain some warehouses. Signs of the city's reappropriation of this territory began to appear in the southern part of the enclave, on the Quai des Queyries, such as the botanical garden (landscape architect: Catherine Mosbach) and the mixed development zone of La Bastide (architect: Ateliers Lion). Opposite, on the left bank: the train station in the south, and, above it, the Place des Quinconces, the Quai des Chartrons and the former wine district; in the north, the wet docks and the submarine base. The quays of the centre have not yet been refurbished by Michel Corajoud.

Park project on the right bank. Opposite the dense historic city on the left bank, the Bastide district is made up of large, irregular buildings on vast plots. The railway line, two major

avenues and the chain of wooded slopes delimit the successive contours to the east.
Along the river, the planting programme penetrates into the industrial strips as they are acquired by the City. The Angéliques Park thus forms a thick green front on the Garonne, which contrasts with the "city of stone" on the opposite bank and unifies the various divisions of the urban plan to the rear. These adjoining operations will be developed one by one by urban planners, in principle around the green branches intended to extend the structure of the park inland.

To the north, at the arrival point of the new Jacques Chaban-Delmas Bridge, the Brazza district (urban planner: Youssef Tohmé) extends its broad tree-lined avenues perpendicular to the river.

The river landscape before the redevelopment project in 2003. The scheduled termination of industrial and port activities has begun to change the historical relationship between the two parts of the city. On the right bank, their departure gradually freed up a vast territory, still underused; on the left bank, freeing up the quays of the "city of stone" to create a new public space (landscape architect: Michel Corajoud) gives access to the water and opens distant views towards the wooded hills.

The proposal to establish, in the long term, a park generating public space that will become the landscape horizon of the left bank is based on these two observations.
Double page, from left to right.
Top row: seen from the left bank, the opposite bank still mixes industrial buildings and the relief of the riparian forest; upstream, facing the historic city, housing developments testify to the first attempts to reclaim this territory. On the right, the Pont de Pierre (Stone Bridge).
Middle row: downstream, seen from the abandoned Quai de Brazza, the Aquitaine Bridge provides a crossing for the motorway while avoiding the quays; the panorama of the historic city shows the persistent disparity between the two sides of the river.
Bottom row: in the Queyries business park, the landscape is fragmented by the last remaining warehouses and their enclosures, between service roads that are often in a state of disrepair.

BORDEAUX RIVE DROITE / BORDEAUX, FRANCE, 2002–

At the same time, we had imagined that behind this riverbank strip, the district could be fleshed out by following the pattern of partitions bequeathed by the former industrial activities. We planted as soon as a fragment became available, creating a structure that might or might not be modified during the subsequent construction phase (the plots were not all freed up at the same time, however a calendar existed in which their probable availability dates were specified). In this way, the urban development would retain the imprint of the conversion process. Since it was a long process, we would use the opportunity to give a landscape presence to these liberated spaces.

Landscape and prototype charter

Traditional urban planning tools – the combination of massing plans and regulations – are rendered ineffective by the complexity of the territory. We preferred a method that combines case studies with the drafting of an empirically tested charter through full-scale mock-ups. We were immediately able to produce full-scale prototypes that were displayed to the public on site. They served to define an aesthetic as the basis of a shared culture. The conclusions of the experiment replaced traditional regulatory documents.

Opposite page: comprehensive map of Bordeaux with, in red, the parcels concerned by the "landscape charter". The Angéliques Park is one of the pieces of a landscaping project conceived as a series of case studies. To the north, between the lake, the botanical garden and the Garonne, the project seeks to reinforce the existing wooded framework. Prototypes were tested, in particular for the refurbishment of the car park at the entrance to the botanical garden (this page). The asphalt surface was landscaped using screens of trees planted in deep draining trenches. This structure extends to the neighbouring plot of land, for the parking area around the new stadium (architect: Herzog & de Meuron), treated according to the same principles.

Angéliques Park

Part of the land purchased by the City is set aside for a park that is not supposed to be "pretty". It functions practically as a forest, extending either side of a large paved road that was preserved in agreement with Bruno Fortier. The plots needed to be decontaminated one by one and planted gradually. Afforestation is a partial solution to this problem: by sequestering some of the soil, it postpones decontamination to when these areas will be reopened to the public. In the industrial territory, broad tree lines are being planted, a strategy that also functions as a water management method. All over the site, there are water channels dating back to the seventeenth-century drainage work conducted by Flemish engineers. Equipped with a flap at their end, they allowed water to be drained into the river at low tide and prevented it from rising up into the land at high tide. We adopted this economy of means (we have an annual maintenance budget of just €1 million, a pittance for a 75 hectare park) and followed the same logic with this programme of rural planting, which legibly alternates "rooms" and masses as one walks along the central path: one moves from volume to void, as if passing a sequence of backdrops.

It is not a false nature, but literally a kind of agriculture, which constructs an explicitly artificial forest mass but on such a scale that it becomes a natural geography. This forest system will very obviously display how old it is, which is not a negative thing, since it makes this very empirical physical process readable. The ages of the plantings will be determined by the release of parcels over time. Their different growth stages will turn it into a mosaic, as in any logged forest.

Opposite page: in the Angéliques Park, paths running perpendicular to the Garonne, lined by poplars, offer views of the river, the protected riverbank vegetation that borders it, and the city. Further north, small, water-based recreational activities are sited along the riverbank.
This page: representation of the park on the right bank in a south-facing aerial view. The riverbank park branches into the new neighbourhoods to the rear, as far as the railway line. The curtain-like planting pattern is structured by the site's narrow parcels.
In the foreground, the new Jacques Chaban-Delmas Bridge links the area of the wet docks on the left bank to the Brazza district; top right, we recognise the Place des Quinconces and, further upstream, the historic Stone Bridge, which links the Bastide to the city centre.

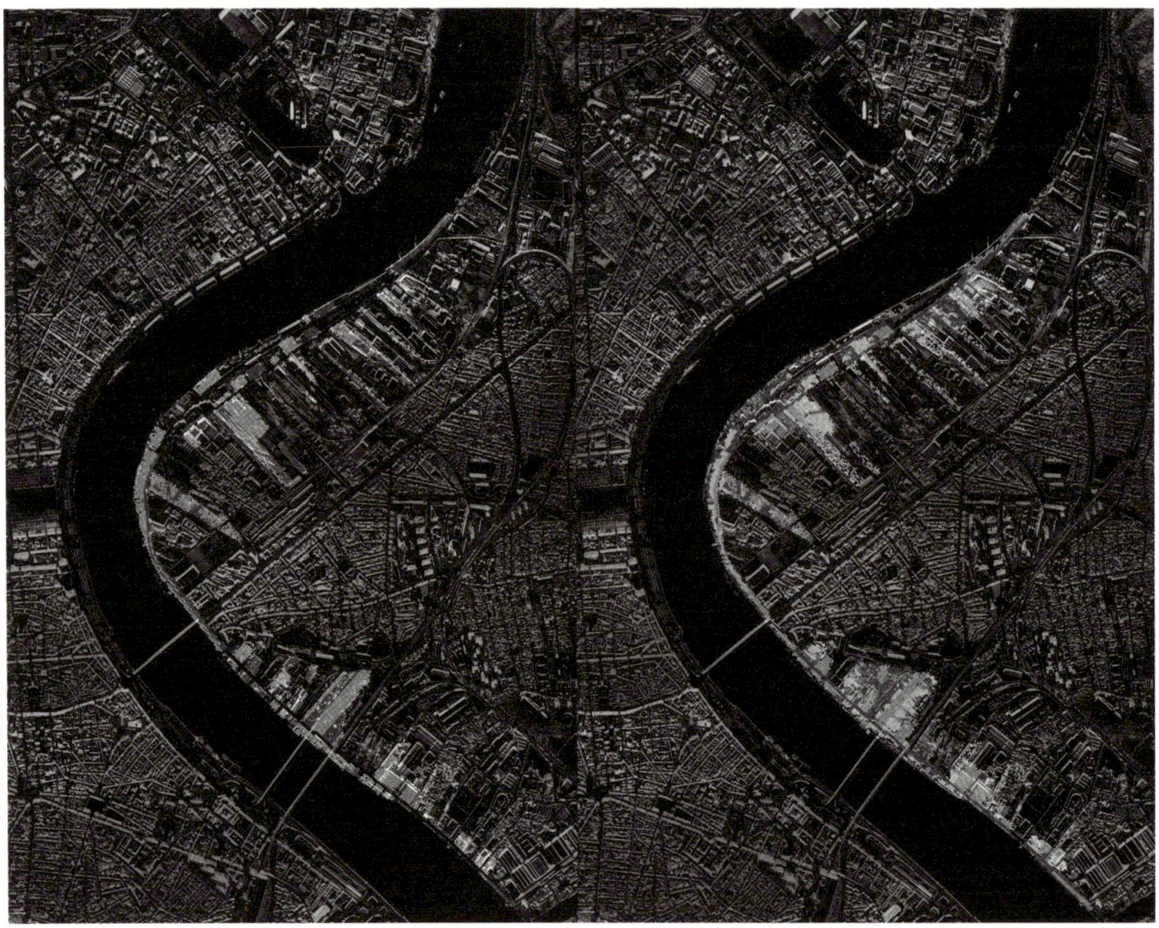

This page: first drawings of the "incremental" transformation process of the old industrial fabric into a ramified park: at the scale of the entire Bastide (bottom), and at the more detailed scale of the Brazza Quay (top).
The landscape project is not based on a phased process, but on the superposition and accumulation of layers of intervention over time. The landscape samples and their abstraction into graphic grids show, in three steps, the anticipated thickening of their textures and grain (aerial photos: Alex MacLean).

Opposite page: the process of densifying the landscape over time involves successive technical steps, site preparation, the creation of nurseries, the construction of paths and plantings, and the establishment of maintained or wild grassy or flowery meadows.

BORDEAUX RIVE DROITE / BORDEAUX, FRANCE, 2002–

Programming method

While work was already underway on the Queyries sequence, the start of the Brazza sequence was delayed by the question of how to programme the park. The six project stakeholders had been asked to list the activities they wished to include on the site. There were so many that they took over the entire public space, leaving little room to establish continuity with the Queyries sequence in terms of vegetation, or to include the essential pedestrian connections with the car parks. The planted surfaces were shrinking away to nothing. To maintain a balance, we set out a few principles: prioritising park-specific programmes and water-related activities; preserving and extending all non-motorised routes; creating public reception areas of various sizes; limiting soil sealing to 25 per cent of surfaces; establishing a 40/60 ratio between activities and "free" spaces. We built mock-ups to help the decision-making process. In each case, in an empirical approach, we proposed a non-definitive representation of the requested activities, which made it possible to visualise the issues at stake. This tool for reflection, in which the various pieces could be moved around, made it possible to arbitrate between contradictory or conflicting uses in this limited space.

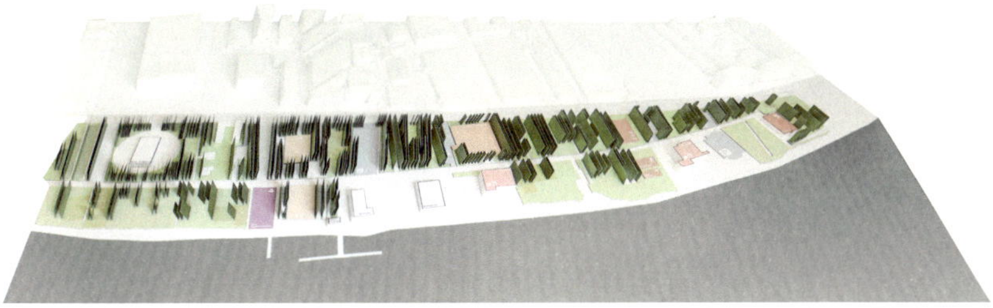

Opposite page: summary plan of the entire Angéliques Park showing the evolution of the project. The need to incorporate activities has transformed the language of "textures" initially envisaged for the park; the scheme has changed to take the functional surfaces into account. The drawing inscribes in space the decisions resulting from the consultation.

This page: examples of site representations using the consultation mock-up. Identification of the uses requested on the Brazza sequence by the various stakeholders (top) and programming proposal (middle). In pink, from left to right: site to host circuses, event esplanade and large open area; small open area and car park; park management building and project information centre, urban farm, sports facilities. Large open areas accompany the tree-lined paths. Three panoramic viewpoints are spaced out along the riverbank at regular intervals.
Below: mock-up of existing uses on the Queyries sequence and revision after programming, drawing on the lessons of the Brazza sequence. The need to incorporate activities led to a multiplication and refinement of the planted "backdrops". Guest houses, restaurants, skate parks etc. (in orange) remain scattered throughout the park; events, water sports and leisure activities are grouped in a cluster on the riverbank (in blue).

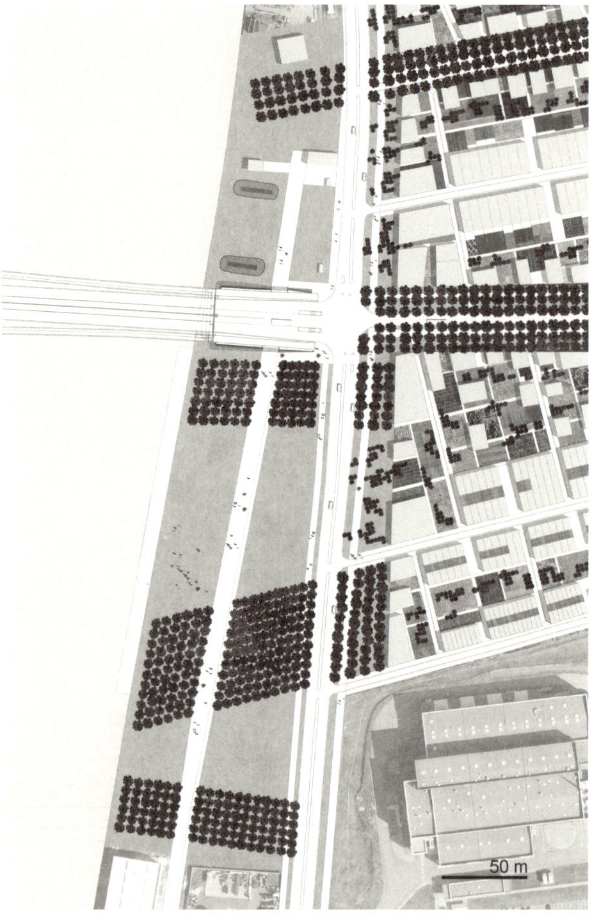

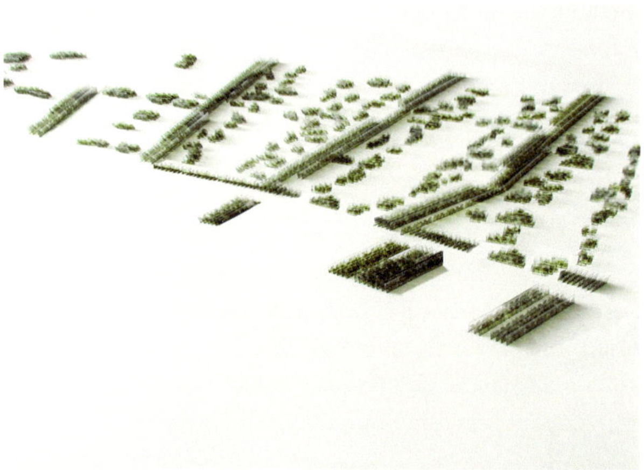

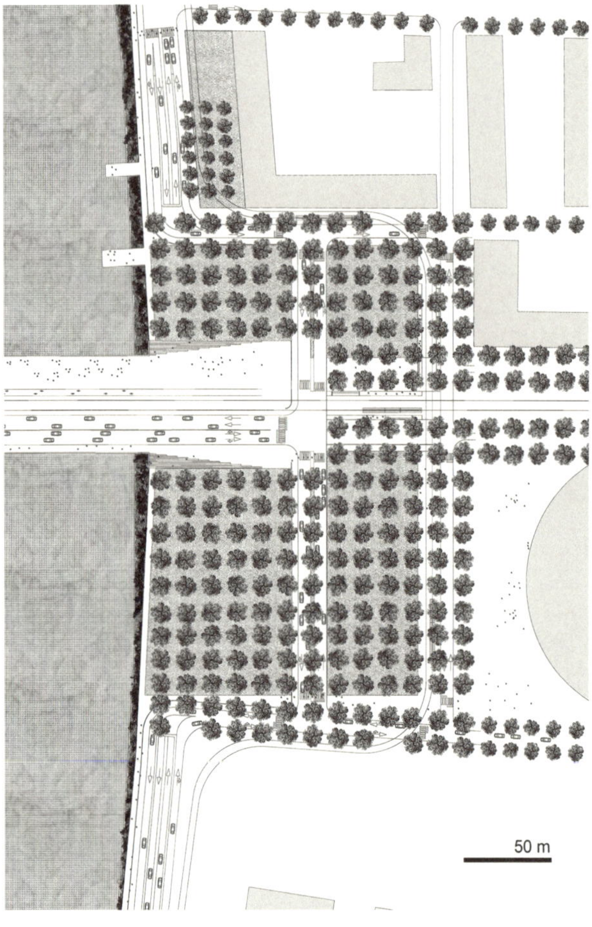

BORDEAUX RIVE DROITE / BORDEAUX, FRANCE, 2002–

Brazza district / Simone Veil Bridge

In 2013, along with urbanist Youssef Tohmé, we won the competition for the Brazza sector, located in the north of Bordeaux. Up to this point, most planners consulted for the other districts had not really understood the common interest of this obvious heritage – linked to the hydraulic system, itself the basis of the local agriculture, and subsequently to the industrial history that developed within these agrarian structures. Instead, they tended to emphasise what they considered to be stronger ideas. This time, on the contrary, the existing division of the land into strips determined the layout design for the future development. Its plan is structured around three avenues running perpendicular to the river, which reinforce the landscape grid while preserving the views on the left bank. The Angéliques Park thus seems to have taken over the interior of the Brazza district. The avenues are flanked by large lawns accommodating a wide variety of uses. Connecting streets provide access to the communal gardens inserted between the strips.

Then in 2014, the OMA team, which we were part of, won the competition for the new bridge that will complete the loop of Bordeaux's boulevards to the south. MDP was tasked with designing the landings. Treated as a broad platform, the bridge connects to land through two public spaces that reflect the contextual asymmetry of the two banks: one more rural, the other more urban.

Opposite page: plan of the arrival of the Chaban-Delmas Bridge in the Brazza Nord district, mock-up illustrating the principle of structuring the site through planting, and representation of a fragment of the sector. Amenities on stilts alternate with housing along paved streets that cross through the district longitudinally. Some plots are left free to encourage unplanned uses. The wooded landscape extends into communal and individual gardens; groves of trees frame views and also align visual connections between neighbouring buildings.

Plan of the Simone Veil Bridge "landing" on the right bank and view of the proposed landscape: the river can be viewed through the grid of a tall poplars with bare trunks planted alongside the bicycle and pedestrian paths. On the opposite bank, a park composed of a series of groves participates in the restoration of the natural riverfront.

This page: the crossing created by the Simone Veil Bridge (architect: OMA) completes the loop of boulevards connecting Bordeaux's two banks.

PLANTS AS A WORKING MATERIAL

Learning to work proficiently with plants has more to do with personal choice than a deductive process. It all started for me in my grandmother's garden in the suburbs of Lyon, when I was a student in natural sciences. Where her henhouse used to stand, I had planted a large thicket of birches, with creeping honeysuckles at their feet – twenty years later, the garden for Renzo Piano's apartment building on the Rue de Meaux in Paris drew from the same fundamental intuition. I also practised a lot in my parents' garden. In the Rhône Valley the soil is stony and it gets very hot in summer: it is impossible to have a lawn, a meadow, or green grass. I had a physical attachment to the many trees I planted at that time.

It instilled an affinity for tree-planting in me, later reinforced when I was learning my trade under the influence of Jacques Simon, a highly inspired character who used tree-planting a great deal in his work. His background was in forestry and photography. He used to plant very dense, miniature woodlands; trees leaning to the side to mimic the effect of the wind, with a magnificent graphic effect; parks that played with circular, perfectly geometric clearings, surrounded by extremely freely planted woods. There could even be a certain brutality to the way he used plants. He would plant one or two species of any kind very densely and in very large quantities, like one finds on railway embankments, playing on volumes and light, without any botanical pretensions. His tree farms were quite similar to the forest plantings of the 1970s, more concerned with production than with creating a living environment. Michel Corajoud was very interested in what Jacques Simon was doing and quickly reinforced and diversified this type of approach through the use of consultants. The Sausset Park in Villepinte, north of Paris, Corajoud's masterpiece of forest park design, demonstrates complexity in its treatment of boundaries and a great knowledge of botany, all the while remaining a small-scale forest sculpted by paths, combining visual, spatial and material components.

Botanically poor plantings can accommodate a lot of spontaneous diversity. In the temporary garden on the Île Seguin on the river Seine, for reasons of economy, we only planted willows; they attracted all kinds of parasitic plants. The Walker Center garden in Minneapolis, one of whose sections we designed, was conceived as a scaled-down version of the Minnesota landscape. It combined planting patterns based on the Jefferson Grid, and other more random systems related to topography; it varied the densities of one or other of these categories, giving rise to infinite modulations in texture. Even a single species can create great variety. Planted trees are a material with a porosity and degree of transparency that can be controlled. I like production forests, such as poplar nurseries, and playing with these systematised plantings. They change by themselves as they grow and a form emerges as they evolve over time. I am fascinated by indetermination, by randomness, where only one adult subject will emerge from one hundred saplings. When you plant very densely along a perfectly orthogonal grid, as some foresters do, the selection process that takes place over the long term means that the geometric order disappears, in favour of an afforestation whose origin can no longer necessarily be detected. The intention is not to produce a false nature, but an almost agricultural-type planting that will gradually acquire a natural form due to the way it is managed. It's about playing on artifice in the hope that the mechanisms of natural reconquest will trigger a process of colonisation gradually leading to an inversion of the starting point: traces of alignment in a forest that seems "natural". These formal games with plants, used as a raw material, always worry our clients somewhat, who fear that the trees will not have enough room to breathe. I study every forest I come across: I photograph them, I measure them, I look for evidence that this practice of dense planting works. On the border between Michigan and Canada, on a miners' island, there is a forest where trees are planted 30 centimetres apart. They can live this way for a very long time, packed extremely tightly. In France, in the traditional language of the park, the tree tends to be seen as a *subject*, and this mass is difficult to accept. In Germany and Russia, on the other hand, they plant very densely, without fear that massing will crush the individual trees.

In some small gardens, complex environments can be recreated in their richness, even if it means distorting them, adding a few species and embellishing them. In Lens, the wooded strips we planted will thin out depending on how the trees develop, radicalising the artificial device. This will enrich the colonisation we set in motion and facilitate the fertilisation of the grid, exaggerating each aspect somewhat. Artifice can also be overcome through use. The car park of the Alésia museum park was planted in a highly orthogonal, offset pattern, but drivers did not follow the circulation plan; the grass, reinforced by a stony substratum, was not enough to stabilise the soil, it was used too intensely due to high visitor numbers. We will therefore redesign the circulation plan following the outline of the car routes, which will blur the geometry of the temporary forest, in the same way as paths do in the countryside.

The objective is clearly to build places that are immediately usable and will continue to be so for a long time to come. In Bordeaux, the trees are planted along lines parallel to the parcel boundaries to constitute a radiator-like pattern that will eventually become a wooded area. This system defines relatively simple clearings that have immediate appeal. Their use or dimensioning was not very precisely imagined, but the density and forms applied allow for a multitude of situations where everyone can find something to suit: a comfortably sized setting, a clearing for a picnic, etc. Like in some spot in the countryside, there's no one telling what you are supposed to do or where to do it. Locals have embraced this lack of sophistication in the design – willows and poplars, lines of very durable perennial pin oaks, and a few rows of ornamental fruit trees, combined with rustic flowering meadows to bring a little animation and colour from the outset.

In response to increasingly pressing demands to over-programme public space, I insist on this non-determination. In our interventions, to create this multiplicity of situations, which should be meaningful in relation to the territory as well as to its history while generating potential use, we need clients who agree to play this game, who understand it, and who have a long-term vision. The city of Montpellier gave us the opportunity to conduct a number of experiments over the past twenty-five years: first with Christine Dalnoky, for the planting of 14,000 umbrella pines; recently, for Charpak Park, where, we began by designing wooded areas around a flood reservoir, later adding further wooded areas, then tree lines, then groves, where a wetland area is being created. Our clients have had us come back periodically to accompany the evolution of the site.

The landscape is a precondition. Very strong structures are created through planting, and buildings then find their place in this structure pieced together from the observation of a larger territory. One of our gardens on the outskirts of Milan is inspired by the Po plain and how it is structured by lines of trees – a plant landscape of boundaries, which, like the walls of a cell, end up forming a landscape. Forests and plant alignments are components in the material composition of the territory on a very large scale. This is clear to see when driving on the N7 from Paris to the south of France, or when walking along the canals of Burgundy, or on the Place des Quinconces in Bordeaux, with its regular grid of plane trees and in which all kinds of uses have long been established. These are very large masses, disproportionate to the volume of the buildings. In peripheral, diluted or destitute territories, our landscapes may be taking on a role in relation to architecture that urban planning has held for a very long time. Plant volumes can impart coherence to isolated buildings, in a kind of recomposition that will make these territories more liveable. This is precisely what is at stake in Saclay: on this plateau, the large buildings built by the architects seem lost in the agricultural territory, even though they are sometimes 200 or 300 metres long! They need a horizon that unites them, that transcends their accumulation. This horizon is linked to the wooded hills that can be read from the plateau as well as from the valley. Based on the distances involved, we designed it in space, in its length, height and volume, while incorporating rhythms and anticipating tree growth. In the more homogeneous, fully formed city, built-up areas are first perceived in terms of masses, then buildings; in the periphery, on the other hand, one sees buildings that seem to have no connection to any collective dimension. Vegetation is what adds this dimension to freestanding constructions.

The danger would be to believe that plants alone suffice, and to turn this into a standardised approach. In Bordeaux, initially, I was more interested in reconstructing a riparian woodland along this age-old river than in revealing the traces of a few decades of industrial activity. In the end, the idea of the forest had the effect of broadening the reflection to the scale of the river and, in this broader perspective, we were able to take the traces of the industrial past into account.

PARIS-SACLAY CLUSTER
SACLAY PLATEAU, GRAND PARIS, FRANCE, 2009–

In 2009, we won the international competition for the project management of the Paris-Saclay urban development plan as lead consultant for a team including urban planners Floris Alkemade (FAA) and Xaveer de Geyter (XDGA). The competition brief was to extend and strengthen this higher education and research site with the aim of transforming it into a hub of the future Grand Paris, linked to central Paris and the services and working zones of the Yvelines and Essonne departments through the expansion of the public transport network.
The Saclay Plateau extends over an area of 5,000 hectares of highly fertile land elevated above valleys to which it is connected by wooded slopes. Fifteen per cent of French scientific research was already located in this area: the CEA (French Atomic Energy Commission) in a facility built in the 1960s, designed by Auguste Perret; the Supélec engineering school; and, since 1973, the École Polytechnique, the Soleil Synchrotron research lab and the Danone research centre among other institutions, and many large objects that appeared on the landscape one by one, somewhat in isolation and difficult to understand. When viewed from a great height, this landscape appeared essentially agricultural; however it was not at all an area of open fields. Its dimensions were very intimidating: we were being asked to think about the future of a territory spanning over 30 kilometres... The whole difficulty lay in *accommodation*: finding the right scale at which to engage with the landscape was not self-evident.
A number of projects had already been realised by French urban designers for the southern part of the plateau. Starting from existing construction, they had produced massing plans ranging from 7 to 8 kilometres in length. However, these fixed plans did not seem capable of endowing these districts with a long-term structure. We preferred the idea of progressively managing the urban development through its infrastructure, in reference to the western extension of Washington, carried out between 1900 and 1950 by Olmsted Jr. The dimensions of Georgetown's university district are comparable to those of the southern Saclay Plateau. At a time when industrial development was causing cities to expand at a rapid pace, Olmsted Jr. worked from an inventory of natural geography to superimpose vast landscape continua over the Jefferson grid, creating a kind of framework for large networks to pass through. He took valleys carved by rivers and made them into parks where people circulate. This amplified geography still works today. The trees have grown, but the legibility of the layout remains extraordinary: water collection, cars, cyclists, pedestrians, everything flows through the valley. The engineering, road and servicing decisions are consistent with the landscape, which confers a logic on the whole.
While these principles are excellent, design matters too. The natural geography of the Île de France is not spectacular; its minimal presence must be preserved and reinforced. It was necessary to establish physical coherence at the scale of the plateau without neglecting the different intermediate levels we were working on simultaneously. We therefore defined three scales of landscape intervention: that of the entire territory (7,700 hectares over a distance of 30 kilometres), that of the urban campus (650 hectares over a distance of 8 kilometres), and that of the neighbourhoods (200–300 hectares over a distance of 2.5 kilometres). These nested scales correspond to the three missions initially entrusted to our project management group: an intervention strategy for the entire plateau, a framework for the development of the southern fringe (the city-campus) and an urban planning mission for the École Polytechnique district.

Aerial view of the "intermediate landscape" under construction, on the edge of the south campus. The land preserved as an ecological compensation for the construction of the cluster forms a large urban park. A chain of retention basins crossed by planted avenues models the space between the reinforced wooded edges (on the left) and, on the right, the École Polytechnique campus, which is currently being densified. In the foreground, the circular buildings of the EDF laboratory (architect: Francis Soler); behind, the comb plan of the Danone research centre. On the upper right, we can make out the twin "horns" of the École Polytechnique lake, which is now part of the new water network.

The Saclay Plateau in the geography of Grand Paris. At the top of the image, one can recognise the capital in the meanders of the Seine, the Eiffel Tower and La Défense; on the left, Versailles, whose fountains and canals drew their water from the plateau's drainage network. Surrounded by wooded slopes, this largely agricultural territory dominates the valleys of the Yvette (to the south) and the Bièvre (to the north). Vélizy, Trappes, Saint-Quentin-en-Yvelines, Palaiseau, Orsay and Gif-sur-Yvette complete the circle of urban entities that surround this vast protected open space.
The Paris-Saclay project, defined as an operation of national interest (OIN) in 2006, covers

7,700 hectares. Its core is the "urban campus" that extends south of the plateau for over 7 kilometres (the same distance from the Louvre to La Défense) between the École Polytechnique (1) and the CEA (2); it incorporates the vast campus of Université Paris-Sud, on the plateau and in the valley (3), as well as that of the National Centre for Scientific Research (CNRS) in Gif-sur-Yvette (4).
The aerial view represents, in white, the archipelago of compact complexes constructed for the south campus by urban planners, each on its own plot: from right to left, the École Polytechnique (230 ha), Corbeville (90 ha) and Moulon (330 ha) districts. This density frees up an "intermediate landscape" between the protected agricultural and natural areas and along them, a thick, programmed border to compose a system of parks that is gradually being implemented.

PARIS-SACLAY CLUSTER / SACLAY PLATEAU, GRAND PARIS, FRANCE, 2009–

Opposite page: collage maps illustrating the natural geography and its wooded continuities (top), as well as the respective proportions of agricultural and urbanised areas (bottom).
This page: the landscapes of the plateau give rise to the coexistence of agricultural territories, marked by the technologies necessary for their exploitation (water management), university or research sites, and service infrastructures.
From top to bottom: a field of crops and the Saclay pond; the École Polytechnique, facing its lake, and the edge of the plateau, seen from west to east, showing the Soleil Synchrotron research lab, Saint-Aubin and the CEA (architect: Auguste Perret) in the foreground; a landscaped road on the plateau near the École Polytechnique, and the A road (RN 118) that links the Yvette valley to Paris-Porte de Saint-Cloud via the Saclay Plateau.

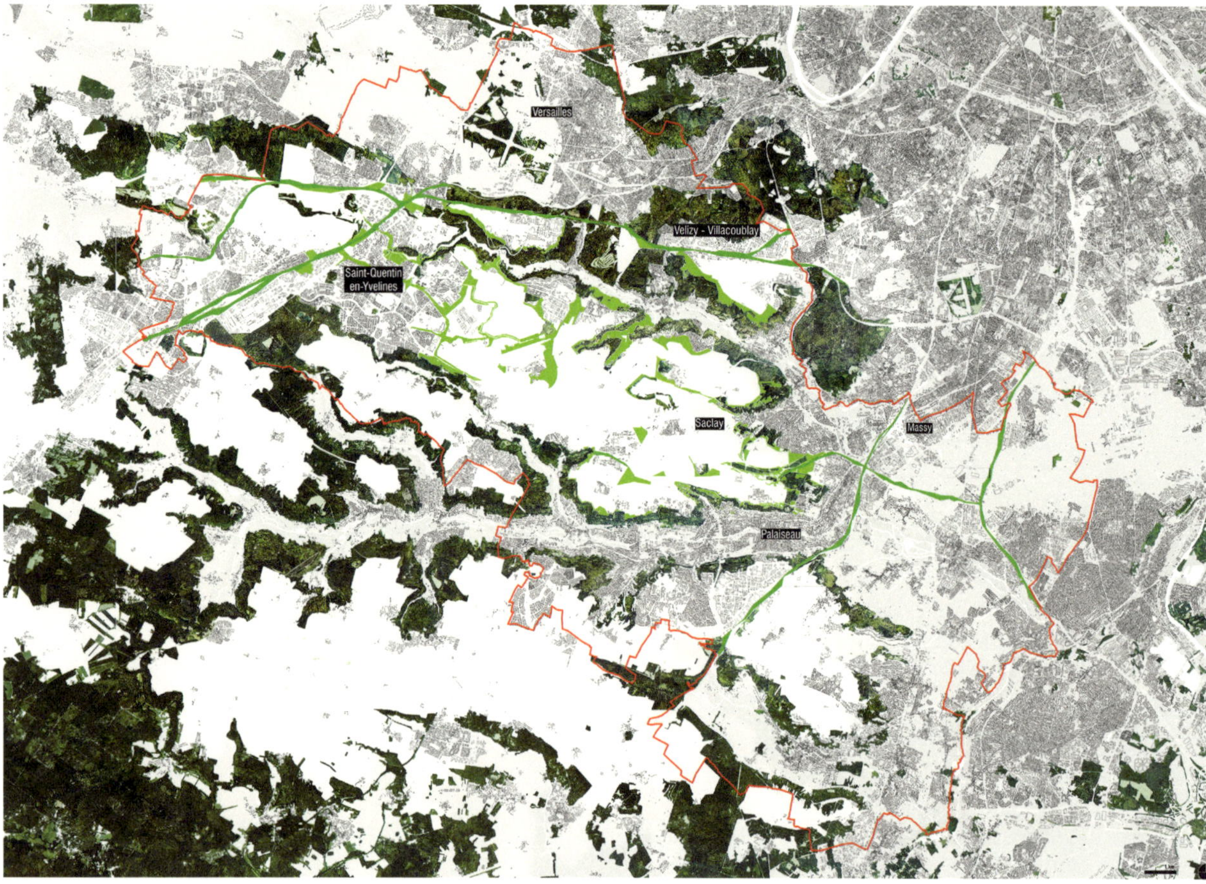
Versailles
Velizy - Villacoublay
Saint-Quentin
en-Yvelines
Saclay
Massy
Palaiseau

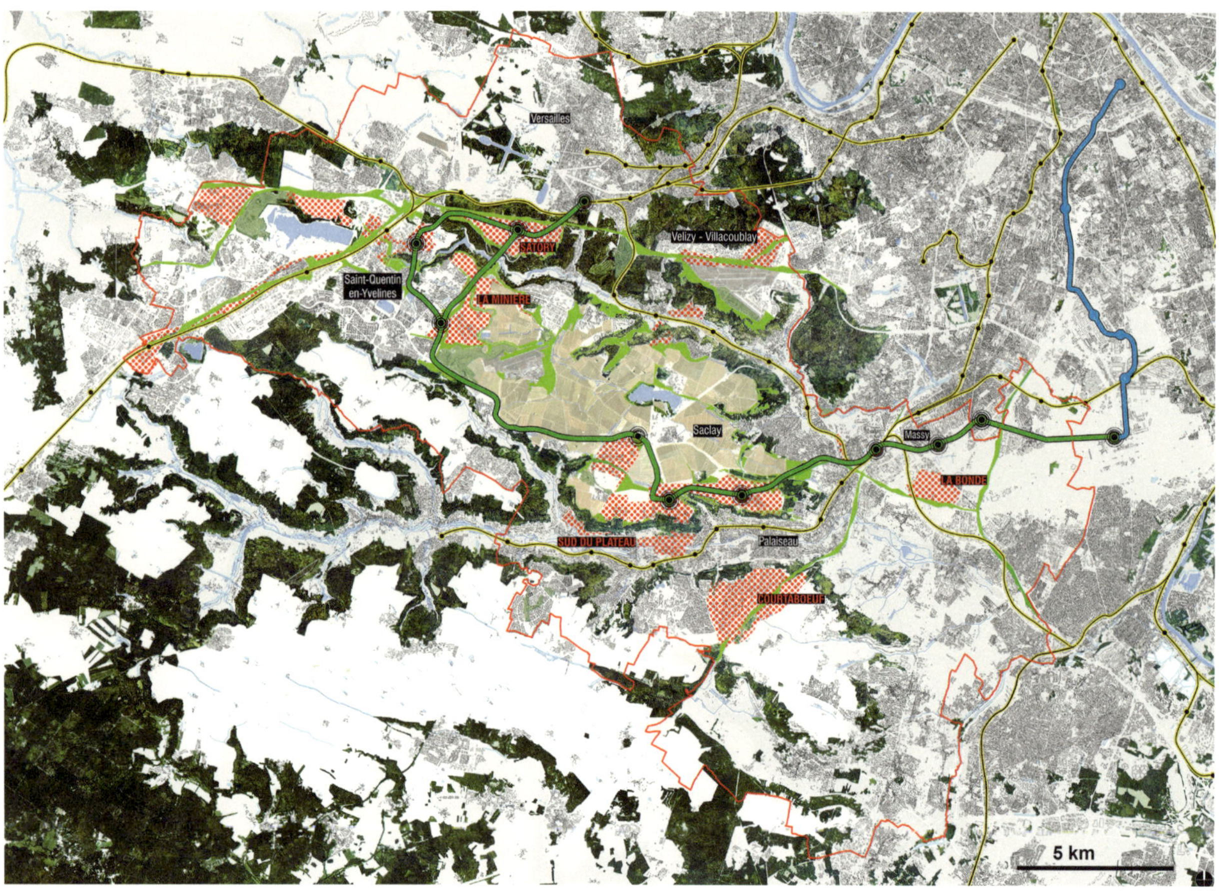
Versailles
Velizy - Villacoublay
SATORY
Saint-Quentin
en-Yvelines
LA MINIERE
Saclay
Massy
LA BONDE
SUD DU PLATEAU
Palaiseau
COURTABOEUF
5 km

30-kilometre scale

The first step at the scale of the entire site: amplify the wooded slopes to reinforce the coherence of the existing districts and improve the quality of the major access roads already present. The future "science cluster" was to be first and foremost a transformation of what already existed: a number of enormous campuses and 2,400 hectares of protected agricultural land. The aim was not to create a new city but to add a number of educational, research and production institutions to the site. The role of the urban planners FAA and XDGA was precisely to inject intensity and compactness into what was not a whole but an inherited archipelago, while preserving the territory's lack of unity rather than filling it in. Of course, transport is the true element of coherence that makes this archipelago acceptable: the loop of the Grand Paris Express, the dedicated bus lanes and the improved RER.

In the existing system, the only readable structures on this scale were the famous wooded hillsides, often located close to the campuses and some of which were listed sites. They form the skyline visible from the valleys, the plateau, the trains, the motorways, and even from planes. We imagined adding a further 3 kilometres of forest, extending it as far as the thalwegs, onto which the districts back and which therefore significantly contribute to delimiting them. Each of these extensions has a geographical legitimacy: they are not green corridors, gratuitous patches of green. All these elements are part of an authentic, coherent and appropriate system.

Opposite page: two "moments" in the development of the landscape on a territorial scale: the amplified landscape settles into the geography and extends it, the "campus parks" back onto it. The arrival of metro line 18 connects these neighbourhoods with each other and with the metropolitan area. In red: the scope of intervention (35,000 ha, or ten times the size of inner Paris) of the Paris-Saclay public company (Établissement public Paris-Saclay, EPAPS). It includes the 7,700 ha of the operation of national interest. The dotted lines indicate the outlines of the eleven sectors of intervention. This page: the geography of the plateau seen from the east, before the project. Between the Bièvre valley (to the north), the Yvette valley (to the south) and their wooded hills, the plateau deploys its protected agricultural zone, punctuated by pockets of urbanisation created on an ad hoc basis for teaching and research activities.

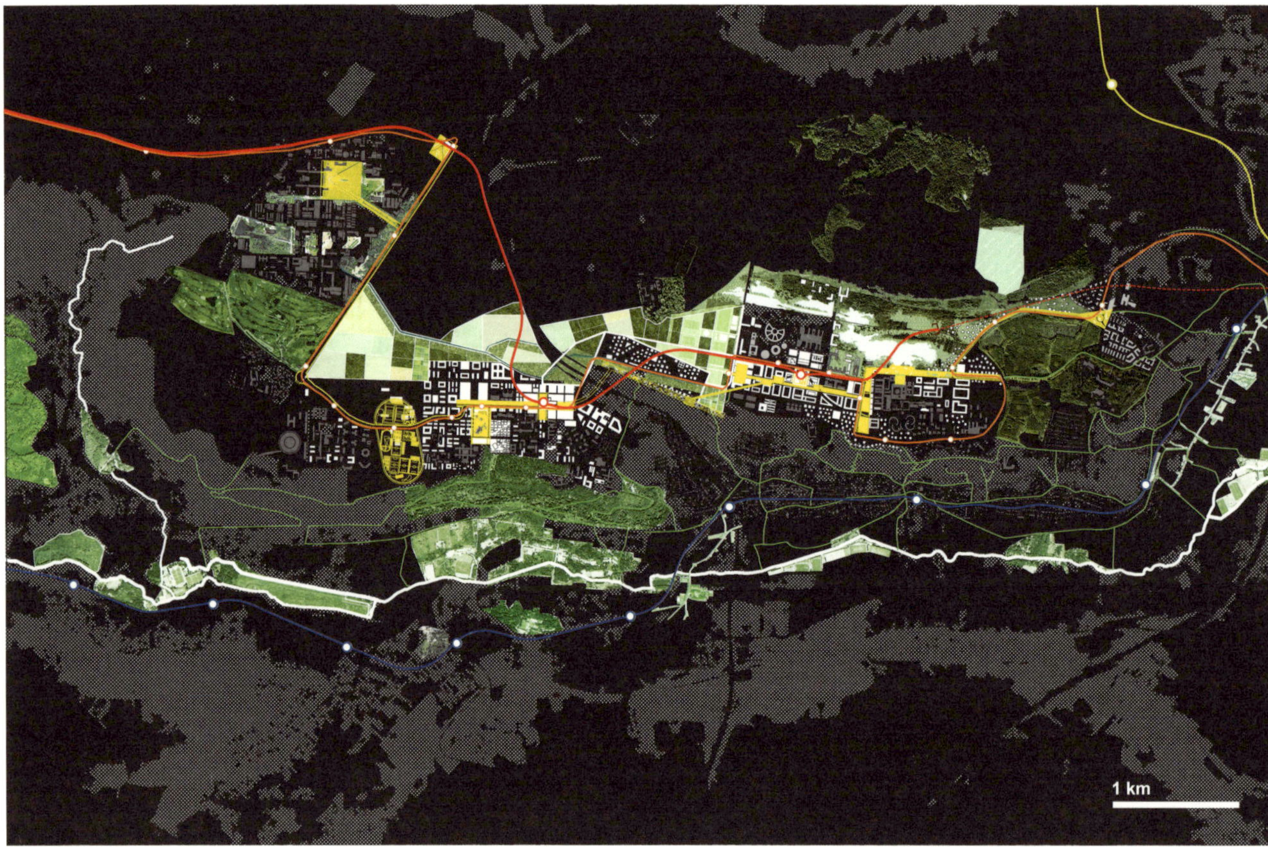
1 km

8-kilometre scale

At the intermediate scale, on the south side of the plateau, the solutions proposed for the overall site are not valid. Spatial planning is not a matter of homothety: the factors that establish coherence vary according to the scales. On this scale, the creation of a series of "edges" over the 250 hectares of the site provides a structuring framework for these intensified campuses. In each of the districts, a public space will be the key component of a chain of "significant places" dotted along the transport system. This is how Brussels was extended eastwards along Avenue de Tervuren and its tramway: planners built public spaces and parks, then the districts developed around these features and became more attractive as a result. Here, we are not building a park, but a kind of landscape between fields and campuses, in a scheme that combines ecology and engineering. It incorporates the ecological compensation required to offset the agricultural land annexed by extending the campus. It hosts shared environmental services (for the management of wetlands and biodiversity), technical and sports facilities, recreational areas, gardens and small-scale agriculture: nurseries, market gardens etc. It also functions as a kind of prototype of what could be created at the edge of the large housing estates of the urban sprawl which, in Grand Paris, represent an 800 kilometre long band between the city and the countryside. Cultivating these urbanised fringes is not so simple; the actors and the economy necessary for that to happen don't exist. In Saclay, we have real actors – agronomists, the National Institute of Agricultural Research (INRA) – and environmental ecology needs. Here, our orchards, maintained by horticulturists, are more ornamental than productive but they contribute to the creation of public spaces.

A landscape is fabricated along the historical drainage channels of the plateau. We are exaggerating them to provide capacity for exceptional floods, merging historical heritage, a hydraulic system and an environmental compensation area into a landscape that is actually used, since a path runs alongside the system on the edge of the orchards. The idea therefore is that the landscape can provide coherence to multiple needs and makes solutions readable, while also representing a potential saving. It is not about encircling the districts with a landscape cordon, a green rampart, but about offering them a "third space" where a reconciliation between two worlds that have long been opposed, the city and the countryside, can take place.

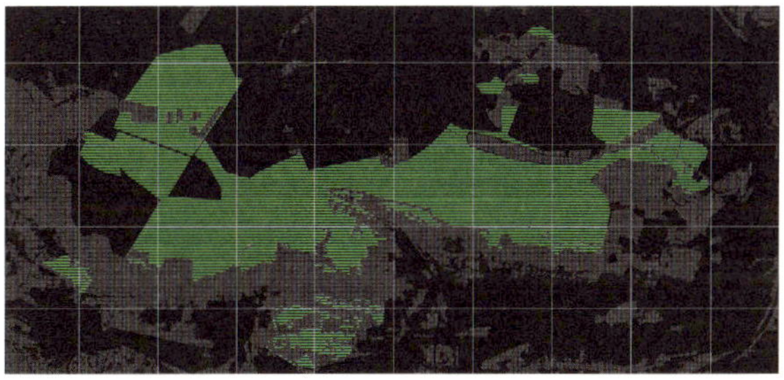

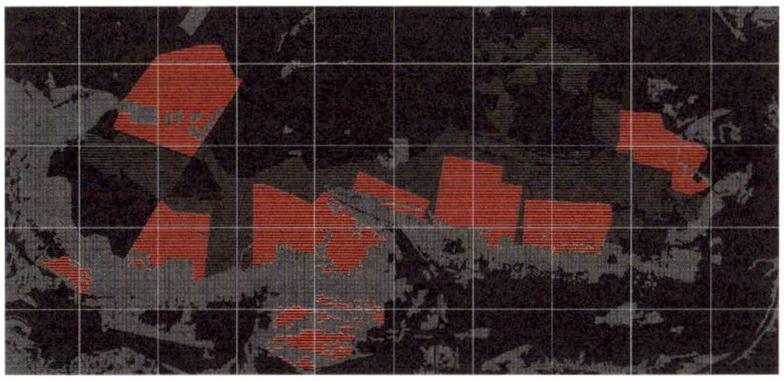

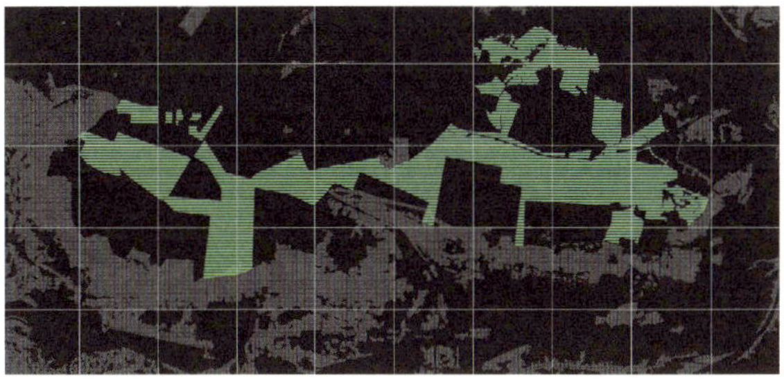

This page, top: the three analytical diagrams show the footprint of the park-campus (in dark green), the high-density neighbourhoods (in red), and the "intermediate landscape" of the northern edge (in light green).
This page, bottom: the study model, built in 2012 with urban planners, represents the urban forms and densities of the park-campus, the connections between the agricultural zone and the built areas through the edge – small-scale agriculture and woodland – the transition of scale and the road network between the extensive agriculture zone and the districts.

Opposite page, top: the conceptual diagram of the south campus shows the integration of the new hubs into the "intermediate landscape" of the northern edge. The chain of "significant places" appears in yellow, the RER B line in blue, the public transport lines on the plateau, including the future Grand Paris Express viaduct, in red.
Opposite page, bottom: the map of the green and blue infrastructure in the same zone highlights how the existing water management network is strengthened through new landscaping, and identifies ecological corridors.

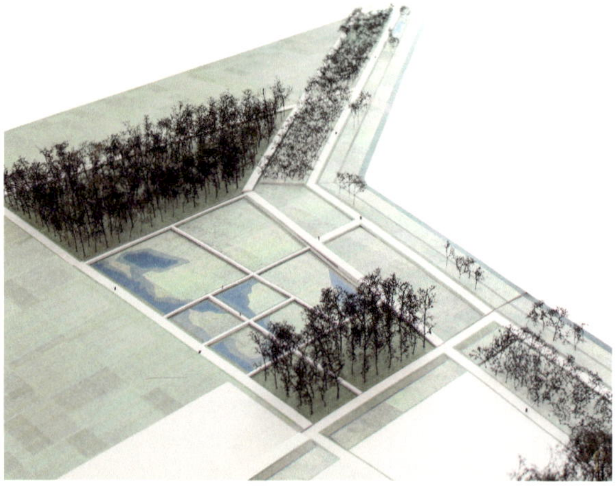

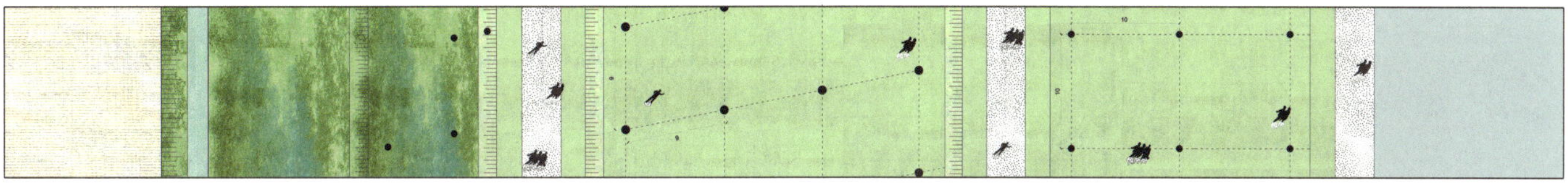

Moulon district

Details of the future landscape of the northern edge between the CEA (opposite page, top left) and the future Moulon district (bottom). The public park is sited on a major component of the old hydraulic system structuring the plateau: the Corbeville channel, an old drainage ditch nearly 2 kilometres in length built in the seventeenth century as part of the major works for Versailles – which borders it to the north. The public space is organised according to a system of basins and plantings, woven together by the paths (pedestrian and bicycle) that connect it to the developing districts.
This page: cross-section of the edge. From left to right: the agricultural territory, the Corbeville channel and its overflow area, the promenade planted with poplars, orchards and buildings. The perspective represents the resulting landscape and coexisting uses: agriculture, walking and leisure.

Progression of development on the northern edge.
Opposite page, from top to bottom: lines of young plantings between the Corbeville channel and the new buildings in the Moulon district; grid pattern of elevated walkways between the retention ponds that extend the tree plantings.
This page, top: preparatory earthworks for the further excavation of the ponds, along the new north-south urban motorway that circumscribes the École Polytechnique district.
Middle and bottom: seen from the new roads bordering or crossing it, the hydraulic landscape already created in the ecological corridor extends the scope of the wetlands, bordered by the forest strip along the RN 36.

Forest cover

Series of ponds

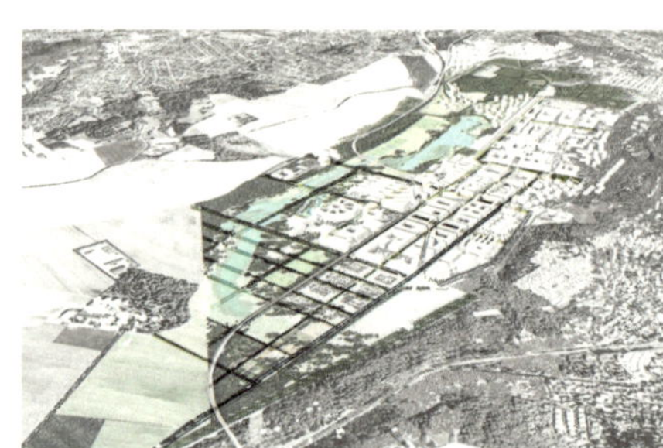

Road network

École Polytechnique district
Close-up of the district and its edges. To the north, the RD 36 marks the boundary between the agricultural zone and the band of forest through which the Grand Paris Express viaduct (line 18) will cross. Connecting the École Polytechnique basin to the vast hydraulic system structuring the park gives continuity to the wetland and strengthens its biodiversity. This page: the forest cover lining the campus integrates the infrastructure; the series of ponds maintains water flows and the continuity of the ecological corridors; the intensity of the planting on the road network densifies plant life throughout the district. Opposite page: sketch by Michel Desvigne. The overall operation proceeds through gradual transitions between the naturalistic park in the north, the "artificial" landscape of the central strip in the middle, and the amplified geography of the wooded hillside in the south.

100 m

This page: detailed plan of the "green". This large public space, which links the "Quai de Polytechnique" to the median strip, forms the central sequence of the chain of significant places, the backbone of the most urban part of the district. On the ground plane, lawns alternate with small mineral plazas (in the perspective of the side streets); these different surfaces are planted with large trees arranged randomly, which gives the landscape its unity and the space its character.
Opposite page: elements of public space design: top, the nursery and its life-size planting prototypes; middle, two views of the swale landscape (landscape architect: Martel & Michel) created in front of the ENSAE (architect: CAB); bottom, on the ground of the central strip, granite paving with two types of finish.

2.5-kilometre scale

If we zoom in on the substance of the districts making up this archipelago, we see that each one resembles a large grid development. The École Polytechnique district is about the same size as the Paris-Rive gauche mixed development zone. Along its northern edge, it includes a series of large basins and ecological structures necessary for it to function properly. Urbanisation and the low permeability of the plateau's soils require the creation of sizeable stormwater storage volumes, which then discharge into very low-flow channels. These basins are grouped into a succession of water features that incorporate habitats for fauna and flora as well as public paths.

The public spaces were designed with FAA and XDGA. Running east-west, a central promenade 18.50 metres wide reserved for non-motorised transport is to become a place of urban life within the urban grid. With reference to the British university quadrangle, such as found in Oxford, this grid is occupied by a particular typology of courtyard buildings, sometimes of very large dimensions – up to 1 hectare – and equipped with densely planted interior spaces. They host a variety of functions: higher education and research, businesses and housing – student housing in particular. In keeping with the American campus model, the landscaping at the heart of this district does not make a separation between parks and gardens, or roads and squares. To break free from the pre-existing logic of state-owned grounds, it composes a geography of institutions in which interstitial spaces are as important as the buildings themselves. The vegetation disregards plot boundaries, overflowing from public space to invade the

interiors of blocks and thereby distinguish the landscape of the campus from that of a city. The strongly unified design of the exterior spaces and its extension into the heart of the blocks transcend the programmatic separation that exists both between the buildings and with public space. In this way, we are implementing an adaptable green infrastructure, which does not overdetermine the spaces but qualifies them, and which evolves in its uses. The central promenade and the green are made up of real lawns, dotted with large trees distributed randomly. An extensive system of increasingly rustic meadows extends beyond. As the built environment becomes less dense, groves of trees appear, gradually leading to the wooded masses of the fringes and hillsides. These landscapes are not cumulative, but are transformed according to the environments through which they pass. All the roadways – the RD 36 to the north, the western boulevard in the centre, the Boulevard Descartes to the south, as well as the avenues running perpendicular to them – are treated as "parkways", i.e. the traffic lanes are separated by lines of trees planted on green strips that generally incorporate swales. Here again, the principle allows for variations. The plant palette adapts to the environments the road passes through: oaks, beeches and hornbeams in urban areas, poplars, willows and alders in wetlands. Our work on the western boulevard and the north-south urban motorways extends over considerable distances – and is slow to implement. We used life-size prototypes to test the roads, materials and species, planting densities and the composition of the wooded strips bordering these ordinary streets, which became readable within a few months but more as woodland than avenue trees.

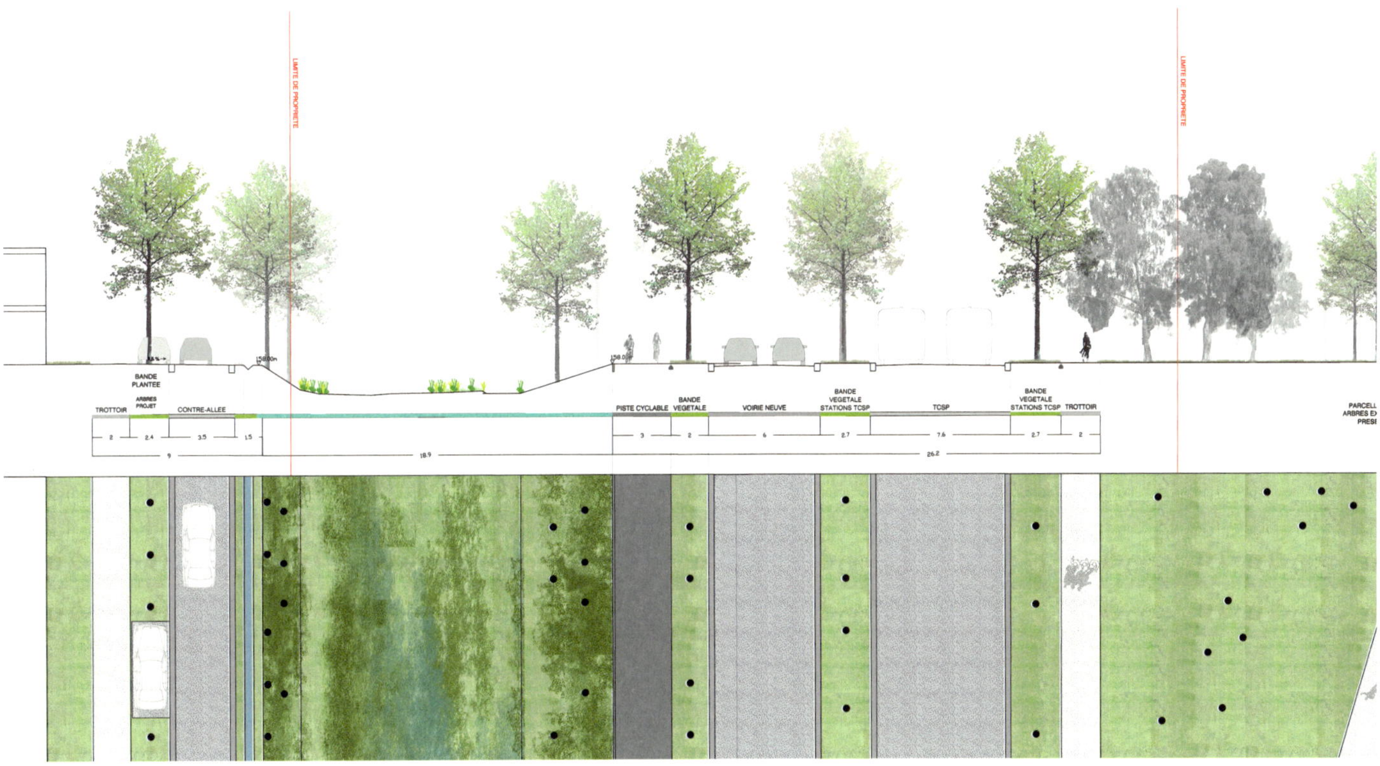

Opposite page: examples of dense plantings along and between lanes in various road situations.
This page: the cross-section on the Boulevard Descartes and the extract from the plan show how the lanes are divided by median strips incorporating trees planted around a wide swale, in the manner characterising the "parkway strategy".

NEW TERRITORIES FOR PUBLIC SPACE

In the near future, our societies will have to deal with several large-scale phenomena, starting with the necessary transformation of agricultural practices. Industrialised agriculture has left us with vast functional expanses, and it will take time for these landscapes to evolve. For example, it will mean leaving land fallow to prepare the transition to alternative farming methods. If we choose to view this transformation as a "grand projet" in itself, it becomes an extraordinary opportunity to improve the quality of these landscapes while tending to the fringes of cities. The work we have undertaken in areas lying between the urban periphery and the territories of intensive agriculture – seeking to restore a kind of public space to both by introducing a number of horticultural practices – would become much more meaningful in the context of a major agrarian reform.

In the 1960s, the mechanisation of agricultural labour brought about the consolidation of parcels, doing away with roads, ditches and hedges in the process. Some landscape architects sought to counter the disastrous ecological consequences of this policy: Claude Guinaudeau, for example – a famous horticultural engineer who worked for a while with the Corajouds, then with Renzo Piano – came up with the idea of a finance bill to encourage farmers to replant hedges on ditches. But this proposal met little success.

Today, sensibilities have evolved. Public opinion is now ripe for this objective to become a reality. The territory will have to be reordered, this is unavoidable, so let us make this necessity serve the interest of our cities by reviving the idea of a "grand projet", even if today labels of this kind seem to cause anxiety and fear, or at least a degree of misunderstanding. Whenever the subject of nature is discussed, it tends to be in defensive terms, with the emphasis being placed on the need for its "protection". I am struck by the fact that in Berlin, for example, the transformation of Tempelhof – the gigantic wasteland left in the middle of the city by the closure of the airport of the same name – was carried out in a piecemeal approach, sometimes brilliantly so, but without any overriding project intention. The contemporary city has developed in an almost insidious way, by sprawling outwards; even mixed development zones seem to be laid out without explicit ambition, without much pride. It therefore seems very important to restore meaning to the notion of "grand projet": not out of a penchant for grandiloquence, but to elevate our ambitions and resources to the scale of the problem.

This transformation cannot be expressed in a drawing – no agricultural landscape has ever been drawn, except perhaps in totalitarian regimes! Instead, quantitative data and new ways of tilling the soil will compose the landscape of the future. The reordering process could be initiated by encouraging small-scale local farming. The outskirts of cities would be well suited to this purpose. But the critical break-even point for farms of this type is not optimal, as can be clearly seen on the Saclay Plateau. The plateau could obviously be planted with something else, such as forests, which will prove increasingly necessary for climate regulation in the Paris conurbation. As it happens, Gilles Clément had made a proposal for experimental agroforestry on the plateau. The woodlands scattered over the large agricultural territory are often haphazard, marking an abandoned field or a game preserve, for instance. Why not give them an environmental and aesthetic purpose by creating much larger forest continuities? To manage this transition it will be necessary to organise workshops that can serve as forums in which to discuss the proposals and rules that have been drawn up and that would arbitrate based on goals, needs and interests: those of the future farmers, the cities and the ecology. Such an approach would be about substituting the notion of landscape protection for that of their production, forging links and continuities with cities, revealing certain places, proposing walks and things to see, and highlighting topographies and views, as we are trying to do in Euralens.

Another vast undertaking that lies ahead, also a legacy of a typical late twentieth-century planning phenomenon, is the transformation of large-scale retail zones that have proliferated over the past thirty years. The outskirts of our cities will undergo a decline of these zones and their gigantic car parks. What is to be done with them? We have been working on this subject in Mérignac Soleil, with OMA, and more recently in Saint-Malo. In the first case, the relative proximity to Bordeaux offers the possibility of replacing obsolete facilities with housing: rather than eating up plots farther out into the territory, let us make use of the fact the land is already serviced and connected to public transport. Nonetheless, in small- and medium-sized cities, this strategy does not work. Other methods will have to be found, perhaps through renaturing, as is already being done to transform former industrial or mining sites. Who will take on this responsibility? It would be wise to ask this question sooner rather than later, while there are still solvent owners. Today, when a contractor opens a quarry, he must also propose a site restoration project for which the financing is already secured. No such measures were implemented in these retail zones, and the surfaces involved are considerable. Can we rely on politicians to take on these often highly powerful regional stakeholders? In Mérignac, it was a public contracting authority that commissioned us to reorder a district: our brief was defined with a view to private owners, who hope to make a profit later by selling their plots.

Agricultural transformation must also be based on a shared vision, placed in the service of the community. We know how to create sustainable "green-blue grids" necessary for water flow and establishing ecological continuity. This infrastructure could be enhanced by paths that let people make use of the countryside: people living in small towns sometimes have to drive 20 kilometres to find a place to go for a walk. However, it is anything but easily feasible to transform expanses of neutral substrate, devoid of insects, saturated with fertiliser and constantly watered, into land used for crops that are not about maximum profitability. Major work will have to be undertaken, and funds mobilised at a level that remains beyond the reach of these municipalities. In some of the projects we were involved in, we were able to convince decision-makers by using the argument that our hybrid "edges" could enhance the value of the diffused city, providing it with the public spaces it lacks. But the resources required to make this principle operational are still too limited. Financial capacity and political vision need to be articulated at a level that goes beyond the scale of proximity. While a local initiative could take on the air of a kind of dissident project – pioneering, valiant but fragile – a major agricultural, national and perhaps even European plan would be needed for a general change to take place that would penetrate all the way to the local level. This kind of public commission has yet to be invented.

The landscape of major transport infrastructure can be added to the list. The city of the second half of the twentieth century was designed by road engineers: everywhere, urban sprawl is structured by the poor "design" of roundabouts. The landscape project could determine the position of roads when they are inserted into the plans, but also guide their "repair", since this is the main task facing us today. We are working with Richard Rogers' office on the future of the expressways and motorways of Grand Paris. Their construction generated a considerable amount of leftover land: on the section of the A1 between Paris and Charles-de-Gaulle airport alone, we calculated a surface of 260 hectares! Nothing has been done about these "leftovers", except to add ridiculous ornamentation. Rather than sticking to the usual reflex of transforming them into urban parks – which are often pointless and out of scale – they should fall under the competence of the agricultural and forestry sectors.

The most worrying wounds caused by territorial planning could therefore be remedied by major landscape projects forged through a comprehensive reflection on the agriculture of the future. Take the example of Switzerland: landscape architects work in these sectors by defining components and rules, and then actively following up on their design and implementation. For instance, a scheme to renature a number of canalised waterways was initiated to combat environmental impoverishment. Georges Descombes was entrusted with one of these waterways near Geneva. In France, landscape architects played a major role in the planning of the *villes nouvelles* in the 1960s and 70s. Michel Corajoud designed a landscape plan for the Isle-d'Abeau, near Lyon. For Cergy-Pontoise, Saint-Quentin-en-Yvelines and some suburbs, Jacques Sgard, Gilbert Samel and Allain Provost proposed projects that were sometimes similar to a park system, inspired by a fairly pronounced ecological vision. Our society needs to give itself the means to inject a new impetus into territorial planning, starting from right now.

BULEVAR DEL FERROCARRIL
BURGOS, SPAIN, 2006–2012

The network of railway tracks that used to weave for 9 kilometres through Burgos was dismantled in favour of a new line that bypasses the city centre, with the station moved to the immediate outskirts. The City commissioned Herzog & de Meuron to transform the disused tracks into an urban boulevard and to develop new neighbourhoods on former railway sites: marshalling yards, unused areas to the rear of parcels, or warehouses enclosed by walls. To escape the stereotype of the urban boulevard as we know it (essential servicing, buildings aligned on either side of a neatly laid-out road with its public spaces, pavements, streetlights and façades) and to avoid urbanisation spreading along it, Herzog & de Meuron allocated specific areas for construction, concentrated where life already existed. These nuclei of relatively dense urban intensity alternate with empty spaces along the trajectory of the former railway infrastructure.
Our first step was to study the areas freed up by the decommissioning of the railway lines, and their relationship to a relatively subtle natural geography. In Spain, urban sprawl is not the same as in France: cities are dense and often have clear boundaries with the countryside. A river passes through Burgos, flanked by a few hills; the railway and its associated infrastructure formed a second system, in parallel to this landscape. We therefore envisaged establishing an imaginary relationship between the two. As the railway tracks had been laid on flat ground, the breadth of their footprint varied in accordance with the topographical conditions; Burgos' hilly landscape, even if not very pronounced, imposed limits on the expansion of the industrial zone towards the periphery of the city. The liberated surfaces therefore looked like the imprint of a natural geography, their horizontality defining a waterline that highlighted the topography.

Since the footprint of the old railway site formed a pseudo-geography, our ambition, from the outset, was to plant it intensely, in order to constitute significant clusters of woodland along the "bed" of this former railway. In fact, a number of large pine forests already existed along the river, having developed naturally in the floodplains. These highly important flood expansion zones formed parks of sorts, or at least forest sites with the potential to become parks. Our thinking therefore shifted from the idea of a continuous boulevard to that of a road whose nature would change according to the built sequences, with lateral landscape expansions forming areas of woodland. Our intention was to plant these areas with forest species – pines, holm oaks – rather than city trees. The project therefore focused, on both sides of the boulevard's traffic lanes, on public spaces designed in relation to the situations through which they passed – squares, paths, pavements, designed in detail – as well as to their scope and specificities, along a continuous, planted road of varying contours. The overall effect brought to mind the continuous plant cover that is typical of a riparian forest.
Public support for this project was strong, as the railway lines constituted a considerable barrier in the city, with few crossing points. The project even managed to survive the property crisis: the clients – the City and a consortium of companies – did not abandon it, however they only realised it partially. Despite everything, the previously restricted area is now a public space. What once were the rear walls of the plots have now become front walls, bordered by promenades and gardens. Even though the project remains incomplete, the city's assimilation of this geographical boulevard has had truly incredible effects.

At the eastern entrance to the city, the public spaces that border the new Bulevar del Ferrocarril open onto the landscape of meadows, woods and hills. Between the young pines, the geometry of the paths delineates areas planted with grasses, walking areas and resting places.

In the old town, the former railway outbuildings and yards have been incorporated by the project to become the "façade" of a new boulevard of untypical contours. The opening up of some neglected areas has favoured the lateral expansion of pedestrian areas and the creation of small public spaces.

The urbanisation of the city of Burgos is limited by its geography. Its industrial development was concentrated around the railway line crossing through the city. Along with its service areas, the railway site composes a system

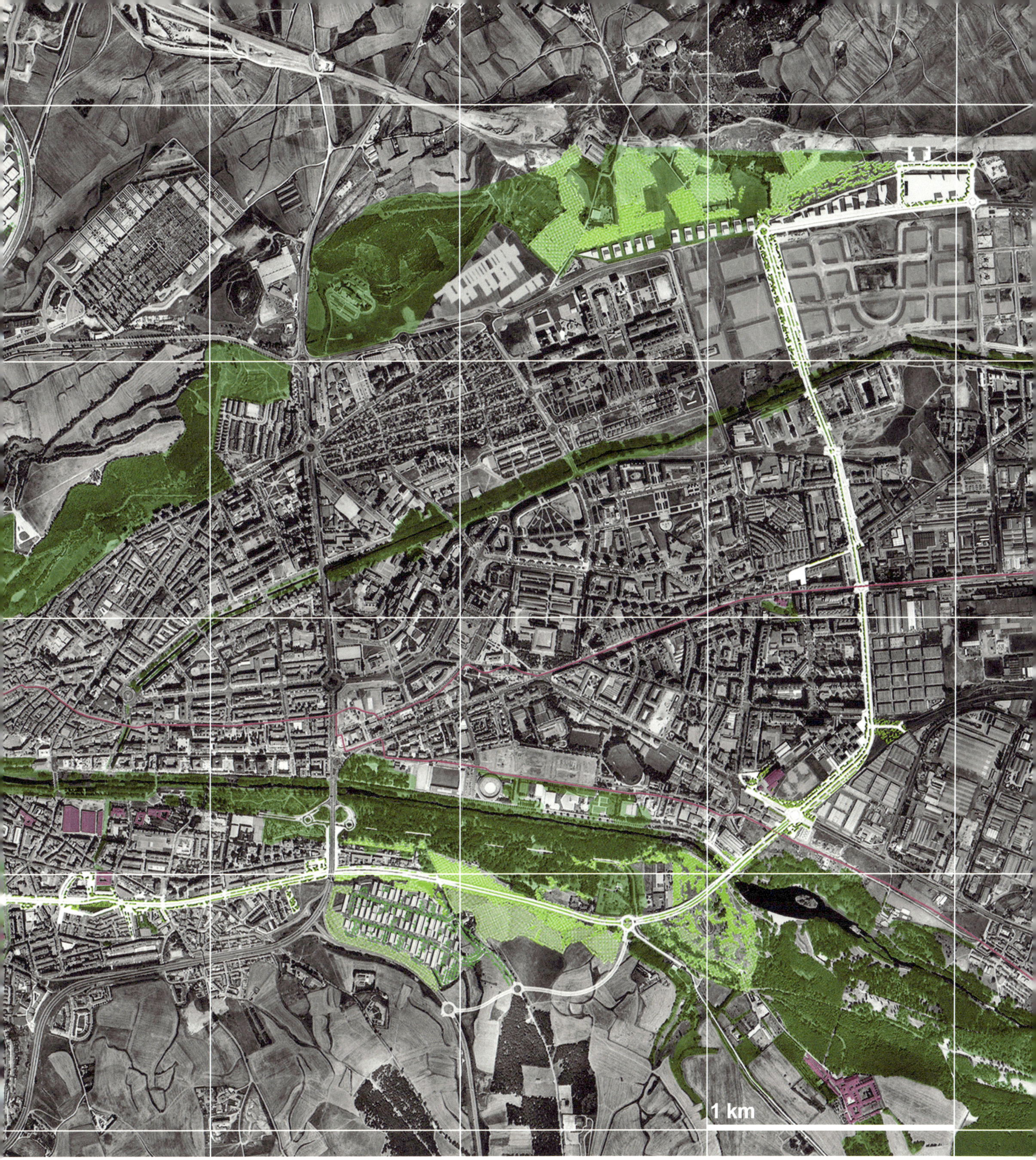

similar to that formed by the river Arlanzon (in dark green): the project exploits this similarity to make the layout of the railway and its infrastructure into a new urban geography (in light green).
In the Herzog & de Meuron project, the boulevard that replaces the railways constitutes the backbone of a new urban plan linking the city's west end with its new station to the northeast. From one end of the site to another, a chain of new neighbourhoods alternates between nuclei of intensity and the empty spaces separating them.
The MDP landscape project comprises two scales of intervention: that of the territory, incorporating wooded areas and meadows; that of existing and future districts, with the development of neighbourhood public spaces.

This page: the railway site before the project: vast brownfields, a landscape distended by overhead lines and railway buildings; a barrier in the city, materialised by the high, blank walls of the industrial yards.

Opposite page: the overview map shows (in red) noteworthy buildings located in the city centre, extended to the system formed by the new boulevard (in grey) and public spaces (in dark green). The creation of paths to the districts connected by the opening up of the former enclave has sometimes required major earthworks. Everywhere, the existing trees have been preserved and supplemented by other plantings: patches of young pines, grasses.

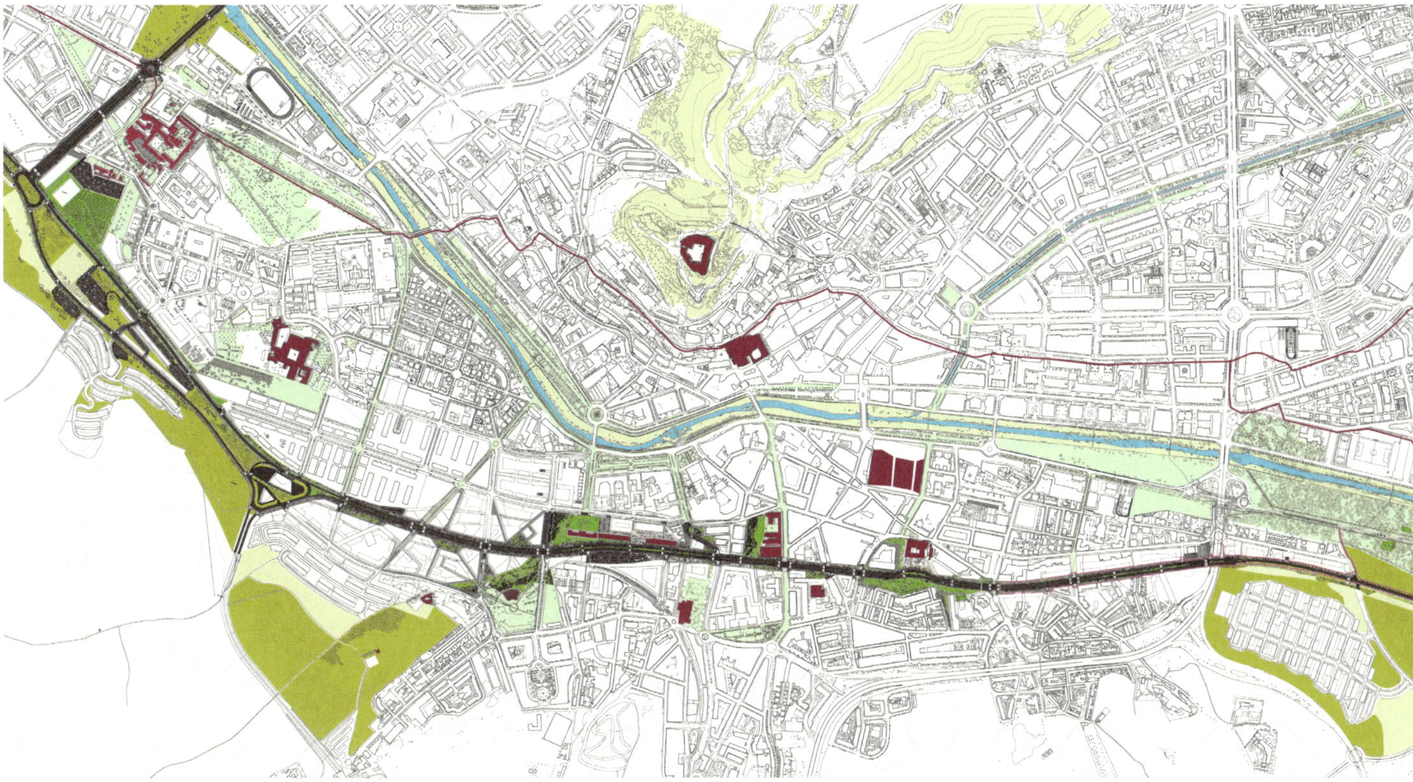

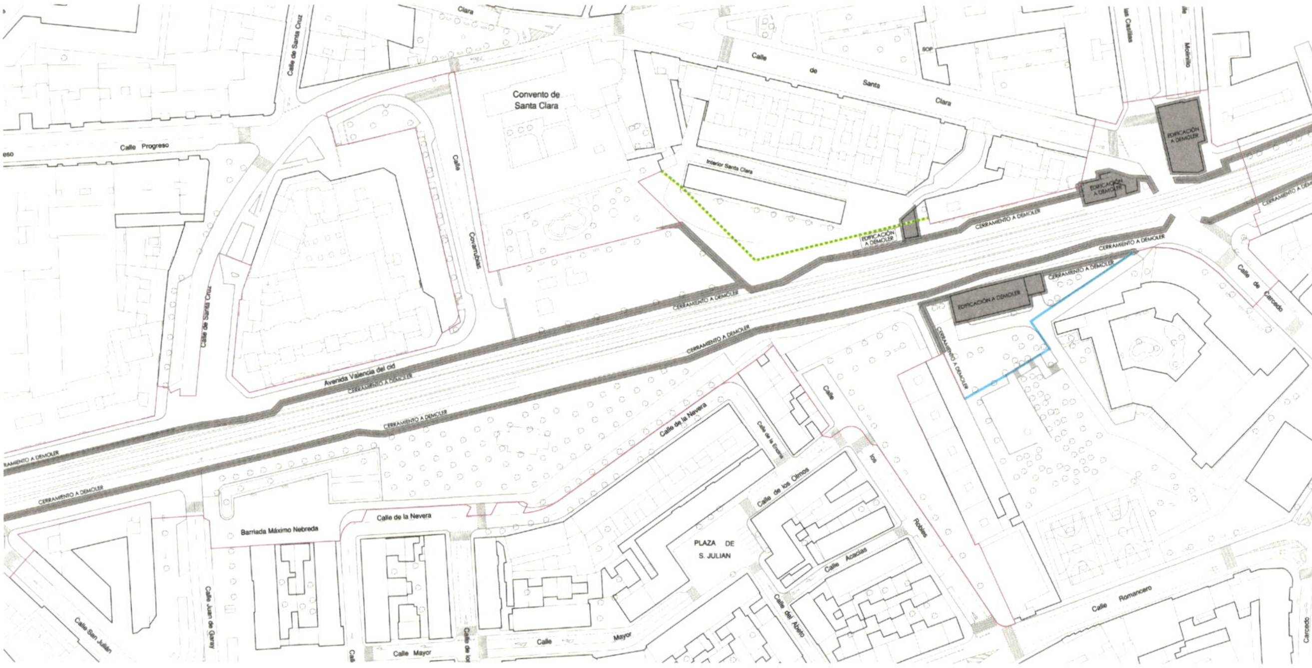

Detailed plan for the development of a central section oft he boulevard. Before the intervention: the railway formed a narrow ribbon, impervious to its environment, delimited by walls that left many parcels of land cut off to the rear of plots. After the intervention, the removal of walls gives prominence to the countryside or adjacent buildings, and the empty spaces opened up on either side of the traffic lanes become an integral part of the boulevard's public spaces. The layout of the boulevard also takes advantage of these opportunities for lateral expansion. For example, the lanes are widened to plant the median strip more generously.

3707
2 PN

On either side of the new boulevard, the removal of the walls, the annexation of industrial and railway yards, and the topographical connection of the side roads formerly cut off by the train lines create specific public-space situations. Open squares planted with holm oaks, parks with lawns shaded by large preserved trees, playgrounds and rest areas, large landscaped slopes: all are accessed on one side by the boulevard and on the other by the new paths.

REPRESENTING OVER TIME

How can we ensure that large-scale thinking anticipates major transformative shifts in territories? Or that it will drive some of these shifts, guide choices, and rise above the history of the project itself because suddenly our understanding of it changes, or because we have to respond to new needs? A long time frame must be taken as an opportunity: there is nothing worse than an endless project where you find yourself acting as the custodian of a dead idea.

In Burgos, a key illustration of these dilemmas, we had drafted a comprehensive plan associating the creation of the boulevard and its adjoining public spaces, the generation of an imaginary landscape around the boulevard and a whole series of new neighbourhoods. Then the economic crisis hit. Only the areas around the boulevard were developed, leaving the large-scale landscape untreated, and we looked back at the images of the original project with despair. It had been driven by a forest concept, based on the presence of a very large nursery in Burgos, a pine forest of fairly urban use. However, of the 250,000 trees planned – a figure that more or less corresponded to the number of inhabitants of the city, to the great amusement of its elected officials – only 5,000 were planted. The development of the large landscape did not take place, none of the districts were built. Only some of the public spaces were initiated. Today, therefore, the constructed reality does not correspond to the one that was designed.

In other words, a significant gap exists between the initial project and the finished reality. "So that's all it came to!" we say to ourselves as we walk through the sites, or browse their images. But it came to that all the same: €48 million of works, roads, a bridge, trees, public spaces, in harmony with the existing and planned landscape. The location, density and character of the neighbourhoods we had imagined will remain in future projections; they will be assimilated by this sequenced, localised vision in relation to a large territory and to the differentiated geographical situations that the project takes into account. But all this is not as precise as we believed. Moreover, the crisis that brought everything to a halt came from this obliviousness: we thought it would be possible to landscape 9 kilometres in one go in a city of this size! We were all caught up by the construction frenzy that had gripped Spain at the time. And yet already, some operations had been abandoned in the city. We had a foreboding of the disaster that would result from Spain's insane over-investment in real estate. But it was all the more difficult to avoid it because the financing of our projects was based on remunerating companies in building rights on serviced land. This legal reality will continue. It is therefore not out of fidelity to a dated drawing that the districts will be constructed. Beyond the urban plan itself, there is something of an invisible and probably inalienable form of ownership that prevails.

Such is the time frame we are talking about, too theoretically perhaps. Beginnings are never grandiose on such a scale. They can be promising, and the idea of promise is integral to the idea of the project. These mega-site preparations, which have a huge impact over time, lack visibility at the outset. The large scale has to be constantly reconquered and reformulated. We must remain steadfast in purpose for fear of appearing indecisive.

In a territory, buildings, roads and public spaces evolve all the time. When we draw a plan, we produce a still image of phenomena that are all in flux. This means we need to constantly update plans that are constantly outdated. For the Skolkovo project, seven people spent months integrating continuous changes into the overall plan. We purport to give a stable image of an unstable multitude and in doing so fuel the illusion that updating a plan is the same thing as having a project.

How is one to tackle the problem? Perhaps by accepting that a plan has *states*, each with its own lifespan, and by combining the representation of the project in a fixed state with notebooks documenting modifications, so as to avoid paralysing the design. Architects are familiar with this method for buildings, but I have only rarely seen it practised on a large scale in landscape projects. We applied this principle to a project in Monaco. The "stable" plan, the one at the beginning of the project design, represents all future transformations, everything is coherent at that moment in time. But as soon as this plan exists as a drawing, it becomes obsolete: on all sides, everything continues to live, to change. So we try to make this stable image independent of all the evolving parts. Doing so means reshaping this image by a series of opportunistic adjustments at the micro level, while maintaining the coherence of the macro-project at all times. The plan, which represents the outdated image – a stopgap intended to evolve until the next plan becomes outdated – permanently coexists with a living set of detail drawings that respond to constraints, of which there are very many since the project can extend to an area of up to 15 hectares.

In Burgos we did not use this method, having only the outdated initial plan intended to act as a single document. To go back to it now would require reviewing the completed parts step by step and updating the overall plan. We wanted to believe in the possibility of real-time coherence between a project and its execution. But a simultaneity of this kind makes no sense. All that exists is a major system of coherence within which one makes constant adjustments. It is the record of the project evolutions, as facilitated by IT, that constitutes the real project. We could even imagine having this method apply to the entire project, at certain scales and at certain times. In Saclay, for example, the sequence of public spaces is still a little open to debate. These spaces could be rethought more independently of each other within the overall picture, which would remain unchanged and then be updated later.

We should look at how the historical references that inspire us were made in their time. Olmsted drew everything on huge scales and to an unimaginable degree of detail. The commissioning of large American park systems could well be re-explored from this perspective. Did these plans also give rise to infinite revisions? Handling large dimensions and a long time frame is not the same as dealing with a finished object. Conversely, we should also ask ourselves: to sidestep this pitfall of ending up with a "half-baked" result, should we not give ourselves the means to render visible, from an earlier stage, what has been composed with geography? At what critical point in its development does the project become useful? When does it become legible? With these questions in mind, in Montpellier, the Charpak Park is conceived as a series of states, each of which is acceptable.

The awareness of our failures requires us to analyse them retrospectively. However, this feeling of failure should not be over-dramatised. Indeed, every project feeds others, including when it is not executed. In response to immense instability, we are constantly developing ideas and convictions, without knowing what will succeed, nor when or how. Our domain is subject to thousands of unforeseen social factors, even more strongly than architecture, due to the scale of our interventions, the multiple actors involved, the scope of the problems – urban sprawl, the limits of the city, shopping centres etc. – to which we seek solutions: how do we restore quality to these mutilated territories, what can we do with them? We develop hypotheses as best we can, we explore in different directions. Since we never know which of our attempts will succeed, nothing is a failure. In its random nature, reality also holds positive surprises in store. When an idea for a project is strong, it succeeds in embedding itself permanently in people's minds, in leaving a long-term imprint; sometimes it is so present that the actors forget to act on it!

Not everyone *sees* the same thing, which can lead to endless misunderstandings. The formulation of the "vision" embodied by the "grand plan" must therefore be simple enough for everyone to form an image of it without being constrained by premature details or a hastily drafted representation. If the representation is too formal, too closed or too cluttered with effects, it will quickly become dated and void of meaning. Politicians need this frozen image, formulated in a universal language that enables them to reach a consensus, or at least a minimal point of agreement. For them, the stable plan means two things: the fact that they have chosen, because they cannot tolerate indetermination, but also the promise of democratic consideration of public opinion. During the public consultation, this plan will also serve as a basis for its own relativisation, since it will be presented as a medium capable of integrating new opinions. We must produce the illusion that will enable us to move forward. The large plan is a *speculative image* induced by a question: in what we draw, what will be true?

CENTRALITÉ AND CHAIN OF PARKS EURALENS, MINING BASIN, FRANCE, 2010–

The stated objective of the Euralens project was to use the momentum generated by the construction of a satellite of the Louvre Museum and a TGV station in Lens to revitalise this former mining territory, in line with the very strong political vision of the President of the Nord-Pas-de-Calais region at the time, Daniel Percheron. The brief was to create a "centrality" for a geographical area of 400,000 inhabitants spanning three municipalities: Lens, Liévin and Loos-en-Gohelle. This project was the latest phase in a conversion process that had been underway since the closure of the mines forty years earlier. Many sites had been renaturalised and transformed into recreational areas. Their uses and people's representations of them had begun to change. A number of slag heaps had been fully preserved and planted; the unique ground-cover flora that had developed on them spontaneously was preserved. But these scattered initiatives did not form an easily readable ensemble. We were commissioned as landscape architects, alongside Christian de Portzamparc as urban planner, to reimagine this territory. In the era when the mines were active, each company to which a concession had been granted built workers' housing in close proximity to its pit. The territory produced by this history can therefore be read as an archipelago in which villages, towns and housing estates form a series of built islands in the landscape. The empty spaces separating these islands are experienced as derelict tracts of land. They comprise slag heaps, preserved in their original state or levelled, as well as extraction sites that have fallen into disuse; the local people consider them the back ends of their towns. Politicians, who, like many of the inhabitants, are the children of miners, still describe these areas as "forbidden", in memory of the time when mine workers were not allowed to enter them as they were suspected of stealing coal. The urban planners consulted on these sites had often imagined using these gaps, filling them in. We chose a different tack, starting from the intuition that this archipelago was an extraordinary urban asset: the gaps between the concessions in fact made it possible to establish infrastructural continuity on a territorial scale. Rather than filling them in by urbanising them, we imagined these gaps as active components of a strong landscape structure that would produce a new centrality on the scale of the three municipalities.

To do this, we mobilised the existing system of *cavaliers*, a series of dykes and embankments built for wagons to transport material in the area and cross roads on bridges. Abandoned for decades, they had become overgrown, bringing unexpected landscape continuities into the towns. These spaces could be restored and enhanced by other teams to structure the overall redevelopment of the landscape. The crescent-shaped network they formed would weave all the major amenities into the planned system of parks: the Louvre (architect: Sanaa), its storage facility (architect: Rogers Stirk Harbour + Partners), as well as sports facilities, the Bollaert Stadium, playgrounds, the university and the TGV station. We therefore conceived this "centrality" as a large web with multiple strands, the network of *cavaliers* providing a framework within which to consolidate land uses, prior to the densification of construction. Thus, rather than re-programme land uses by using existing roads or by creating urban boulevards, we redistributed them based on these lines criss-crossing the landscape. Hidden from view, they form a continuum of paths that reshapes the territory. From background they become foreground and so the emblems of the site's decline become vectors of its transformation. This approach is not about restoring the existing fabric but extending it. The aim, however, is not to substitute a "black archipelago" with a "green archipelago" – which would be equivalent to painting over a difficult heritage in new colours – but to take advantage of this particular configuration, experienced as a political fact.

Boulevard Émile-Basly opens up a perspective on the twin slag heaps of Loos-en-Gohelle. Their monumental artificial geography (186 m in altitude, the highest in Europe) is a major landmark in this flat area.

The bird's-eye view shows a territory where urban pockets alternate with large green voids. On either side of Rue Paul Bert and the railway line: the Bollaert Stadium (right) and the Louvre-Lens (left) with its adjacent park.

The footbridge that crosses the street (in the foreground) provides continuity to the pedestrian path between the TGV station (out of frame, bottom right) and the new museum. The outline of this "fake *cavalier*" can be identified by its light-coloured narrow strip and the patches of dense vegetation covering it.

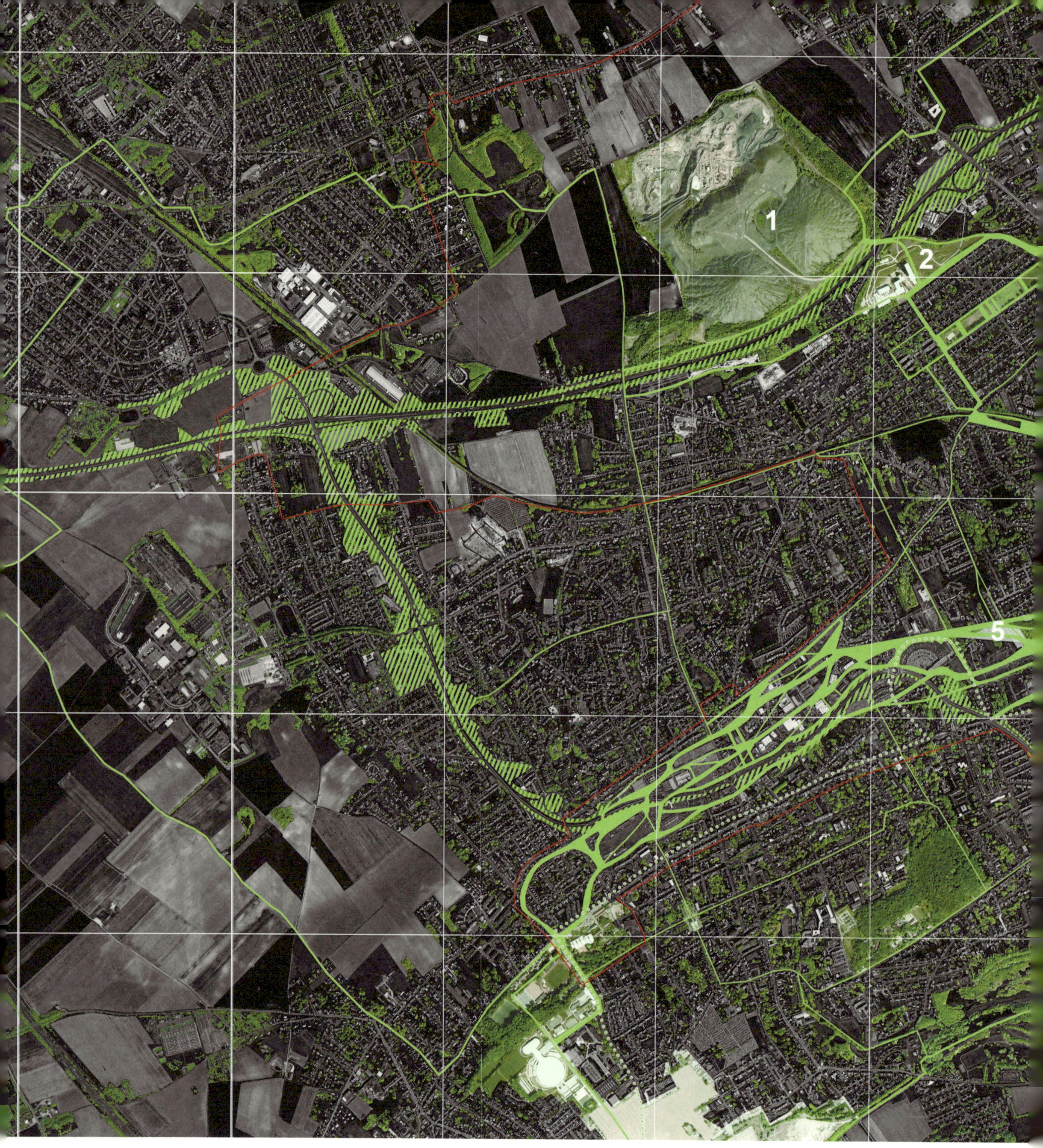

The project transforms the tangle of *cavaliers* into landscape infrastructure; once essential to mining activity, they are now considered as a resource for the entire territory. The vestiges of this industrial transport system overlap with the current street layout with a certain independence. They potentially constitute a network of walks giving access to certain sites, in the first place to the Louvre. Sited on a former pithead, the museum marked the first, symbolic

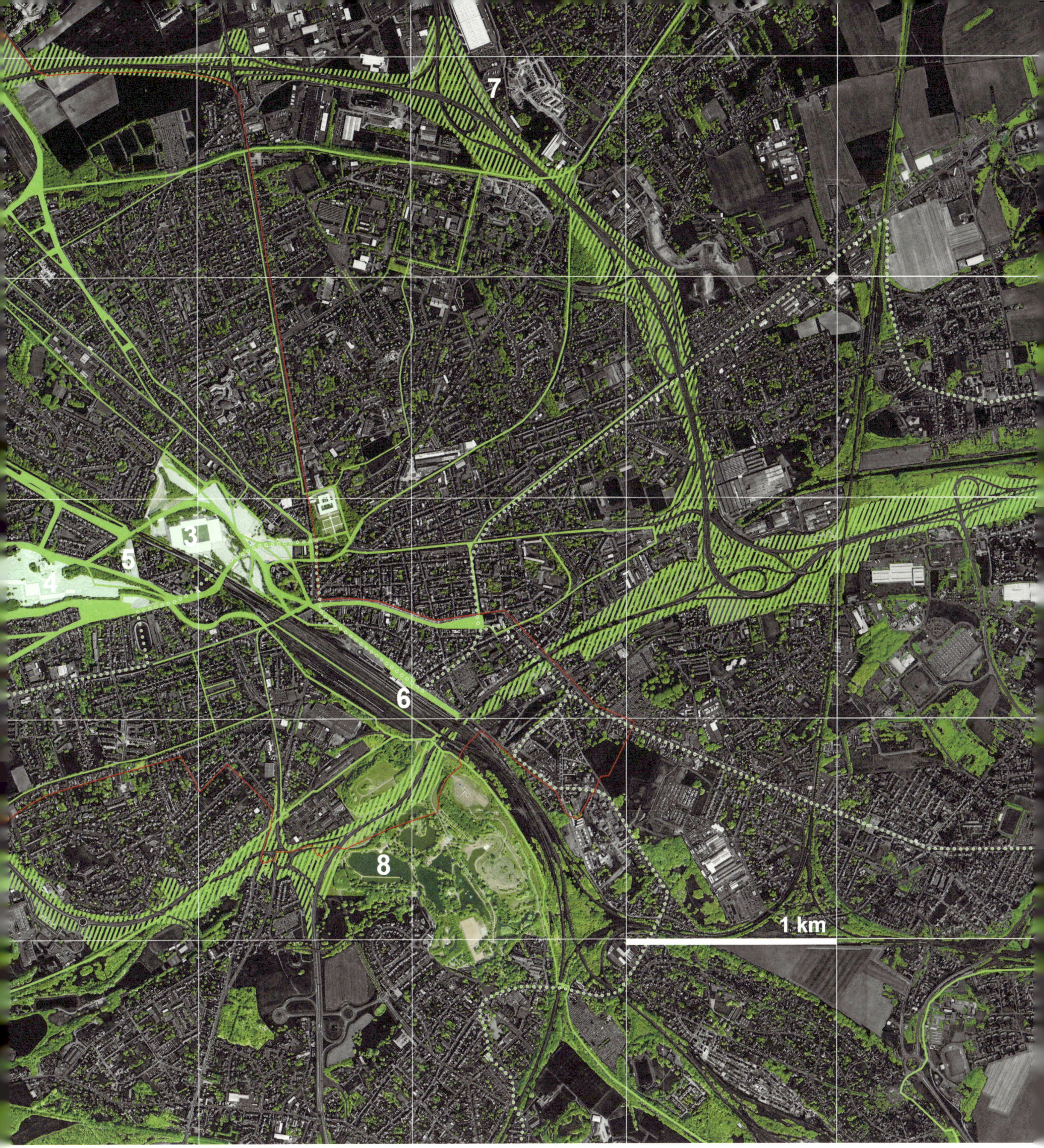

phase in the project to reclaim the "islands" between the *cavaliers*. In red: the perimeter of the project, which extends over three municipalities. From northwest to southeast: the twin slag heaps of Loos-en-Gohelle (1), on the fringes of the latter, pit 11/19, a former excavation site rehabilitated as an environmental and heritage education centre (2), the Bollaert Stadium (3), the Louvre-Lens with its adjacent park (4), the Louvre-Lens car parks (5), the TGV station (6). The landscaping plan incorporates the areas lining the existing motorway infrastructure, such as the bypass through the mining basin (7), redesigned on the parkway model. It connects multiple green spaces, public parks or woods, and takes into account previous developments such as leisure parks (8).

SAUF BUS
ET SERVICES

Strips of woodland

Based on these principles, coherence is built on a territorial scale through the implementation of planting and material procedures and palettes. To supplement the network of restored *cavaliers*, we added "fake *cavaliers*", designed according to the same model. Together, they will eventually form a continuous web of "tree-lined paths" intended to transform the way people live and travel between the pieces of the archipelago. This first phase of the project had a twofold objective: to contribute to the creation of good conditions for the opening of the Louvre-Lens, and to kickstart the transformation of the territory by giving a reality to the first offshoots of the green network.

The need to give immediate presence and clarity to the system was emphasised. To begin the process, we undertook a series of very straightforward operations: we defined pathways and planted 5,000 trees. This represented a budget of €20 million and six years' work. The strips of woodland are formed of very closely planted forest trees; this extreme density makes them look like clumps that have grown spontaneously rather than alignments. The selected species are compatible with the soil, which makes ecological sense; they vary according to the situation of the planting – proximity to water, slope of an embankment etc. – but always participate in the overall search for coherence and the goal

Opposite page, top: an example of an abandoned and inaccessible *cavalier* (left), subsequently reclassified as landscape infrastructure (right). To give these former mine transport routes a landscape status, the naturally growing tall vegetation was preserved on either side of a hard-surfaced road bordered by grass verges.
Bottom: before and after views, three examples of "fake *cavaliers*": the "Euralens pathway" near the TGV station; Rue Jean-Létienne, before intervention and three years after its delivery; in the vicinity of the Bollaert Stadium, two situations showing the transformation of the road by the introduction of planted reservations (central and side, with or without cycle path) and by the densification of vegetation on existing embankments.
This page: mock-up to study layout and intensities of plant infrastructure around the landscape circuits of the Louvre-Lens and the Bollaert Stadium.

of producing the image of a forest. The density of these plantings is somewhat forced so that, from the outset, paths can be created in a context that is very difficult to read: we are literally fabricating corridors and backdrops. Inserted between the buildings, they take on a strong visual role. Water management is essential in the mining basin. The mining operations have extracted considerable volumes of matter from the subsoil – of which slag heaps are only a small part – and caused gigantic collapses. As the galleries were dug, the ground slowly subsided, sometimes by 10 or 15 metres. As it sinks, it becomes submerged: the water in the mine galleries must be pumped permanently to prevent it from rising and forming lakes. Surface water drainage is crucial, as runoff must not add to the groundwater. This is always an effective tool for us: ditches irrigate our plantings, water flows into the ditches and joins the rivers. Here, the *cavaliers* also contribute to hydraulic management.

Opposite page: the bands of woodland are made up of a mixture of young forest trees – hornbeam, ash, oak etc. – planted very closely to form thick screens. The choice of species is adapted to the different types of soil. The paths are made of stabilised or light-coloured asphalt.
This deliberately reduced plant and material palette combines with the diversity of road situations to create a wide variety of routes for non-motorised traffic, from *cavaliers* to paved pathways. Most of the runoff water is collected in the tree pits in the bands of woodland.
This page: mock-up of the *cavalier* landscape. Forming 6 metre high embankments, they function as planted dykes. These long, planted "filaments" compose a green landscape throughout the territory, with multiple horizons, which is very noticeable during long journeys.

CENTRALITÉ AND CHAIN OF PARKS / EURALENS, MINING BASIN, FRANCE, 2010–

Densification of the housing estates

Due to their low density and the gradual abandonment of their vegetable gardens, mining town housing estates hold great potential for construction, especially since their land is often controlled directly by the community. They contain public spaces that have been beautifully designed by engineers – streets lined with regular rows of trees, planted avenues, squares, small parks. These are important features, and we respect them. Our proposal is to complement them, within the blocks, with "planted paths" that serve as vectors for the densification of the various "islands" of the archipelago but also for the transformation of the way people live and travel between the three municipalities of Euralens.

Imagining processes by which to densify the existing built fabric averts the temptation to fill in the gaps in the landscape while preserving the architectural and social heritage. The project made me recall the lanes that run along the rear of terraced houses in the Victorian suburbs of Paddington, in Sydney. These spaces – mews – used to contain old garages and utility buildings, which have since been adopted for residential use. Along with Christian de Portzamparc, we adopted the same principle to create new streets behind the houses, which will give access to garden sheds now transformed into housing: we use the existing structure to give intensity to the territory.

This page: densification samples in three mining housing estates out of the five around the Louvre earmarked for transformation into "eco-cities": Cité des Provinces, Cité du 9 (two samples), Cité du 4. On the bottom right: the web of railway line and the TGV station, higher up, the Bollaert Stadium and the Louvre-Lens to the left.
Opposite page, top: axonometric view of the proposed densification of the Cité du 4. While respecting the existing building heights, new constructions are concentrated around the network created inside the block. Gardens that were once food-producing are now enhanced with hedges and fruit trees; planted with ornamental vegetation (flowering trees, climbing plants), the public spaces are becoming fully fledged "linear gardens", at the same time access paths and promenades but also water management devices. Examples of hydrographic enhancement of the transformed sectors: bottom left, aerial view of swales running through the Jaurès car park in Liévin; bottom right, proposals for the Cité du 9 eco-city and for the restoration of the Seignier ditch.

CENTRALITÉ AND CHAIN OF PARKS / EURALENS, MINING BASIN, FRANCE, 2010–

Chain of places and connections

The mining basin features a constellation of industrial heritage sites, each one of which is independently managed: each small municipality has its own slag heap, its own nature area, its own embryonic path, the sum of which does not form a structure. While observing this landscape from the top of a slag heap with Daniel Percheron, we realised that the artificial relief created by the mine, with the new parks connected by the restored *cavaliers* at its feet, potentially composed a chain of public spaces of incredible richness. Walking areas, sports and leisure facilities, biodiversity refuges, major cultural or memorial sites: each site, with its distinct character, could play a role in the daily lives of the inhabitants and contribute to enhancing the image of the greater area if it were linked to the others.

The local people's enthusiasm for this idea gave rise to many requests, which were evaluated on the basis of the potential organisation and accessibility of the sites in question. Car-free itineraries provided a medium for daily activities (cycling to school or work, Sunday walks etc.) as well as for tourist activities (cycling tours through the mining basin). They form a green corridor that encourages the discovery of the territory's natural, sporting and cultural spaces.

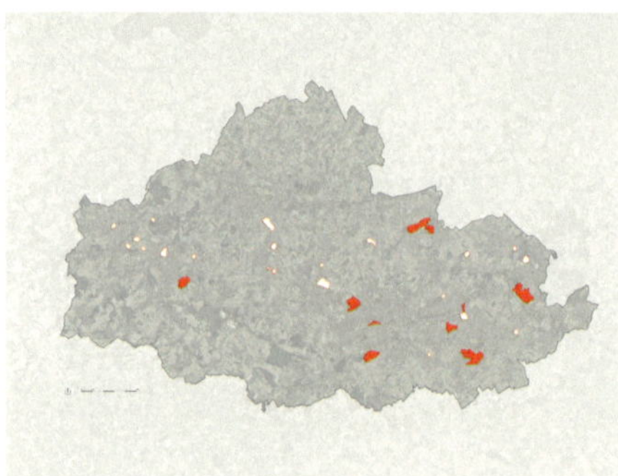
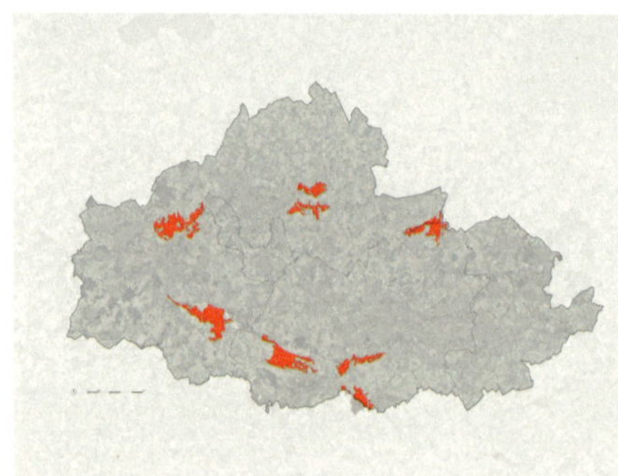
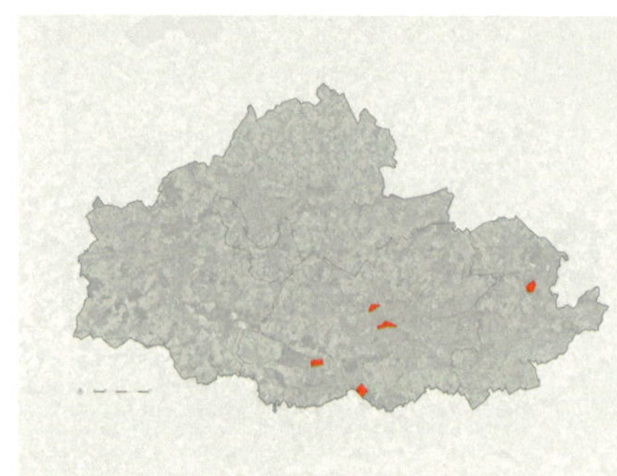

Previous page: geography and industrial "monuments" of the mining basin. Three "strata" stand out in this landscape: on the ground, the green voids; the thickness of the shrub layer; and protruding from the surface, slag heaps and other artificial artefacts.

The former mining basin has been listed as a UNESCO heritage site. The project to create a chain of parks extrapolates, on a larger scale, the strategy implemented for Euralens Centralité. The vestiges of the basin's industrial past have been photographed, mapped and classified according to six themes.

These pages, left to right: 1/ slag heaps, 2/ woods, forests and wetlands, 3/ key locations, 4/ *cavaliers*, circuits and paths, 5/ hydrography, 6/ entry points. Each of the parks becomes a major public space around which urbanisation develops. When linked, they add up to potentially form a whole that structures the entire territory.

The maps opposite show, on an enlarged fragment of the mining basin, the car-free paths created to connect the existing parks around Euralens Centralité (left) and the entire "chain of places and links" (right).

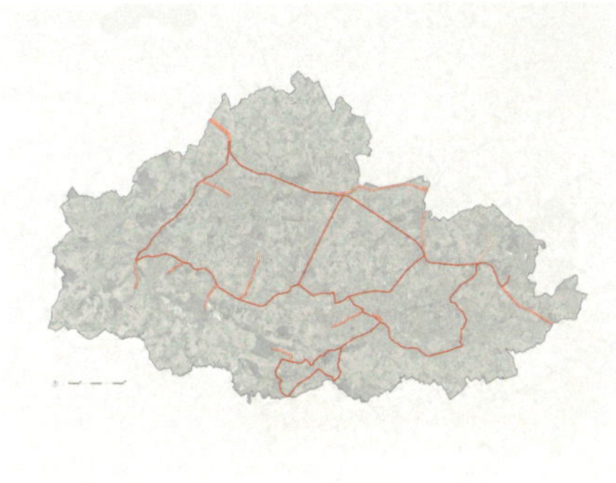
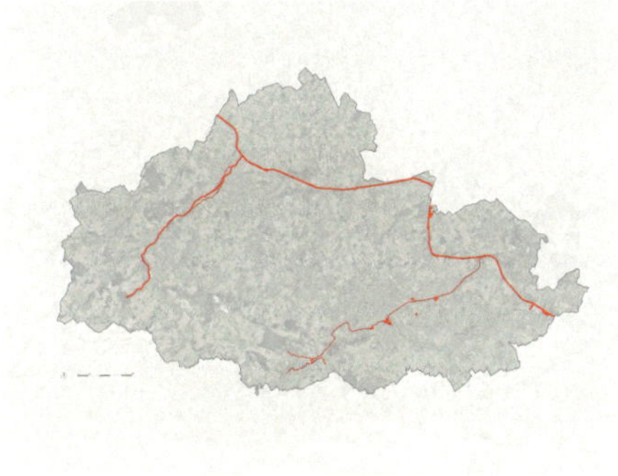

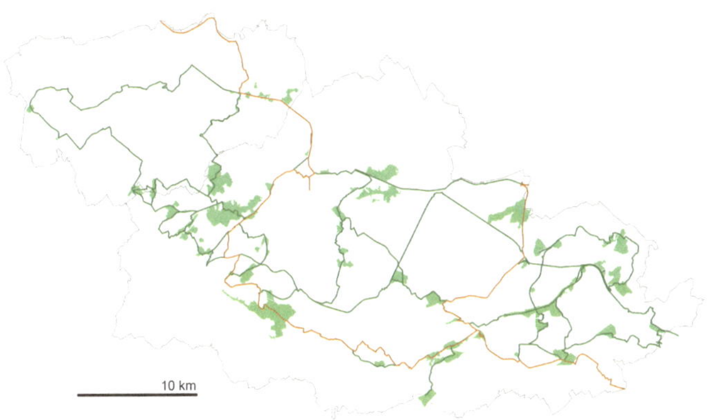
10 km
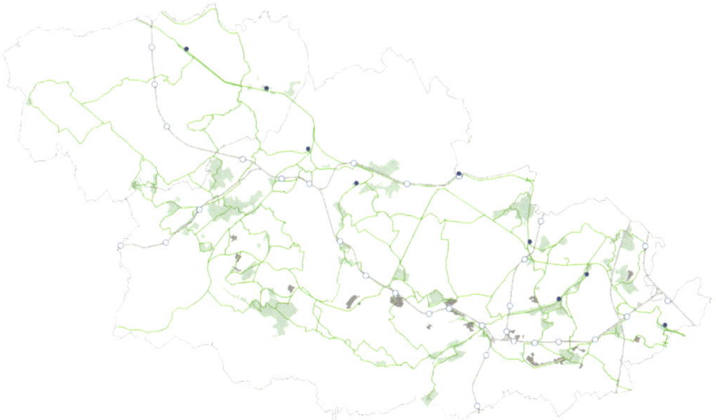

This page: examples of interventions on some downstream sites of the Souchez, in the Souchez valley, near Loison-sous-Lens, where the Lens canal meets the Deûle canal. Top: improvement of the towpath and the former mining viaduct spanning the canal at Courrières. Middle: reinforcement of the continuity of road refurbishment and connection with adjacent urban areas along the canal in Harnes. Bottom: facilitating access to the chain of parks from the west of Harnes, by the path that crosses the Lens canal.
Opposite page, top: landscaping of the access routes to the Fouquières-lès-Lens slag heap site on the RN 43. Middle: expansion of pedestrian routes in Montigny-en-Gohelle; on Boulevard Pierre-Bérégovoy, a thin roundabout pavement becomes a walkway connected to the landscape. Bottom: redefinition of a former *cavalier* in Barlin.
Opposite: map of the entire park chain. The colours show the eleven major operational units.

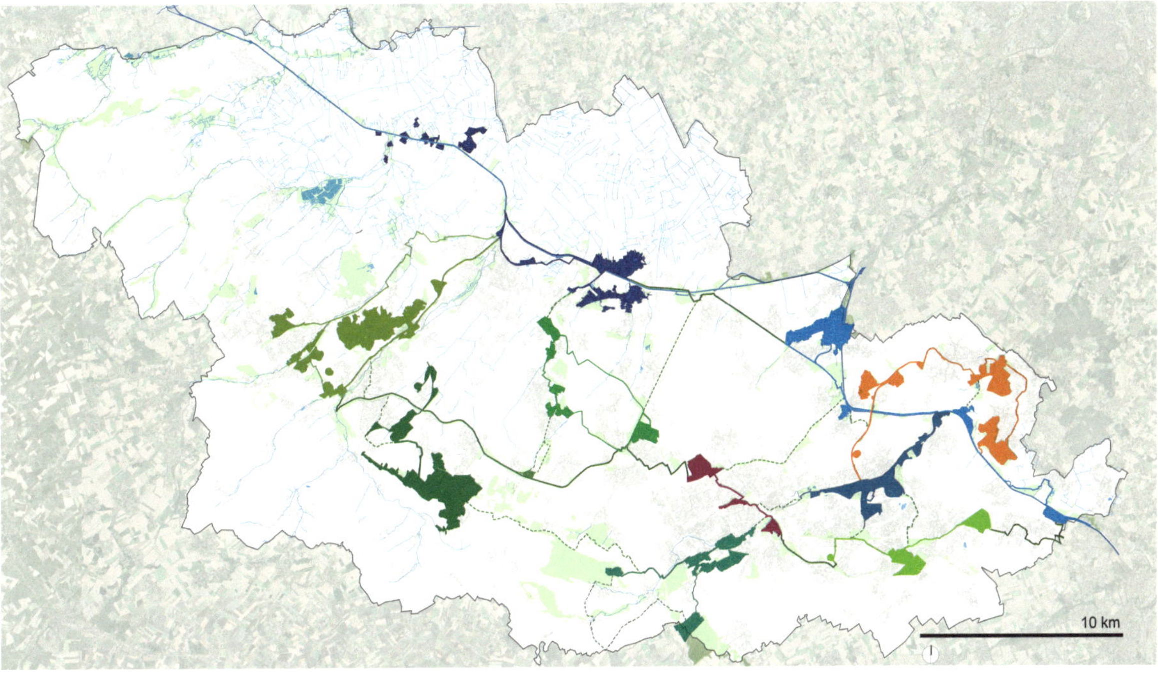
10 km

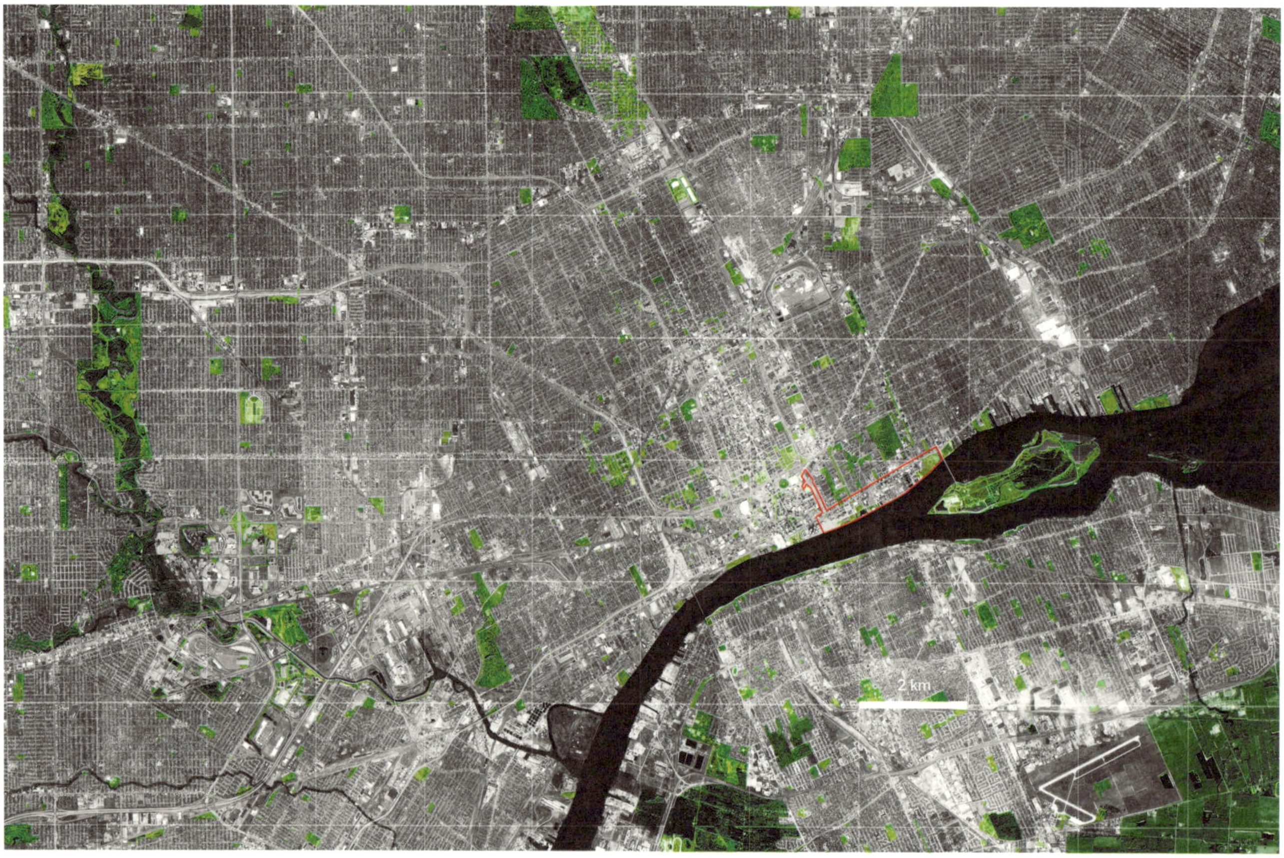
2 km

2 km

EAST RIVERFRONT
DETROIT, MICHIGAN, UNITED STATES, 2016–

Too often, a horrified or romantic fascination with the ruins and wastelands of central Detroit has prevailed to the detriment of a more comprehensive vision of its metropolitan area. Yet this area encompasses a population of more than 4 million. In the 1950s, jobs shifted to outlying districts inhabited by a wealthy middle class, while the city centre remained overwhelmingly working-class and predominantly black. Race riots, followed by the industrial and real-estate crises, accelerated the inner city's decline.

I was contacted by Detroit city planner Maurice Cox to submit a proposal for the 3 kilometre long redevelopment competition for the riverfront of this devastated city. Under the City's refurbishment programme, Cox had already launched a series of projects to test interventions on public space through large prototypes. The City was now asking us to propose a comprehensive landscaping plan that would help repopulate the centre and its abandoned first-ring suburbs.

It has become relatively rare in the United States for a public body to have the authority to design on a territorial scale, so it was decided that European know-how in this field could be useful. The specifications required that we partner with a large team to conduct surveys, draw up inventories, and implement the programming and consultation. We asked the American agency SOM to take charge of this phase, within a relatively short time frame.

In keeping with a pattern found the world over, Detroit's riverfront went into decline when industry abandoned its urban sites. The land remains largely in private hands, meaning the City must negotiate with the owners. In the saturated city centres of Europe, where open space is sorely lacking, a void of this kind would practically be greeted as a godsend. In Detroit, however, there is an overabundance of empty space. Nonetheless, the European model does not hold all the answers, for if we fully urbanise the site, we will have forgotten how to think about Detroit's public spaces on the scale of the riverfront. Worse, we will have merely reproduced, in a shorter time, the planning strategies applied in European cities, where they have made urban life difficult. In this recomposed city centre, densification is certainly an urgent matter, but at the same time we must find a balance that preserves the significant presence of the natural geography, which we know to be precious.

Even in this situation where we were under pressure to build as much as possible, a forward-looking plan based on preserving the riverfront void convinced urban planners, all the landowners and, most importantly, the population. Our East Riverfront Framework Plan includes the creation of a riverfront park, Creek Park. On one side it overlooks the river, along a continuous walk, and on the other it works its way into the void-riddled fabric of the centre through landscaped ramifications. Lafayette Park, the residential complex designed by Mies van der Rohe in the late 1950s, also finds itself commandeered into the project, as does a highway that enters the centre and breaks off into the orthogonal grid of the road. This general principle was negotiated by the City and SOM on a plot-by-plot basis with the owners. We participated in some consultation meetings, particularly with the people who were still residents on the site, a poor population that had been through many hardships. All feared that in turn they too would be excluded from this territory, and they were not going to let anyone pull the wool over their eyes. The consultations were conducted in a very methodical manner, as a genuine, structured democratic process, in which everyone could express themselves. The project progressed slowly due to both a lack of money and a lack of public culture: when the City of Detroit went bankrupt, its public services disappeared, including the city planning department. A change is occurring now, with companies beginning to show a willingness to relocate their offices downtown, and their executives considering living there: this evolution was unthinkable ten years ago.

Opposite page, top: satellite view of the city and its main recreational areas. Natural geography has practically disappeared under the grid plan covering the territory. A notable exception to the west is the Rouge river park system. Bottom: at the same scale, the hydrographic diagram before urbanisation. A series of "historic" tributaries drained the marshy banks of the Detroit river.

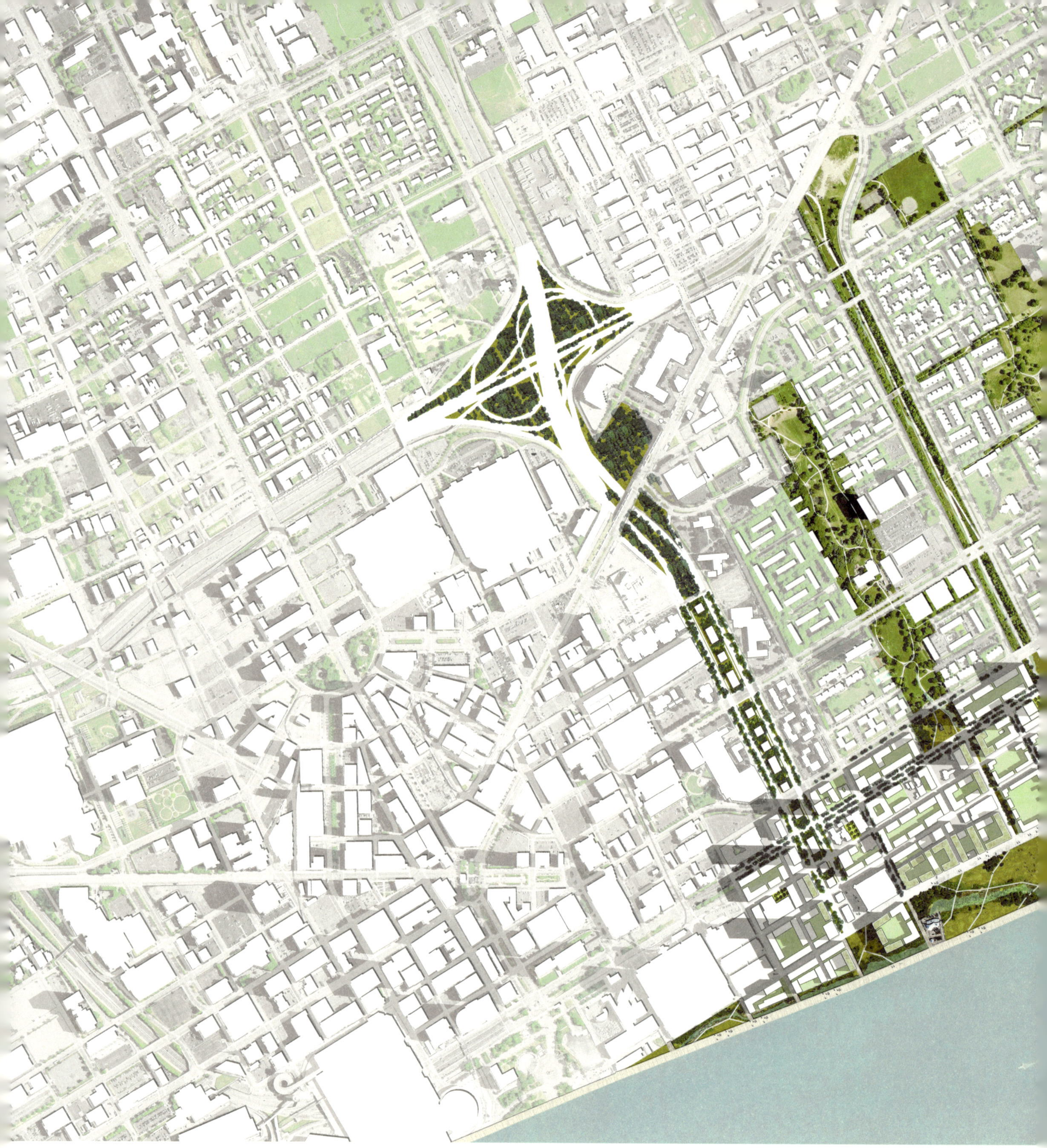

The project makes use of the gaps left by deindustrialisation, takes advantage of land opportunities and amplifies the traces of existing geography to form a ramified park system.

On the riverfront, Creek Park recreates a large wetland landscape. It is irrigated by rainwater channelled from public spaces that open at right angles to it. These branches develop on either side of the rehabilitated Jefferson Avenue, which links them. They include, from west to east: the Chrysler Freeway ramp, part of Lafayette Park, the straight line of Aubin Street, the green spaces of several residential developments and the large cemetery.
Creek Park incorporates existing parks and the marina in its western part; its eastern part takes advantage of the large brownfields that flank the bridge landing. Between the two, continuity – interrupted by large privately owned plots – is provided by a walk along the waterfront.

As these formerly industrial parcels are all contaminated, the site must remain protected from flooding. The landscaping of the brownfields and freed areas along the Detroit river is deliberately rudimentary, moulded closely to the urban stormwater collection system.

The park is imagined as a large wet landscape traversed by trails conducive to biodiversity. The white volumes suggest the location and massing of the densities to be built to compensate for the preserved voids. In the background, the towers of the Renaissance Center.

The continuous path along the upper part of the riverbank takes the form of a wide walkway, left unprogrammed to encourage a variety of uses. Tree alignments form a screen of vegetation that gives a foreground to the park being built on the site.

The guardrail, a very important element due to the dangerousness of the river, was imposed by the City. To prevent it from altering the visual relationship with the river from the promenade, it runs along a slightly lowered path that forms a step on the water.

Riverfront park

A few adjustments had been made prior to our involvement. At one end of the site, the headquarters of General Motors had been renovated, in part by SOM, to become the Renaissance Center. Around this building, work had begun on a small and incongruously luxurious public park – a paradox explained by the fact that it was not financed by the City, which has no money, but by a kind of semi-public company (the East Riverfront Conservancy) capable of collecting private funds and even donations. The river has a reputation for being dangerous because of its strong currents; people stay away from it and, of course, don't go swimming in it. For some of the local residents, therefore, this little park represented their only possible relationship to nature and water. A small pond with footbridges had been built for school children to experience this element.

In the end, on a city scale, the riverfront area is not all that long. We proposed creating a wetland that would generate a kind of natural environment, with marshes that would restore the presence of a natural geography that has disappeared. The rain collection system makes use of the slope between Jefferson Avenue, at the rear, and the riverbank running parallel to it. Runoff is collected in sedimentation and purifying tanks as it is prohibited to discharge water directly into the river, a measure intended to attenuate the risk of flooding.

Creek Park is broken up by privately owned properties. But a continuous walk, like a wide quay, goes past them along the river. The City did not want an empty and unsheltered walkway – the climate is very continental, burning hot in summer and freezing in winter – nor a boardwalk, which would have required an expensive wood to survive in this very harsh environment and would also have given it a seaside look. The available funding for this Uniroyal Riverfront Promenade is only sufficient for an industrial or port-type treatment: we will therefore surface it in concrete.

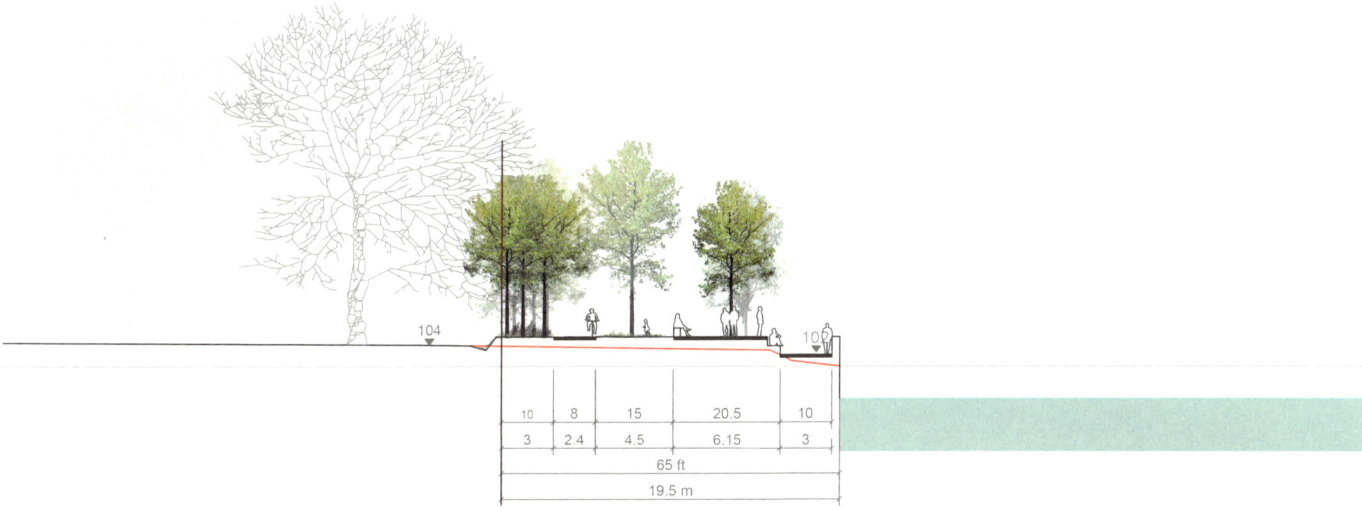

Ramifications

The river once had many tributaries flowing into it at right angles. Their beds have been lost with urbanisation. Since people cannot approach the water, we thought of reinstating it where it used to be, to suggest – although not to restore – geography through the urbanised condition. Other landscaping agencies had imagined ecological continuities extending into the blighted urban fabric further back from the river. We proposed a series of interventions within the urban grid that create continuities on a larger scale. These ramifications of the riverfront park take the form, for example, of public passageways through certain built blocks. We also proposed making Jefferson Avenue, with its eight rows of cars and car parks, into a more welcoming, practical and urban place, by anticipating the arrival of public transport, which the city does not yet have the means to invest in. It was also necessary to free up volumes for construction, so as to finance public space. We adopted the solution of a large boulevard, planted abundantly with large ornamental fruit trees. The model we had in mind was the boulevard in Boston that runs from Commonwealth Avenue to Back Bay and overlooks the Common. This reference space is part of Olmsted's park system for the city; his management of tree masses creates beautiful discontinuities in the plantings. Here, in Detroit, there are some miraculous places where Jefferson Avenue touches Creek Park. To manage the transition between the two, the architect Inessa Hansch designed esplanades and large urban public spaces that could accommodate café terraces.

Detroit was founded by a Frenchman on a strait – *détroit* in French, hence its name – between two of the Great Lakes. The plan was inspired by the one drafted in 1791 by engineer Pierre-Charles Lenfant (1754–1825) for the Federal City that would become Washington, D.C. The island park (Belle Isle) was designed by Olmsted. It therefore seemed apposite, for the development of the riverfront, to refer to Olmsted as well, to his typology of design principles intended to reveal a specific geography, to his early conservationist writings and his naturalism. With his simple language, his use of plants and his understanding of the distinct qualities of topography and hydrography, the park systems he has bequeathed to many large American cities are not in fact iterations of a fixed model, but resemble a pre-existing nature.

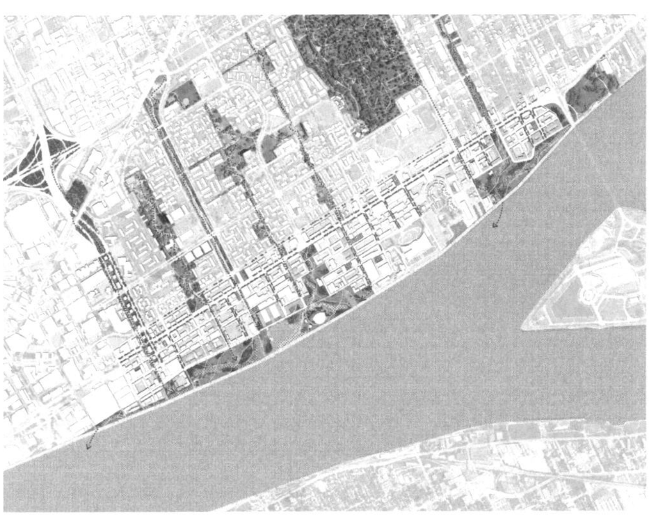

Opposite page: principle of one of the "ramifications". Top, the district in its current state: between the wide cuts of the avenues, a small park, some housing and former industrial buildings and warehouses lie surrounded by empty parcels. Bottom, proposed process and condition: recuperation of car parks and brownfields, demolition of buildings on certain parcels, implementation of a continuous planting scheme incorporating the small park. Future construction is concentrated around Jefferson Avenue.
This page: stormwater management plan. The ramified planting systems collect precipitation and channel it to the settling ponds that form the Creek Park wetland landscape. Any surplus is discharged into the Detroit river.

LANDSCAPE AS A REFERENCE

When I was a second-year student at the École nationale supérieure du paysage in Versailles, I made a discovery that represented a decisive broadening of my landscape culture. Michel Corajoud had found an internship for me at Renzo Piano Building Workshop. The Workshop had an extraordinary library, with titles that were carefully selected. It contained publications that were almost impossible to find in France at the time, in particular the magazine *Process*, which Nori Okabé, one of the architects, brought back from Japan. Some issues featured works by landscape architects, primarily American ones, including Peter Walker, Robert Zion, Lawrence Halprin, Paul Friedberg and Dan Kiley, all of whom were unknown to us students. At our school, twentieth-century landscaping was considered non-existent or lame, dismissed as nothing more than landscaped parks designed by municipal engineers. All of a sudden, I became aware of the existence of these American landscape architects who had produced a lot of surprising projects, most often in fairly simple, well-proportioned forms. They invoked the space of classical gardens but in a style that struck me as modern: in short, they proposed a modern interpretation of classicism. In France, where we are convinced that there is no salvation outside the public commission, this work was looked down upon because it was considered too corporate. So, thanks to Japanese designers who had trained in England and were working in Paris for an Italian architect, and to what was for me their new way of looking at things, I took a more relative view of the credo upheld by our school, according to which landscaping could only be reborn through radical reinvention. It was also at this time that I learned about the work of Olmsted.

Our topography classes were illustrated by stereoscopic aerial views, in which two images are combined to create the illusion of a third dimension. We had to reconstruct the topography of the sites being studied by drawing a plan of their contours. In my personal museum, aerial photography continues to play a major role, but before Google Earth, these images were quite hard to come by. We had two sources at the time. First the flying clubs, where we worked out deals with the pilots: we would pay for a few hours of the flight time the pilots needed to get their licences, and in return they agreed to take us up with them. In this way, I took all kinds of views of our project sites, all purely documentary, free of any aesthetic intent. To understand urban systems and their logic, we also used tourist guides that provided "bird's-eye views" of cities and territories. At the time, I used to systematically buy these guides everywhere I went. The snapshots generally tended to be crude, but very inspiring; there were also some very beautiful ones. I remember, for example, the photos of Georg Gerster, who, long before Alex MacLean, demonstrated an intuitive understanding of the systems of coherence that governed the areas over which he was flying.

In our school projects, we analysed these aerial photos in detail: vegetation, path structures, the partitioning of the land in relation to topography. When the analysis of natural relief is correlated with that of land ownership, one can understand almost everything. With a rudimentary approach based on tracing paper, a pencil and a binocular loupe, we were able to acquire an understanding of the correspondence between the topographies and the structures superimposed on them, rather than just considering them as forms to provide us with inspiration. Our generation learned, as geographers did, to connect all these visible structures. Today, Google Earth is an extraordinary tool provided it is used as a basis for site analysis, without losing sight of scale, and without being fascinated by the figures it reveals. When one designs a project, there is inevitably a temptation to engage in formal games or even to project models onto the plan; the risk is that they replace a real command of space acquired by understanding reality. How many cubist paintings have we seen projected on the ground by landscape architects? Or how many landscape plans reduced to one-liners? Such plans may showcase the promotional cleverness of certain purely visual manipulations, but seem deprived of an intimate understanding of the mechanisms they reveal, and even disconnected from the technical necessities from which they proceed.

The third facet of my landscape culture is of course, and perhaps most importantly, the places and gardens where I have spent time. Versailles is the benchmark: its park, the valley, the city and the King's kitchen garden – places in which I have lived, since that is where the school is located. I know the reference spatial structure, I have mastered it, it is physically embedded in my landscape design training. The garden of the Villa Medici, where I lived and worked for several years, is another yardstick to which I constantly refer to. Having lived in Boston, and as I return there often, I am also very familiar with American park systems. I have tested them in their substance and I appreciate them for a simplicity that drawing fails to capture: grass, trees, a few paths – sometimes not even that. They are not so defined, and yet: thanks to this matter, their space is always extremely readable.

I knew all these parks when they were in a state of relative ruin. Before the great storm of 2009, the one in Versailles was almost abandoned; all that remained was the framework, an organised forest where the imprint of the original plan was visible in negative. When I was in residence at the Villa Medici, many trees were broken in the barely pruned and almost spectral gardens; plant matter existed in its elementary state, without details, without effects, without sophistication. Because of, or owing to, their poor condition, these parks were spared the frills of ornamentation; it is said that Le Nôtre hated "embroideries", those cumbersome boxwood trimmings the king asked him to add.

I also like the nineteenth-century gardens one finds in Belgium, kinds of woodlands sculpted with glades, located in loose valleys, a little exaggerated by their designers and crossed by paths along the edges: the Tervuren Park and its arboretum, a collection of trees organised around large recessed clearings, or the Woluwe Park, designed by the French landscape architect Élie Lainé. All these examples are references to me for their dimensions. I work by going back and forth between the scale of my project and the scales of these sites, to which I have to occasionally return in order to take them in again visually. This spatial, material and physical reference must be constantly renewed. Unlike computer software, whose abstraction makes everything interchangeable, this practice always holds surprises. Going back to these places always produces a pleasure mixed with strangeness, like when you rediscover your own apartment after a long holiday. The sense we have of the space we design – its size, orientation and our physical experience of it – is essential.

And then there is my collection of more personal landscapes, whether known and frequented or just seen. In the Chevreuse valley southeast of Paris, I always go for a walk along the same path to put myself through a gymnastics of the eye and the body that is indispensable to re-tuning the system. As I travel a lot, my collection is enriched by ordinary places related to my work: the landscape between an airport and a city, nondescript public spaces. Reflection on the project develops by associating similar experiences. The experience of a physical situation brings to mind another, reference situation, which, to become operative, also requires the distance that is provided by its aerial view. In the course of these random confrontations, triggered by some unknown device, something appears, without the process being purely deductive. In the case of Novartis Park, the images of archipelagos came to me right away. Although they suggested fragmentation, they also seemed to hold the potential of making a coherent landscape. In Lens, the curves, height and density of the *cavaliers* stood out almost immediately a delta-like landscape. Suddenly the image of a convergence of rivers and oxbow lakes conferred a possible logic on the dyke fragments scattered throughout the mining territory. This simple analogy with a waterflow system became the basis for something different. The near identical nature of the configurations led to the possibility of another development. Typologically, many landscapes are quite similar. Situations are different, but the causes that shape territorial forms are not so numerous, whether in natural geography or human geography. So, in the end, a project is imagined through geography in order to transform the history of a site.

Drawing, this organisation of thought through the movement of the hand, is very important in this process, which is neither linear nor deductive, but circular. Moving from one reference to another, the drawing carries out a transformation, but it is strongly based on the awareness of space: that of the site to be transformed, and that of the example references. When one looks at something, one compares it to possible futures. With experience, one develops the ability to almost physically feel the moment when a system of coherence appears. An ethnologist who taught at Versailles used to tell us about distant populations that perceived sixty shades of green where we saw only one. The more words and references you have, the more you see. We are shaped by all these acquisitions.

NOVARTIS CAMPUS
EAST HANOVER, NEW JERSEY, UNITED STATES, 2013–2016

The pharmaceutical giant's American headquarters is located on a 56 hectare site about 40 kilometres west of New York, in a very industrial region set amongst vast landscapes. The entire site, which contains an eclectic array of large manufacturing and laboratory buildings, is due to be converted into a research campus. Our brief is to assist this process over several decades while anticipating an increase from 7,000 to 9,000 employees, who will continue to work on site throughout the operation. Novartis CEO Daniel Vasella is an architecture enthusiast; he oversaw the transformation of the Basel flagship campus with Milanese urban planner Vittorio Lampugnani. The latter had proposed a mass plan for the East Hanover campus before our involvement. He tightened up the new construction plan and integrated certain existing buildings into a 500 metre long U-shaped layout, arranged around three sides of a 23 hectare park, the surface area of the Jardin des Plantes botanical garden in Paris. This proposal adapted very well to the variations of the programme. It also meant that we were starting from a long-term vision, articulated before our project began. We consequently had to come up with stratagems to control, through the landscape, the changes this central space would undergo over time, so that people would be able to continue using and enjoying the site through each phase of the project.

The competition for the park commission pitted us against West 8, James Corner, Günther Vogt and the current landscape architect, Michael Van Valkenburg. We won it with an "incremental" strategy – it was not all going to be done in one go – combined with a physical vision of a potential long-term condition. Our proposal started from images of winter sports resorts in the United States, landscapes where numerous ski slopes cut through the forest to carve out a kind of archipelago of little wooded islands. Skiers navigate between these islands, which movement and perspective constantly recompose as landscapes. The experience also brought to mind memories of sailing in Stockholm Bay, a former glacial moraine dotted with little islands that are almost invariably covered with beautiful pine forests. When moving through this type of space, on skis or by boat, the skylines constantly change due to the shifting presence of these island blocks; the landscape is very unified but the void is always a surprise. These are kinetic spaces.

To imagine that the large campus park would be composed by successive "blocks" was therefore almost self-evident: the concept of the wooded island and the spatial qualities it implied made sense in the New Jersey landscape. But above all, we knew in advance that we had to play with the existing components of this park: some would have to be removed, others added, others replaced. There were certain contingencies to the order of the transformations planned by Lampugnani: it was impossible to implement a scheme based on a rigid geometry. As a conceptual tool, the forest island enabled us to imagine a physical structure of known qualities and capacities. Our proposal had presented an image that projected into the long term but also recommended, in the short term, refurbishing roadways, pavements, access roads and car parks through afforestation. Woodland therefore both signifies the long-term transformation and provides an immediate improvement, even if just temporarily, to the daily lives of users.

These scattered plantings were carried out as work was beginning on the construction of a large landscape. The planned research buildings are imposing; even if their design will surely be entrusted to high-quality American architectural practices, their dimensions can seem terribly

The future East Hanover campus from the sky. This vast and varied complex comprises large autonomous buildings – the most recent of which were built in 2010 – associated with numerous car parks. Groves of trees are scattered throughout the centre of the site, while others on its periphery screen the surrounding environment. The expressway providing access from the north separates the site from a large shopping mall.

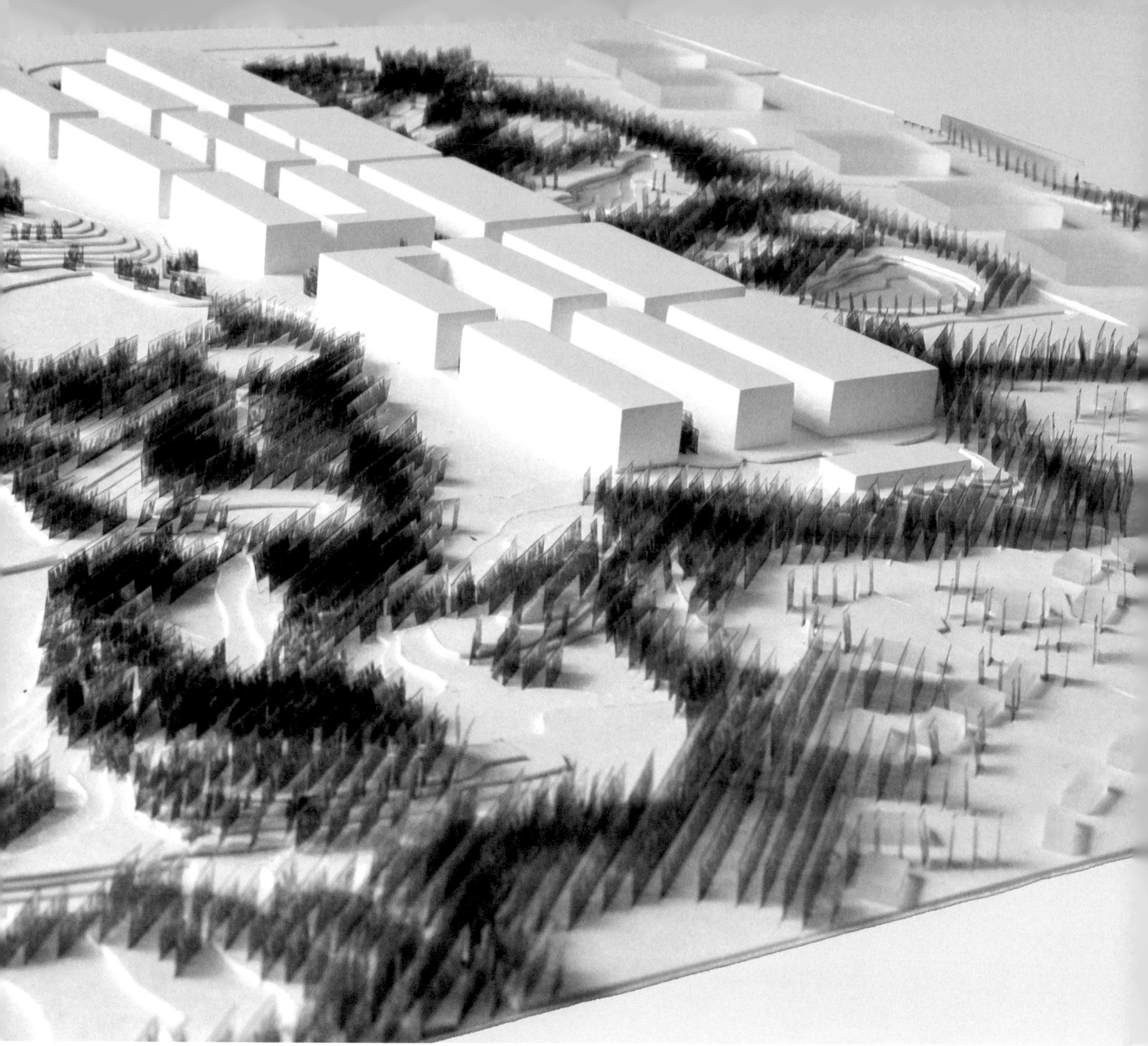

Concept model illustrating the park design strategy. Between the three built sides, drawn into alignment by the U-shape of the urban plan, the site, which slopes steeply southwards, will be planted in successive phases and these plantings will eventually form a wooded archipelago. The reference for this scheme, along with the sought-after kinetic effect, is drawn from aerial images in which patches of woodland are demarcated by ski slopes winding through the snow. These highly targeted "pioneer projects" create successive nodes of intense vegetation that are immediately used.

daunting. On the other hand, this excessive quality can also be highlighted. A park always seems small to me; I tend to look for solutions that make people lose the sense of its size, that amplify space. This is one of the fundamental recurring themes of parks and gardens: if they appear as they really are, one is inevitably frustrated. Le Nôtre's success stems to some degree from the fact that we do not fully grasp the scale of his parks. The way Olmsted plays with this aspect is also decisive in his work. If we extrapolated a visual proposal designed for a small-scale park to a large one, it would seem incongruous. The scales have different speeds; artifice can be maintained when it remains small, but when it comes to a landscape, an outright fantasy cannot sustain any historical dimension: the result seems "off"– like cogs grinding in a gearbox when not correctly aligned. Being equivalent in size to a large city district, the transformation of the Novartis site presents similar characteristics to any urban transformation. However, the clearly defined situation and the stable conditions it presents – a limited surface, a small number of stakeholders, a private status, an economic rather than political decision-making process – likened it to a scientific experiment.

An archipelago in time

The site includes some pre-existing woodlands – vestiges of the surrounding nature – a number of historic buildings, a number of new buildings, a protected hydraulic zone and endless car parks and warehouses. It is a difficult, highly fragmented setting. The terrain is steeply sloping – 20 metres from north to south – and the seasons are very contrasting in this region. Furthermore, demolitions on occupied sites are subject to many constraints. The idea is to install an archipelago of forest blocks and a succession of clearings that weave a sort of infinite fabric in which people will move easily from place to place. This system seeks to encourage walking between buildings, to have people cross the park between the places where they work, meet, get information, do research, and eat. To stimulate activity in the park, it will have a number of pavilions housing amenities such as a library and meeting places.

We thought we would manage the construction process by setting up temporary structures and implementing a phasing plan. But no one accepted the idea of temporary works that would have to be dismantled afterwards. And phasing by geographical zone did not necessarily make it possible to establish the readability of the continuities we were looking for. The client proposed to proceed through "pilot" or "pioneer" projects: every year we would implement a piece of a representative but permanent project, which in itself would be a miniature of a park system. The addition of these pieces would gradually produce a fabric that would colonise the site.

Opposite page: the principle of successive implementation of pioneer projects. Designed to be immediately effective in their programming, the aim is for them to eventually colonise the entire site in an accretive process. To generate activity in the forest "patches", the architect Inessa Hansch proposed associating each one with an amenity, conceived in relation to its specific site.

This page: illustration of the principles upon which the park's image is founded: grassy hills undulating between patches of woodland. Roads run along the edge of these patches. A functional link between the various sectors of the campus, the park is also an inhabited landscape where people can walk, meet or take a lunch break.

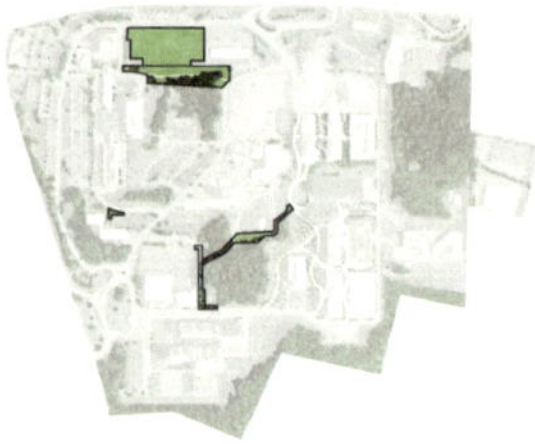

2015-2016

2016-2017

2017-2018

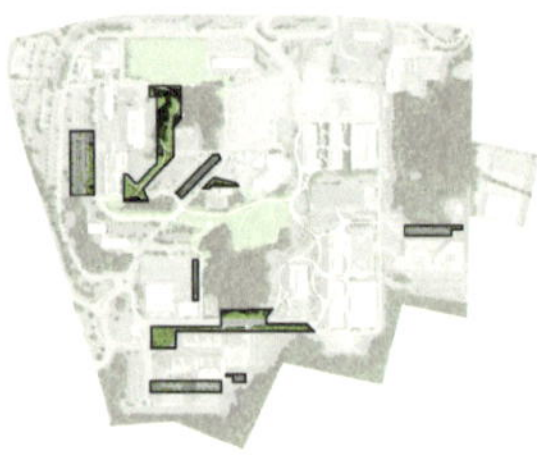

2018-2019

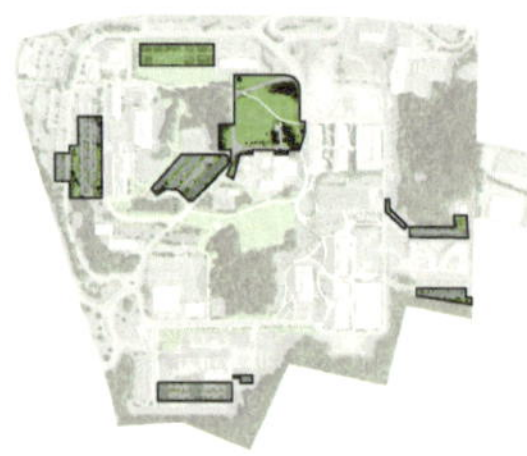

2019-2020

2020-2021

2015-2021

"Pilot" projects

As these pilot or "pioneer" projects are intended to endure, they will gradually produce a system of valleys despite the persistent presence of large chunks of industrial fabric or car parks. We were entrusted with a thirty-year mission and, since 2013, several "pilots" have been devised. The first one has been completed. It slips in between the car parks and then extends into the plantings so that you no longer know exactly where you are – it is already a small park, 600 metres long but not very wide, with a path and patches of woodland that prefigure the sense of space we are trying to instil. This pioneer project is not based on a geometric partition of the site, it is not the partial realisation of a whole: it is firmly established, immediately modifying uses and enhancing the site.

To construct this oversized archipelago, we looked to a few early twentieth-century parks in Brussels, in which an initial path framework was designed and subsequently filled out with lawns and woods. We have given a lot of thought to the positioning of our paths, and how clearings and micro-forests would be woven together. We are composing a network of valleys rather than an accumulation of interventions. The atmospheres and scales are determined, but the system is flexible; it is up to us to play with the rhythm of the plantings over time.

While the long-term plan foresees the development of large swathes of woodland, initially we can only establish their boundary line. The idea is to establish a well-defined and fast-growing forest edge, a first layer of afforestation that is part of the archipelago, which will be completed and thickened after the demolition of the industrial buildings. To what extent do we have to exaggerate the density of the line so that this backdrop makes the space of the future valley readable? We made prototypes of this pilot project to see if the edge was working. To make the void exist immediately, it is fundamental to obtain a screen effect that has a beautiful presence for users. It is a "reverse" landscape that starts from the edge and then thickens.

Opposite page: plans for the actual progress of interventions on the site; examples: first plantings on the edge, establishment of a planted path, plant colonisation of a car park. This page: a boardwalk – one of the amenities designed by Inessa Hansch – passes through a wetland grove. This walk presents variations that generate particular situations (walkway, bench integrated into the guardrail etc.) in relation to the natural setting.

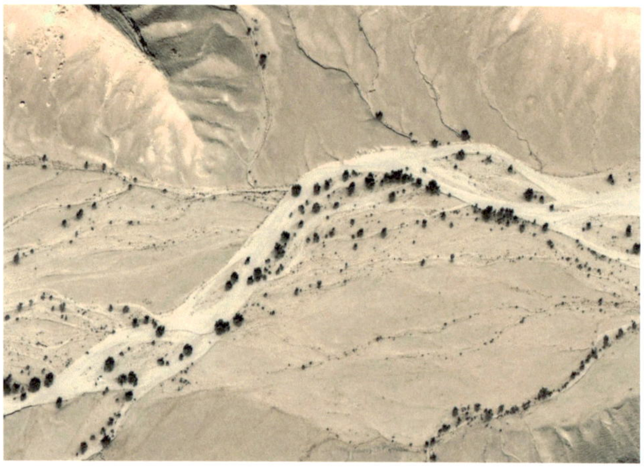
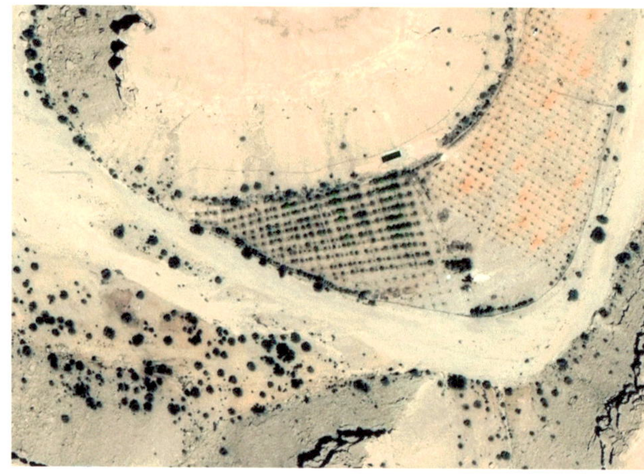
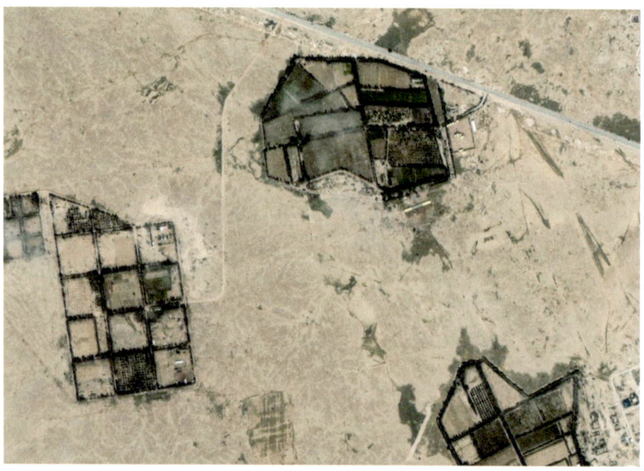

DOHA COASTLINE
QATAR, 2008–2016

Through a succession of opportunities, we designed a series of very large urban interventions for Doha, the capital of Qatar, on sites spread over such a large area that one can almost speak of a territorial project. We did not start from an overall vision to be subsequently broken down point by point, as in some of our European projects, but rather from an accumulation of commissions that forced us to take the territory in the broad sense into account. The first of our projects was for the new National Museum, whose architect Jean Nouvel had commissioned us to design the gardens. Our scheme was composed of large flowerbeds in the shape of wheels, a somewhat alien form in this context, which extended the very particular, disc-like design of Nouvel's building. To our great surprise, the Emir of Qatar said: "No, we have a culture, and that's not it." He was shocked by the idea of this park being built around large abstract discs, as if simply placed on a blank page, and there was also the fact it resembled the irrigation systems sold by the Americans to Saudi Arabia.

We studied the Qatari landscape more closely, seeking out elements that could nourish a landscape project located in the city. As always, natural geography yields particular forms and situations, which include agricultural and urban practices. The dry rivers, the famous *wadi*, sometimes carry runoff water and concentrate a little moisture the rest of the time. A thin but specific vegetation develops in this environment, producing shapes, flows and meanders. Agriculture has created dykes, reservoirs and canals, whose logic and geometries are superimposed on natural geography and topography. Many of the mangroves growing on the coast, where they form a precious ecosystem, have been destroyed in the Gulf by port, industrial or tourist developments, although some have survived. There are also dunes, the places where they touch the water, lagoons etc. In short, there is a territorial culture in Qatar that we did not initially notice.

We therefore reread the landscape, its history and practices, and transposed it into the museum garden. The consistency of the method and approach established a vocabulary for the projects that followed, sometimes at other scales. Nouvel had us participate in a competition for the entire Doha corniche. This was followed by a major commission from Architecture Studio, which entrusted us with the responsibility of public spaces and parks for the Lusail district, located to the north on the edge of the desert. Then we were called on, directly but in association with Pei, for the transformation of the grounds of the Museum of Islamic Art. We also did a large number of competitions and studies for OMA: the University of Qatar, the airport perimeter, including an amusement park, then Endurance Village and, on a very large scale, a highway landscape. Most of them have remained at the study stage. Why get involved in all this? Because it is exciting to carry out large-scale operations over a short time frame. These are the public spaces we should have built in French suburbs: the scales are the same as in Saclay, for example, where we were never able to project continuously over a distance of 10 or 15 kilometres. Being associated with construction projects of this size is fascinating, even if their scale is still much smaller than the work carried out in Boston in the nineteenth century.

Some typical landscapes of Qatar and their associated territorial forms: the natural geography of the dry desert riverbeds (*wadi*), where the vegetation radiating between the dunes hints at the underlying moisture (top); the agricultural irrigation systems and the regular geometry of their dykes and reservoirs (middle); on the coast, deltas and lagoons, with their mangrove ecosystem and the meanders of their sand and water landscape (bottom two rows).

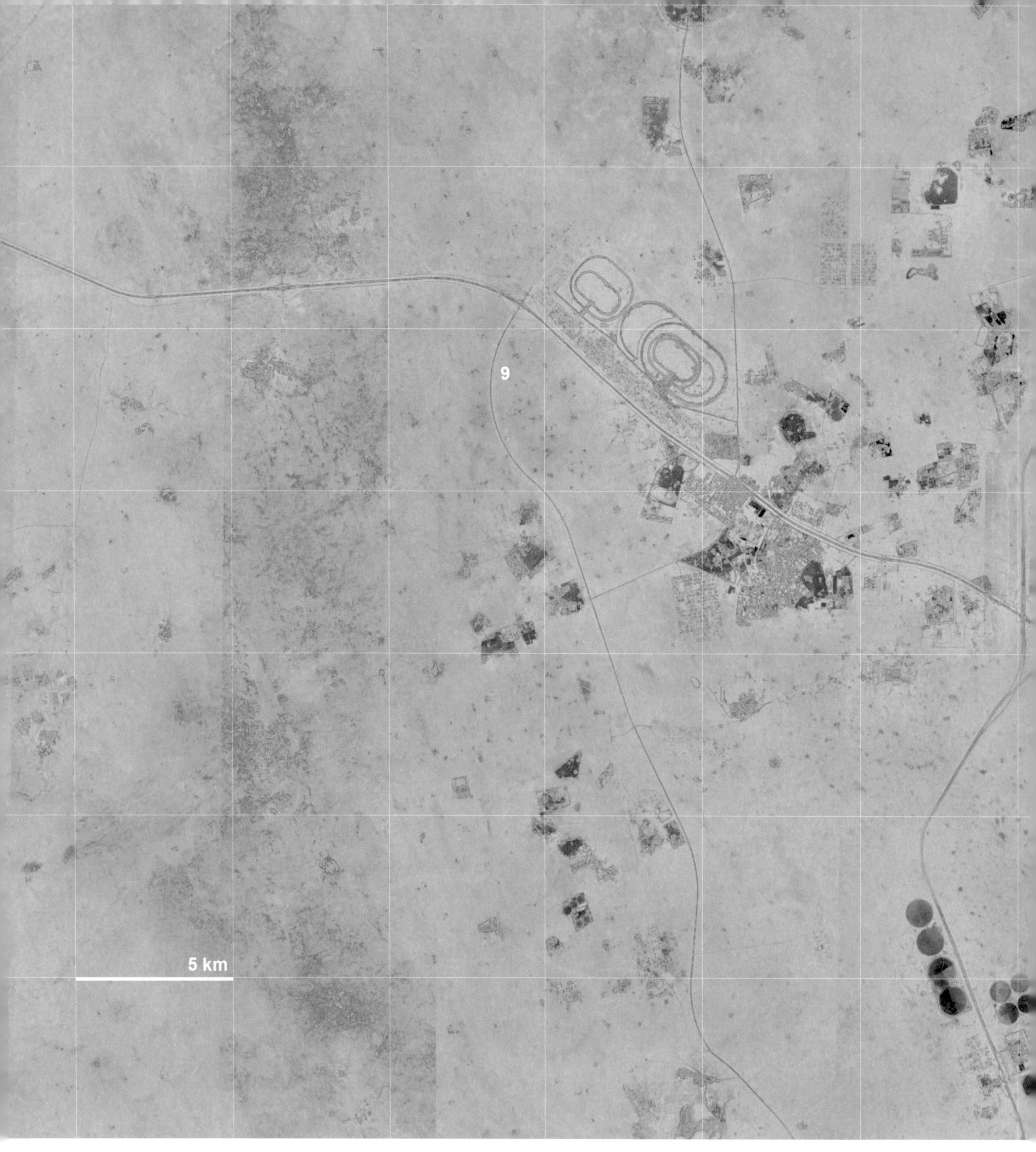
9
5 km

An accumulation of major projects, on the shores of the rapidly changing Gulf coast. From south to north: in Doha, the gardens of the National Museum of Qatar (architect: Jean Nouvel) (1), a proposal for the development of the corniche (2), the park of the Museum of Islamic Art (architect: I.M. Pei) (3), the public spaces of the Lusail district (4), the university (5), Wadi Park (6), Lusail marina (7), Lusail Olympic Park (8), the highway (9).

National Museum of Qatar

The museum garden was used as a testing ground in which to define this atlas of landscape forms. Jean Nouvel's "desert rose" is set in an arid landscape. The surrounding garden had an encyclopedic function, it was supposed to evoke the landscapes and agriculture of Qatar – but, for budgetary reasons, it was not realised. We had imagined a network of artificial dunes, a large landscape embedded with a whole series of gardens, as we had observed in the cultivated hollows of the territory. We wanted to stage, on a small scale, a number of "pseudo-agricultural landscapes". The transposition would have been very artificial. The plan shows the elements previously described: a lagoon, whose bed was deepened to provide a foreground to the museum behind the existing corniche, whose concrete edges transpose the curves of the dunes that continue into the sea.

It is a recurrent idea in the history of gardens to reinterpret the landscapes in which they are set. Food-producing gardens preceded ornamental gardens. In Europe, Renaissance gardens were significantly dedicated to growing vegetables. This dimension only gradually gave way to decorative concerns, before the classical period brought about a change of dimension. In Japan, the garden is still a miniaturised transposition of a large landscape. In the large English gardens, the owners also owned the surrounding countryside and had it redrawn as if they were composing paintings. There is always a relationship between landscape, territory and gardens.

Opposite page: representations of the initial project of the museum garden. Top: perspective simulation and sectional principle of the artificial dune landscape and its planted strata; bottom, overall plan of the garden surrounding the "desert rose" buildings designed by Jean Nouvel.
This metaphorical landscape sets the museum complex in an undulating topography, between a lagoon environment and a series of botanical, food-producing and ornamental gardens.
This page: detail of the plan showing the geometries involved in the project; model details presenting two examples of planting grids applied to the relief of artificial dunes.

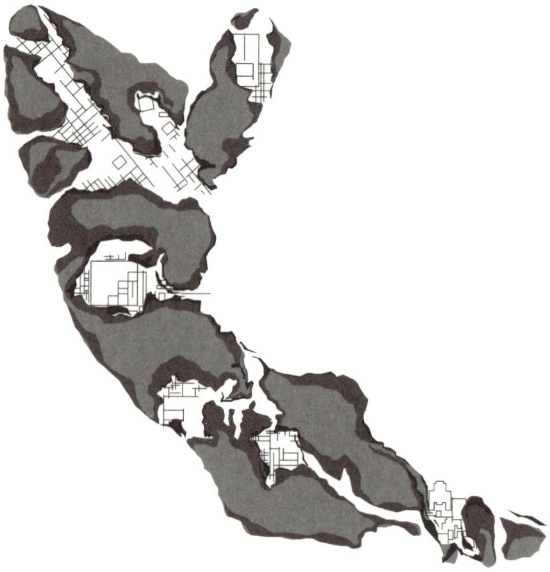

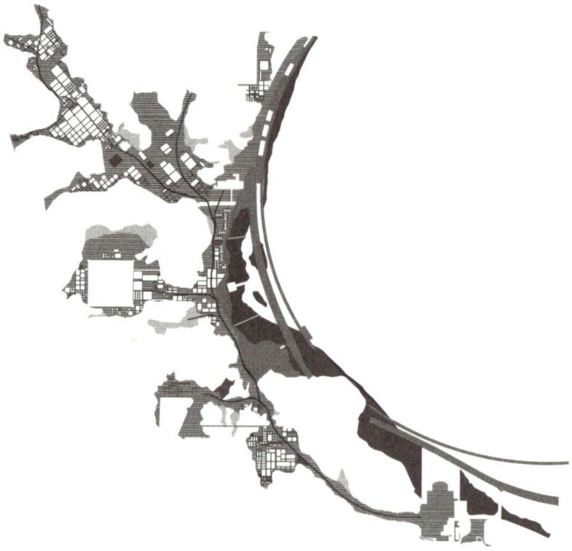

500 m

Doha corniche

Again in collaboration with Nouvel, we reflected on the landscaping of the corniche on which the Museum of Islamic Art (architect: Pei Cobb Freed & Partners) is sited. Our proposal was to endow this vast road landscape, which extends over 3.5 kilometres, with an overall consistency, based on the idea of transposition present in the museum garden, but this time perhaps more to scale. For the 300 hectares of the "Central Park", we identified the landforms and hollows that could form valleys. Exaggerating the features already present on site enables us to identify the empirical process by which these territories were developed. A lagoon is connected to the rear of the corniche by small dykes that pass through the line of dunes. To avoid literally reproducing the existing landscape scheme, we reversed it: what should have been dry became green, but while following the morphology of the site. Vast meadows take over the hills, which will extend according to water availability. Urban operations occupy the valleys, with their public spaces whose highly ordered plantings are modelled on agrarian patterns.

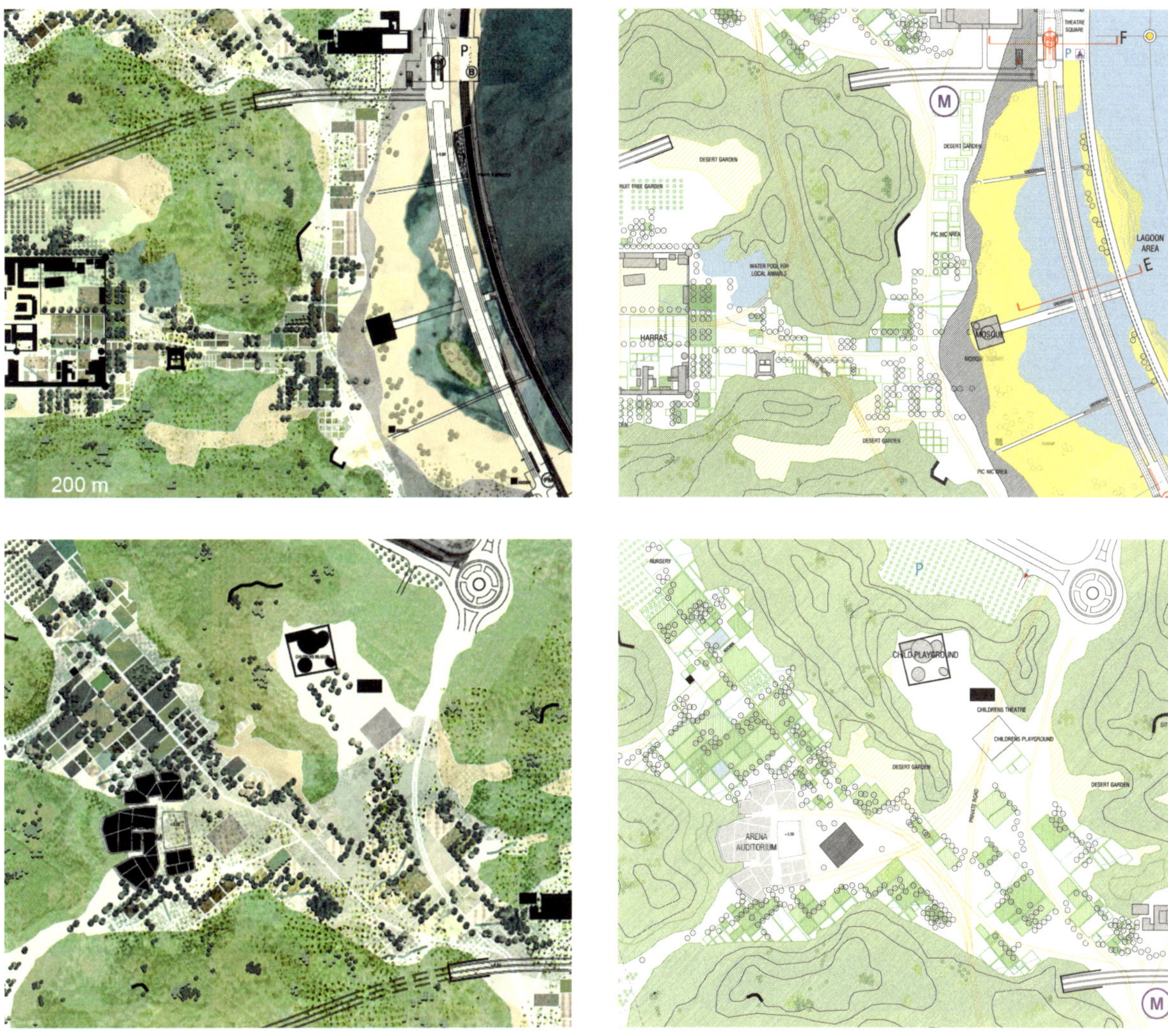

Opposite page: behind the corniche, the park structure is based on the figure of the *wadi* – torrential rains sculpt the bed of the *wadi* and between floods it is lined by small agricultural plots. Reversing the order of things, long, dry "valleys" in which gardens form shaded alcoves have been dug out on the site. These hollows accommodate a variety of amenities, while the hills that separate them are treated like large planted surfaces.
The valleys, traversed by roads, converge towards the bay. They open onto an artificial lagoon and then to the Gulf, with a beach stretching along the 3.5 km of the corniche.
This page: detailed plans of two of the valleys, with the distribution of their plantings on the left and their topography and programmes on the right: top, stud farms, orchards, a mosque, sports facilities, and road-dykes that cross the lagoon towards the corniche; bottom, a sports arena/auditorium, the National Theatre, various playgrounds and a performance arts venue for children.

Park of the Museum of Islamic Art

The construction site of the museum designed by I.M. Pei had left a considerable amount of excavated material. We reused it to create the artificial topographies of this 14 hectare park, which extends to the sea. We started from real dune designs that we made constructible by transforming their undulations into facets. The green slopes of the three dunes, planted in the manner of meadows, alternate with "valleys". These hollows host cafés and their terraces, events and outdoor performances, under metal canopies designed by engineer Jean-François Blassel and the Pei agency.

The site can be "used" in two ways: either by entering the valleys and finding somewhere to sit under the canopies; or by climbing from behind the artificial dune, on a very gentle slope, to reach a ridge from which the city is suddenly revealed. The setting is highly appreciated by residents, who come to relax on the slopes in the evening to enjoy the view of the skyline and its skyscrapers. One can then go down to the quayside and walk as far as the viewing point at the end of the corniche, where a huge sculpture by Richard Serra has been installed.

Offsetting the little semicircular corniche and its regular rows of palm trees, the park's undulating dunes are free of any ornamentation. They are planted with lawns or grasses and a soil irrigation system keeps their faceted slopes green. The gaps in between them host small public amenities, sheltered under large canopies.
From the top of the dunes, visitors can contemplate the panoramic view of the Doha skyline on one side and, on the other, the corniche and the two attractions to which it leads: the museum on the city side, and Richard Serra's sculpture beside the sea.

200 m

Wadi Park

The existing urban plan, designed by a British firm, provided for a 3 kilometre long park from the sea to the interior. As it happens, the site follows the course of a former river, therefore a dry valley, which had been largely neglected and was even derelict. The hypothesis was to re-establish the presence of the dry river in this long corridor, to exaggerate the existing topography and to have components of the Qatari landscape feature along its length – the interplay of dunes and, in the wettest part, agriculture – and even, in one third of the park, to reintroduce the idea that it could be overgrown by mangroves. The canyon's presence is reinforced by excavating it to create a dune on one side, in reinforced sand, which offers a walk and views. Dykes, which also serve as walkways, are built in the valley. They determine wetter areas in which small gardens are nestled, but also larger programmes including an educational farm. Plantings develop sometimes naturalistically at the foot of the dune and sometimes in a more organised manner, in the form of cultivated plots. The mangrove swamp, which was restored by excavation, is also crossed by dykes, like those we had identified on existing sites. These landscaping works are not just backdrops: they create conditions for nature to take root.

Opposite page: the park is a 56 hectare ecological corridor structured by a *wadi* that stitches together the different districts of the new city of Lusail. It is crossed by a number of roads that define five sequences with specific landscape qualities, planted with local plant species. The park is at once a place where different natural environments meet, a complex hydraulic infrastructure, and the setting for light amenities. The segments of the longitudinal section show the evolution of the relief and plantings between the arid parts in the west and the marshy banks with their mangroves in the east. This page: excavation work on the mouth of the old river. Protected from the sea by a temporary dam, the mechanical diggers excavate the sand and rock to shape the landforms on which the mangrove swamp will be sited.

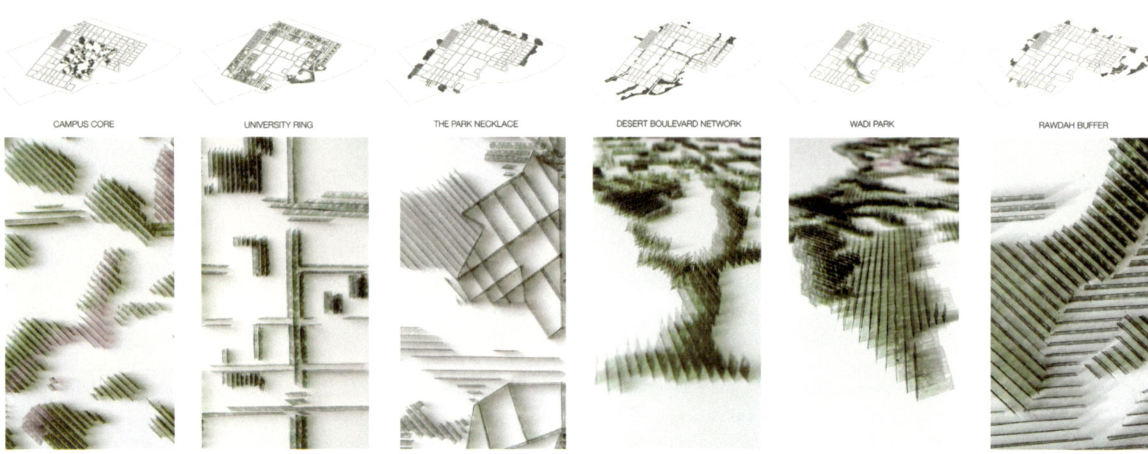
CAMPUS CORE
UNIVERSITY RING
THE PARK NECKLACE
DESERT BOULEVARD NETWORK
WADI PARK
RAWDAH BUFFER

Lusail Olympic Park and Qatar University

The new city of Lusail, 15 kilometres north of Doha, is expected to eventually cater for a population of 200,000. The aim of the urban plan is to produce a high-quality living environment – in which landscaping is a factor – coupled with a strong mix of programmes. These two projects for major facilities are located in cultivated areas. In both cases, the agrarian territorial structure provided us with a planting and traffic plan, into which the sites receiving the programmed functions were assimilated. Lusail's Olympic village is located 20 kilometres north of Doha on the agricultural belt irrigated by a *wadi* that directs runoff water towards the bay in the east. A grid of hedgerows defines a plot where the sports facilities and the Olympic village are located, completed by screens of casuarina and eucalyptus. The university occupies 8 square kilometres of countryside, in a highly attractive location between the residential districts to the west and an opulent neighbourhood of villas and gardens along with a golf course to the east. To preserve this threatened rural fringe, the strategy anticipates future urban development based on the characteristics of the site. The planting scheme for public spaces is derived from the existing topography and irrigation networks, which channel water to the lines of trees shading the paths.
The edges are divided by canals into landscaped, planted or cultivated plots.

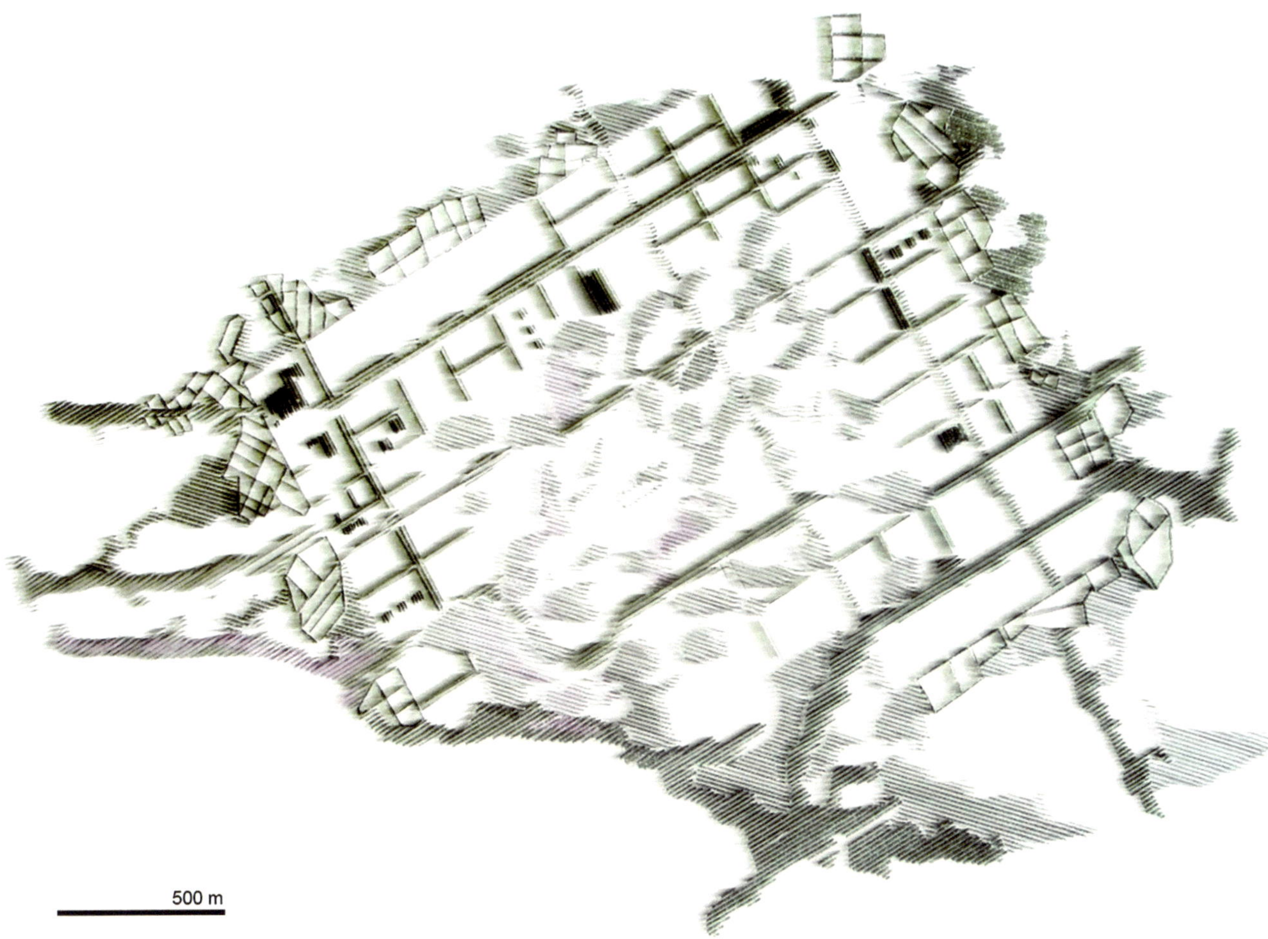

Opposite page: model of the Olympic district and perspectives to illustrate the atmosphere of the gardens planted along the grid (left column); aerial view of the university and conceptual models of the screen planting (right column).

Bottom: the addition of strategic typological actions – at the heart of the campus, on its successive peripheries, across the site – generates an overall vegetation plan (this page) that intensifies the characteristics of the setting.

The planting grid is colonised by more capricious vegetation, whose growth pattern corresponds to the underlying presence of water.

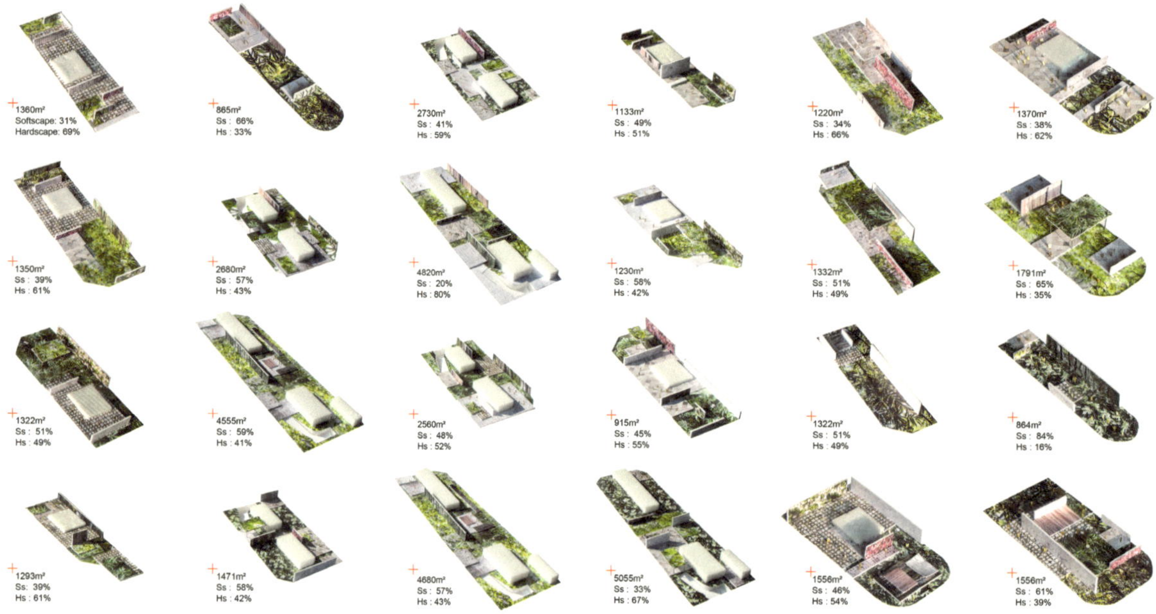

This page: twenty-four "pocket gardens" (top) of various sizes express the principles of the Arabian garden: an enclosed courtyard, flanked by shaded arcades, featuring vegetation and a water source in its centre.

The mock-up photographs show the fundamental components of the project for public spaces: a palm tree grid of varying density and "block gardens", forming oasis-like figures on a mineral ground plane. The unity of the light granite contributes to the district's specific identity.

Opposite page: the grid of granite pathways contains "block gardens" of variable density. The plant species, which can withstand very high temperatures, protect people from the sun and hot winds while providing the necessary coolness for the development of outdoor activities.

Lusail marina district

Lusail's marina district encompasses the entire seafront. We have realised almost all its public spaces. The scale of intervention is enormous. When the Emir asked for a prototype, it was 600 metres long! Granite – enough stone for the ground plane of an entire city – was ordered in huge quantities from China. Guided by the "park-city" concept, to frame the possible expansions of construction with vegetation and to immediately create a unified landscape, the landscaping design is based on a grid of planted streets and boulevards, and on "pocket gardens". These small enclosed spaces, derived from the traditional Arabian garden, the *sahn*, offer places to rest and play away from the hustle and bustle of the big boulevards.

The abundance of planting is quite unusual for a quay. It recalls some of our urban projects in which the composition is not based on tree lines, but on alignments of blocks and voids that, from simple geometries, create places people can appropriate. Underground stations all lead to small gardens. Like variations on "neo-Modernist" design, these gardens appear to be set on mineral surfaces – a little like what some American landscape gardeners did in the 1950s – and endowed with an overabundance of plants. We argued for this density because it creates environments that provide an essential environmental quality in cities. In this type of urbanisation, a surface water table gradually forms, making it unnecessary to water the trees.

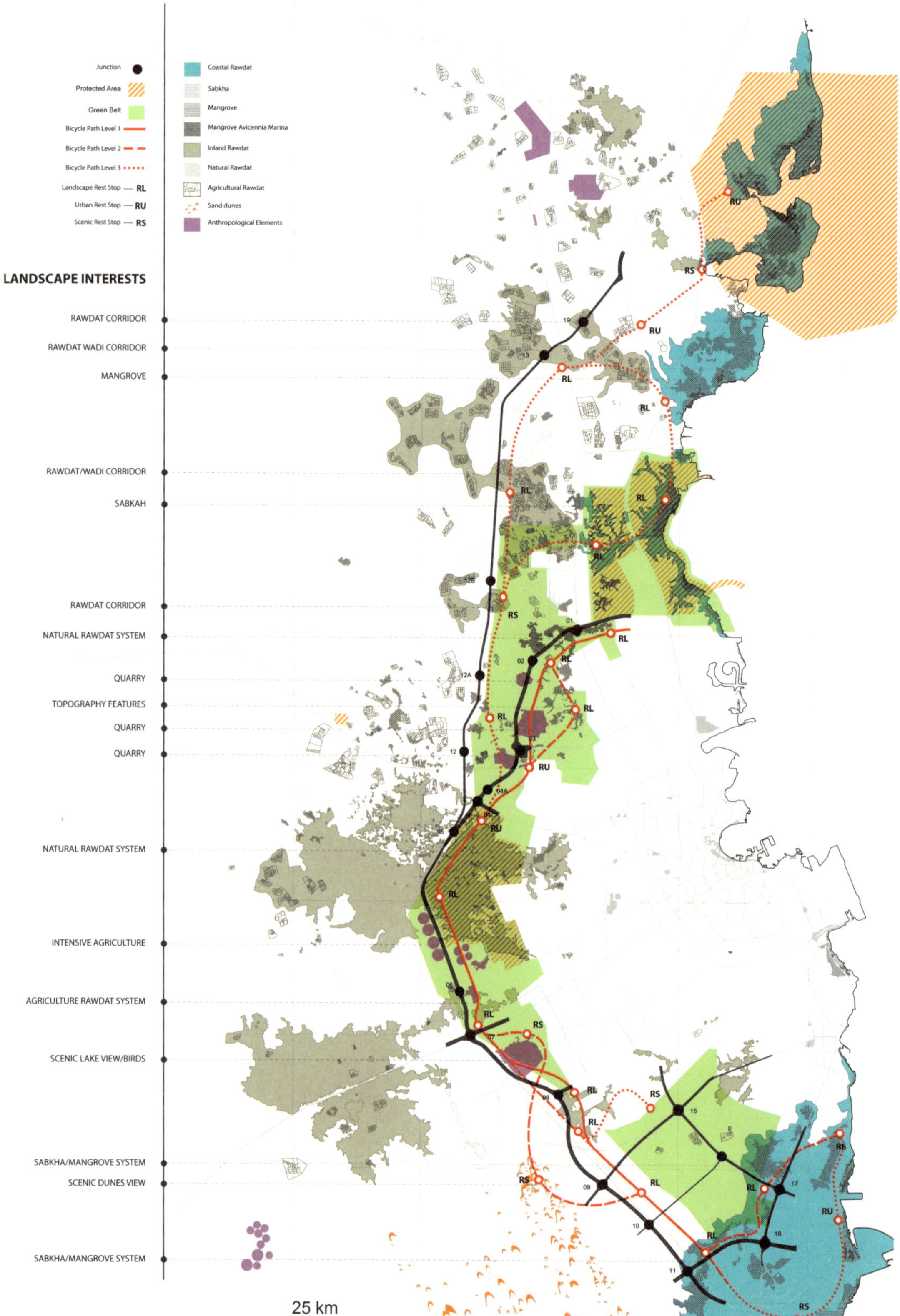

This page: overall plan of the motorway and identification of its noteworthy existing landscapes. The highway also has the function of containing Doha's westward urbanisation. It passes through six major landscape features: the desert, then the salt marshes of the Persian Gulf coast, residential districts, the urban periphery of Doha, the *rawdat* (the system of interconnected micro-depressions by which water flows to the sea), and mangroves whose survival depends on this fresh water supply. Opposite page: arranged as closely as possible to the road, six specific plant and topographical sequences correspond to the different landscape features: they reveal their diversity, bringing their geomorphological and ecological characteristics to the fore. The twenty-two major interchanges occurring the length of the highway each represent a special moment. In each case the landscaping design aims to establish a dialogue between the interchanges' immediate surroundings and the more distant landscape.

Greater Doha ring road (Orbital Highway)

This massive infrastructure project is intended to connect Qatar from north to south. Its roundabouts and their landscaping had already been designed. OMA was asked to conduct a study, with our team as landscape architects. A highway forms an obstacle that disrupts the functioning of the geographical and ecological systems of the territory it crosses. We proposed extending the treatment of the landscapes along the route far beyond the line of the highway itself. The principle consisted in enhancing these landscapes, by amplifying the typological phenomena – continuities, dry valleys, agricultural features, and so on – we had identified at the territorial level by recreating the logic of the large landscape rather than by a decorative embellishment of the roundabouts. We worked on two scales of perception: the land immediately adjacent to the highway, and the projects that extended this intervention into the hinterland. The "artistic actions" followed the same approach: taking into account the ecological dynamics of the site and bringing them to the fore, to connect the perception of the highway to natural systems and thereby facilitate orientation.

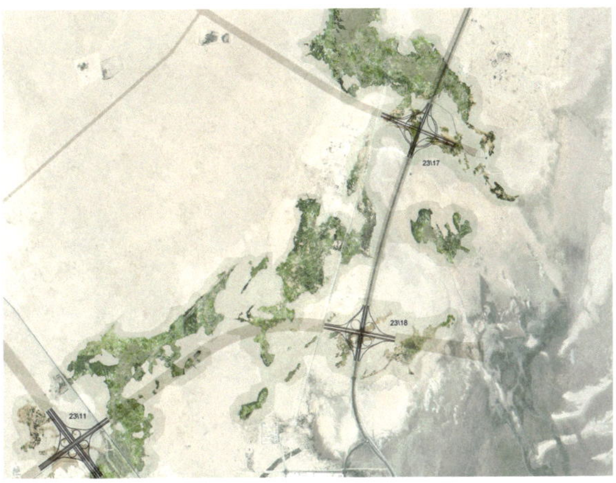

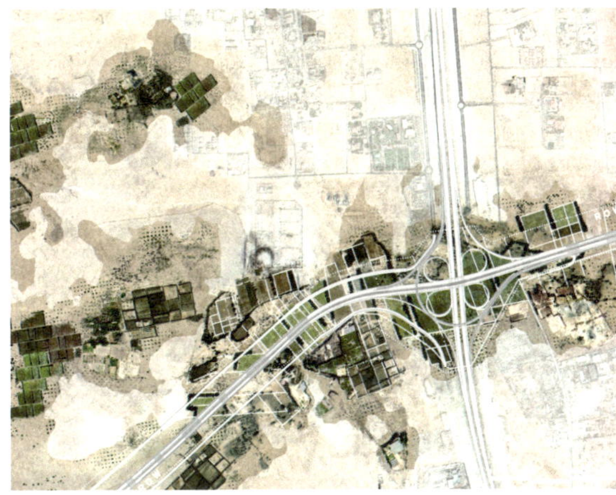

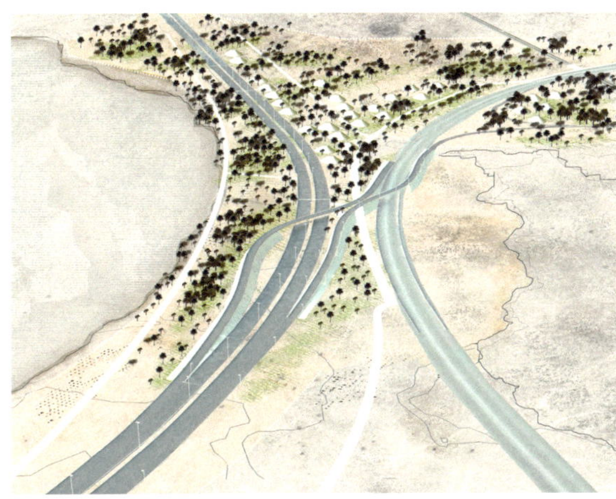

PROJECT CREDITS

MARSEILLE FRANCE

MARSEILLE OLD PORT
2012–2016
Client
Communauté urbaine Marseille Provence Métropole
Team
MDP Michel Desvigne Paysagiste (lead consultant)
Foster + Partners, architect
Tangram, urban designers
Ingérop, engineering
AIK / Yann Kersalé
MDP project managers
Justine Miething, Enrico Ferraris

MARSEILLE CHAIN OF PARKS
2012–2014
Client
Communauté urbaine Marseille Provence Métropole
Conseil général des Bouches-du-Rhône
Team
MDP Michel Desvigne Paysagiste
MDP project manager
Justine Miething

MARSEILLE FRAMEWORK PLAN
2012–2014
Client
Communauté urbaine Marseille Provence Métropole
Team
MDP Michel Desvigne Paysagiste (lead consultant)
Tangram, urban designers
Ingérop, engineers
MDP project manager
Mathieu Labeille

MARSEILLE CITY-CENTRE PUBLIC SPACES, 2018–2022
Client
Métropole Aix-Marseille-Provence
Team
MDP Michel Desvigne Paysagiste
Tangram, urban designers
Ingérop, engineers (lead consultant)
MDP project managers
Guillaume Leuregans, Carla Maria Greco

MONTPELLIER FRANCE

PORT-MARIANNE FRAMEWORK PLAN
1991–2002
Client
Ville de Montpellier
Team
MDP Michel Desvigne Paysagiste, associated with Christine Dalnoky, landscape designer
SERM, developer (lead consultant)
MDP project manager
François Neveux

AVENUE PIERRE-MENDÈS-FRANCE
1993–2000
Client
Ville de Montpellier
Team
MDP Michel Desvigne Paysagiste, associated with Christine Dalnoky, landscape designer
MDP project manager
François Neveux

LEZ PARK
1992–2000
Client
Ville de Montpellier
Team
MDP Michel Desvigne Paysagiste, associated with Christine Dalnoky, landscape designer
Adrien Fainsilber, architect-urban designer
MDP project manager
François Neveux

LIRONDE GARDENS
2001–2014
Client
Ville de Montpellier
Team
MDP Michel Desvigne Paysagiste
Christian de Portzamparc, architect-urban designer
MDP project managers
Pauline Way, Guillaume Leuregans

CHARPAK PARK
1998–
Client
Ville de Montpellier
Team
MDP Michel Desvigne Paysagiste
MDP project managers
Pauline Way, Guillaume Leuregans

LYON FRANCE

QUAI DE SAÔNE
1999
Client
SAEM Lyon-Confluence
Team
MDP Michel Desvigne Paysagiste
SIOAH, engineer
MDP project manager
Pauline Way

LYON CONFLUENCE 1
2000–2005
Client
SPL Lyon-Confluence
Team
MDP Michel Desvigne Paysagiste
François Grether, architect-urban designer (lead consultant)
MDP project managers
Pauline Way, Anne Gaillard

LYON CONFLUENCE 2
2009–2012
Client
SPL Lyon-Confluence
Team
MDP Michel Desvigne Paysagiste
Herzog & de Meuron, architect-urban designer (lead consultant)
MDP project manager
Ana Marti-Baron

LYON CONFLUENCE 2
CENTRAL SQUARE, 2009–2012
Client
SPL Lyon-Confluence
Team
MDP Michel Desvigne Paysagiste
Herzog & de Meuron, architect-urban designer
Christian de Portzamparc, architect
Cap Verde, engineer
MDP project managers
Ana Marti-Baron, Guillaume Leuregans

LYON CONFLUENCE 2, BLOCK A3
2013–2017
Client
Icade
Team
MDP Michel Desvigne Paysagiste
Herzog & de Meuron, architect-urban designer
Tatiana Bilbao S.C.
Manuel Herz Architekten, architect
Christian Kerez
AFAA
MDP project managers
Ana Marti-Baron, Taro Ernst, Guillaume Leuregans

LYON CONFLUENCE 2, BLOCK B2
2015–2019
Client
Ogic
Team
MDP Michel Desvigne Paysagiste
Diener & Diener Architekten, architect
Clément Vergély, architect
Étamine BET, engineer
MDP project managers
Guillaume Leuregans, Taro Ernst

BORDEAUX FRANCE

LANDSCAPE CHARTER, 2002–2005
GARONNE FRAMEWORK PLAN, 2003–2004
BORDEAUX RIGHT BANK, 2005–2006
Client
Ville de Bordeaux
Team
MDP Michel Desvigne Paysagiste
MDP project manager
Sophie Mourthé

ANGÉLIQUES PARK
2008–
Client
Ville de Bordeaux
Team
MDP Michel Desvigne Paysagiste (lead consultant)
IHA Inessa Hansch Architect
Artelia Bordeaux, engineer
MDP project managers
Sophie Mourthé, Ana Marti-Baron, Anne-Fleur Aronstein, Guillaume Leuregans

DESCHAMPS SECTOR
2008
Client
Ville de Bordeaux
Team
MDP Michel Desvigne Paysagiste
Christian de Portzamparc, architect (lead consultant)
MDP project manager
Sophie Mourthé

BASTIDE BRAZZA NORD DISTRICT
2012–
Client
Ville de Bordeaux
Team
MDP Michel Desvigne Paysagiste
Youssef Tohmé, architect-urban designer (lead consultant)
Ingérop, roads and utilities engineer
MDP project managers
Ana Marti-Baron, Guillaume Leuregans, Sara Maillefer

SIMONE VEIL BRIDGE
2013–
Client
Ville de Bordeaux
Team
MDP Michel Desvigne Paysagiste
OMA, architect (lead consultant)
WSP (EGIS group), engineer
Lumières Studio, lighting designer
MDP project managers
Ana Marti-Baron, Guillaume Leuregans

SACLAY PLATEAU GRAND PARIS, FRANCE

PARIS-SACLAY
1ST FRAMEWORK AGREEMENT (2009–2015)
Client
Établissement public d'aménagement public Paris-Saclay (EPAPS)
Urban and landscape project management group
MDP Michel Desvigne Paysagiste (lead consultant)
XDGA-FAA / Xaveer De Geyter, Floris Alkemade, architect-urban designer
Arep, Sogreah, Setec, Altostep, Tractebel
Technical project management for public spaces
Ingérop
Confluences
Sol paysage
Technical project management for edge
Artelia
Confluences
MDP project managers
Sophie Mourthé, Ségolène Merlin-Raynaud

2ND FRAMEWORK AGREEMENT (2015–2021)
Client
Établissement public d'aménagement public Paris-Saclay (EPAPS)
Urban and landscape project management group
MDP Michel Desvigne Paysagiste (lead consultant)
XDGA-FAA / Xaveer De Geyter, Floris Alkemade, architect-urban designer
Concepto, lighting designer
Technical project management for public spaces
Ingérop (2015–2016) / Tugec (2017–)
Confluences
Sol paysage
Technical project management for edge
Artelia
Confluences
Sol paysage
MDP project manager
Ségolène Merlin-Raynaud

BURGOS
SPAIN

RAILWAY BOULEVARD
2006–2012
Client
Consorcio para la gestión de la variante ferroviaria de Burgos
Team
MDP Michel Desvigne Paysagiste
Herzog & de Meuron, architect (lead consultant)
Hydra, consultant botanist
MBG Ingenieria y Arquitectura SL, engineer
MDP project manager
Ana Marti-Baron

EURALENS
FRANCE

EURALENS CENTRALITÉ
2010–2019
Client
Euralens
Team
MDP Michel Desvigne Paysagiste (lead consultant)
Christian de Portzamparc, architect-urban designer
IHA Inessa Hansch Architect (street furniture)
Sogreah Lille
Artelia Group
Buro Happold
MDP project managers
Guillaume Leuregans, Mathieu Labeille, Hugo Bruley

EURALENS CHAIN OF PARKS
2013–2015
Client
Euralens
Team
MDP Michel Desvigne Paysagiste (lead consultant)
IHA Inessa Hansch Architect
Pro Development, project planning engineer
Biotope, ecology consultants
MDP project managers
Guillaume Leuregans, Mathieu Labeille

ARTOIS CHAIN OF PARKS
2018–
Client
Pôle Métropolitain de l'Artois
Team
MDP Michel Desvigne Paysagiste (lead consultant)
IHA Inessa Hansch Architect
Pro Development, project planning engineer
Biotope, ecology consultants
MDP project managers
Guillemette Dumars, Guillaume Leuregans

DETROIT
MICHIGAN, UNITED STATES

DETROIT EAST RIVERFRONT
2016–
Client
Detroit Riverfront Conservancy, Inc.
Team
MDP Michel Desvigne Paysagiste
SOM, Skidmore, Owings & Merrill LLP (lead consultant)
IHA Inessa Hansch Architecte
MDP project manager
Taro Ernst

EAST HANOVER
NEW JERSEY, UNITED STATES

NOVARTIS CAMPUS
2013–2016
Client
Novartis
Team
MDP Michel Desvigne Paysagiste (lead consultant)
IHA Inessa Hansch Architect
MDP project managers
Justine Miething, Hugo Bruley

DOHA
QATAR

NEW QATAR NATIONAL MUSEUM
2008–2012
Client
Qatar Museum Authorities
Qatar Petroleum
Team
MDP Michel Desvigne Paysagiste
Atelier Jean Nouvel, architect (lead consultant)
AIK / Yann Kersalé
Arup, engineer
MDP project manager
Ana Marti-Baron

LUSAIL DEVELOPMENT
2008–2013
Client
Qatar Diar
Team
MDP Michel Desvigne Paysagiste
Architecture Studio, architect (lead consultant)
SOGREAH, engineer
MDP project manager
Sophie Mourthé

DOHA CORNICHE
2009
Client
Qatar Petroleum
Team
MDP Michel Desvigne Paysagiste
Ateliers Jean Nouvel, architect (lead consultant)
MDP project manager
Justine Miething

MUSEUM OF ISLAMIC ART
2008–2013
Client
Qatar Petroleum
Team
MDP Michel Desvigne Paysagiste
Pei Cobb Freed & Partners, architect
Richard Serra, sculptor
MDP project manager
Justine Miething

WADI PARK
2011–2015
Client
Qatar Diar and LREDC
Team
MDP Michel Desvigne Paysagiste
Architecture Studio, architect
Artelia, engineer
RFR, structural engineer
AIK / Yann Kersalé
BWS, quantity surveyor
MDP project managers
Elinor Scarth, Mar Armengol-Reyes

QATAR UNIVERSITY
2012
Client
Qatar Diar and LREDC
Team
MDP Michel Desvigne Paysagiste
OMA, architect-urban designer (lead consultant)
Mott Macdonald, engineering, infrastructure and equipment
WSP / RWDI, environmental engineer
Licht Kunst Licht (LKL), lighting designer
Mijksenaar Signage & Wayfinding
De Leeuw, quantity surveyor
MDP project manager
Elinor Scarth

OLYMPIC PARK
2012
Client
Ashghal - Qatar Public Works Authority
Team
MDP Michel Desvigne Paysagiste
OMA, architect-urban designer (lead consultant)
Mott Macdonald, engineering, infrastructure and equipment
WSP / RWDI, environmental engineer
Licht Kunst Licht (LKL), lighting designer
Mijksenaar Signage & Wayfinding
De Leeuw, quantity surveyor
MDP project manager
Elinor Scarth

LUSINAS DISTRICT IN LUSAIL, 2010–2013
LUSAIL BOULEVARDS, 2010–2013
Client
Qatar Diar and LREDC
Team
MDP Michel Desvigne Paysagiste
Architecture Studio, architect (lead consultant)
Artelia, engineer
RFR, structural engineer
SNAIK, lighting designer
BWS, quantity surveyor
MDP project manager
Elinor Scarth

POCKET GARDENS
2011–2013
Client
Qatar Diar and LREDC
Team
MDP Michel Desvigne Paysagiste
Architecture Studio, architect (lead consultant)
Artelia, engineer
RFR, structural engineer
SNAIK, lighting designer
BWS, quantity surveyor
MDP project manager
Elinor Scarth

LUSAIL WATERFRONT
2010–2012
Client
Qatar Diar and LREDC
Team
MDP Michel Desvigne Paysagiste
Architecture Studio, architect (lead consultant)
Artelia, engineer
RFR, structural engineer
SNAIK, lighting designer
BWS, quantity surveyor
MDP project manager
Elinor Scarth

ORBITAL HIGHWAY
2014–2016
Client
Ashghal, Qatar Public Works Authority
Team
MDP Michel Desvigne Paysagiste
OMA, architect-urban designer (lead consultant)
Hyder, engineer
RWDI, environmental engineer
Licht Kunst Licht (LKL), lighting designer
Space Agency, signage
MDP project managers
Taro Ernst, Mar Armengol-Reyes

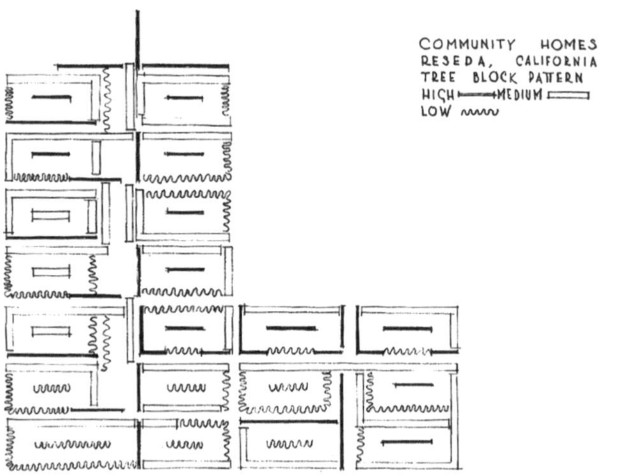

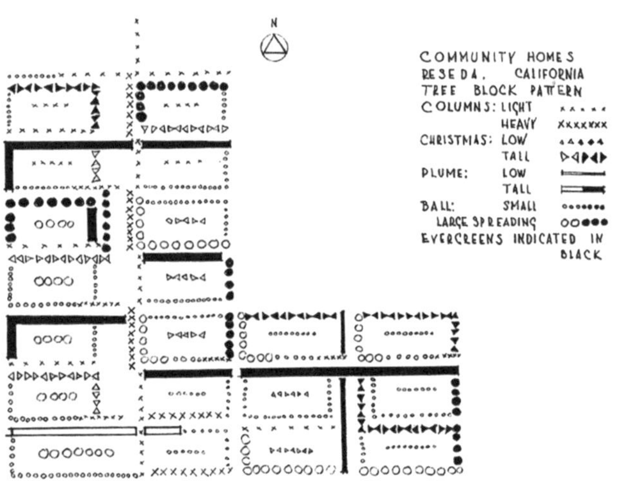

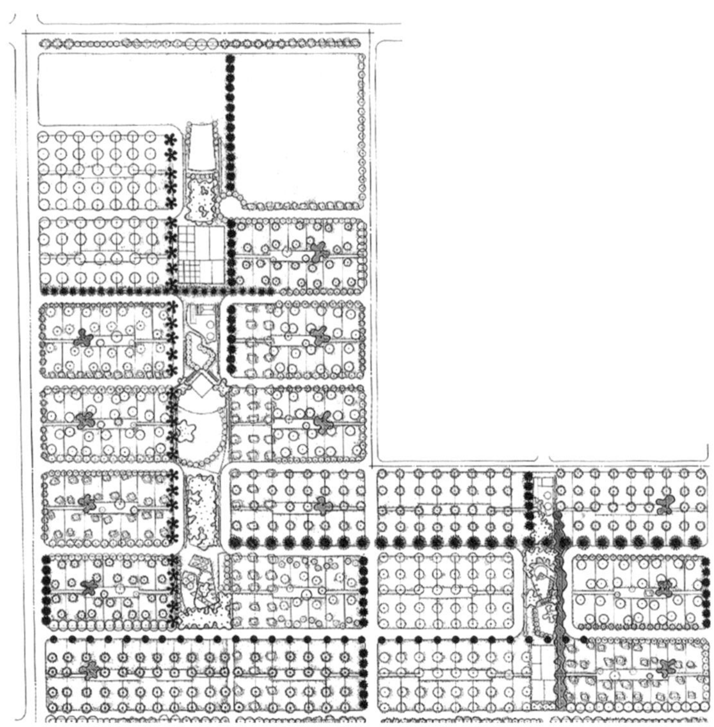

Garrett Eckbo (1910–2000), cooperative housing project for Community Homes, with Gregory Ain, Joseph Johnson and Alfred Day, c. 1948.

Top: view of an apricot orchard in the San Fernando Valley in 1929.

Dorothée Imbert
A TERRITORIAL ATTITUDE

Michel Desvigne has argued over three decades of practice against the "recognisable design" of the fashionable park and the patterned promenade, yet has managed to develop a highly recognisable body of work. His idiosyncratic use of landscape elements – the band of trees, orchard or forest archipelago – evokes a matter-of-fact system to be deployed across scales and programmes, from garden to territory.[1] The landscape project is an experimentation on space and time. The results are in the making, the moments are measured, the process is ongoing. This essay contextualises Desvigne's "landscape attitude" by teasing out themes and historical resonances across the reading and shaping of landscapes, and establishing connections with the disciplines of urbanism and geography.

Offering an alternative to the narrative of landscape as finished product, Desvigne's structural and seemingly neutral elements define spaces and mark time. The parallel bands of his Parc aux Angéliques on the Right Bank of Bordeaux address current uses and future development across a thirty-year framework plan. The bands loosely structure the 4 kilometre long riverbank, bringing to the fore the relation between element and scale, and between the generic and the site-specific. To use one of Desvigne's preferred qualifiers, this is a "dumb" landscape. The tight banding of young oak, pine, cherry and elm suggests a hybrid between nursery and forestry practices. It is a cheap, simple, yet curated, urban forest, thinned and manipulated over time.

Desvigne's use of closely planted young trees as a spatial matrix forms an analogy with the work of American landscape architect Garrett Eckbo (1910–2000). To answer the needs of migrant workers during the Great Depression, Eckbo and fellow architects and planners at the Farm Security Administration (FSA) designed camps across the Central Valley of California and other western agricultural landscapes. Seeking maximum effect with minimal means, Eckbo drew "large tree patterns at the baroque scale on cheap rural land" to create a sense of place for displaced populations.[2] The planting schemes spatially articulated districts and programmes, from school grounds to baseball diamonds. Most notably, his bird's-eye views promoted an environment structured by lines, bands, clumps and blocks of trees. Eckbo's visions were contemporary *and* timeless, drawing from his nursery experience, the agricultural context, and art and architecture. A few years later, a project for the cooperative Community Homes (1946–49) in Reseda, in the San Fernando Valley north of Los Angeles, displayed a similar vegetation strategy. Eckbo organised the 40 hectare site by drawing from the "still rural character of much of the valley around it", with its extensive orchards and nurseries.[3] A series of tree diagrams documents a wealth of variations in space, texture and opacity according to scale and use, from the civic recreational spine to the semiprivate strip park and the individual backyard. Eckbo's tree schemes – investing the most in the simplest landscape unit – expressed a belief in landscape as an agent of social change, and as a shaper of future communities.[4] Stressing the interrelation of theory and practice, he described theory as a scientific process "based on constant observation and experience", to be developed by "analysis, hypothesis, and experiment."[5] The formal analogy between Eckbo's attitude and Desvigne's can be extended to such theory of practice. The reliance on trees as structural elements, the mutual relationship between observation and intuition as a generator of design, and the shift from inspiration to scientific experiment, all find echo in Desvigne's process and interest in empirical research.

Desvigne cites two major influences as defining his working method. The first is the sequence of Observation,

1. Desvigne traces the "landscape attitude" that shaped his entire practice to an early interest in empirical research. See "Conversations with Michel Desvigne", in Dorothée Imbert (ed.), *A Landscape Inventory: Michel Desvigne Paysagiste* (San Francisco: Applied Research and Design, ORO Press, 2018), p. 20.
2. Garrett Eckbo, "Community Recreation Space in Ceres, Central Valley, California, 1940", in *Landscape for Living* (New York: Duell, Sloan and Pearce, 1950), p. 179.
3. Eckbo, "Co-operative Housing in the San Fernando Valley, Los Angeles, California, 1945–49", in *Landscape for Living*, pp. 218–221.
4. For a discussion on the FSA camps and Eckbo's 1940s and 1950s housing projects, see Dorothée Imbert, "The Art of Social Landscape Design", in Marc Treib and Dorothée Imbert, *Garrett Eckbo: Modern Landscapes for Living* (Berkeley and Los Angeles: University of California Press, 1997), pp. 106–167.

Frederick Law Olmsted (1822–1903), view of Back Bay Fens (1887) and map of Boston's "Emerald Necklace" linking the Common and Public Garden, the Fens, Jamaica Pond, the Arnold Arboretum, Franklin Park and Marine Park.

Hypothesis, Confirmation/Refutation established by French physiologist Claude Bernard (1813–1878), which Desvigne discovered while a student in botany and geology in the late 1970s. He traces his early explorations on the shaping of landscapes by natural phenomena to his awakening in empirical research and geomorphology. The other influence came from architects and collaborators Renzo Piano, Richard Rogers and Norman Foster. Desvigne recalls how they launched any design by venturing a hypothesis that was subsequently challenged by "every possible means of experimentation – model, drawing, or discussion."[6] To young Desvigne, the dynamic exchange between hypothesis and confirmation or refutation was far richer than the formal design inspiration that typically drove landscape architecture practice.

Less prominent in Desvigne's narrative, yet equally generative, was the École nationale supérieure du paysage (ENSP) in Versailles, where he studied under Michel Corajoud and Alexandre Chemetoff. Established in 1976 as an institution of higher learning and research within the École nationale d'horticulture (ENH) and under the umbrella of the Ministry of Agriculture, the ENSP inherited a faculty and a pedagogy marked by a significant horticultural tradition.[7] The curriculum combined classes in the humanities and sciences, with design, drawing and art history as well as hydrology, forestry, botany and soils. After three years of instruction and a nine-month internship, students received a professional degree in landscape architecture. Applicants with a degree in agronomy were granted advanced placement, reinforcing the perception of landscape architecture as an extension of agriculture and horticulture.[8] Despite being small, the school was rife with debates on the nature of landscape architecture, and its relation to scientific research. Desvigne enrolled in 1979, at a time when Michel Corajoud was staking a claim on design studio pedagogy with his Atelier Le Nôtre, in opposition to Bernard Lassus's Atelier Dufresny, named after the proponent of a proto-picturesque transformation of the gardens of Versailles.[9] Although Corajoud understood landscapes as vessels of the past and projections of the future, he rejected the nineteenth century for what he termed its flabby nature, as well as the postwar landscape of generic *espaces verts*. Alexandre Chemetoff, with whom Desvigne studied and apprenticed, embraced the nineteenth century and its synoptic view of technology. Chemetoff's classes on grading and drainage, planting, and soils combined lectures by specialists with the study of treatises such as Jean Darcel's Études *sur l'architecture des jardins* (1875) and Édouard André's *L'Art des jardins: Traité général de la composition des parcs et jardins* (1879). Both had been professors at the ENH. In addition to offering techniques for a wide range of landscape operations, these manuals eschewed disciplinary boundaries to promote instead a hybrid landscape architect-engineer-urbanist, equally at ease with planting design as with road alignment. Chemetoff recalls how teaching at the ENSP was informal and experimental. Neither Corajoud nor Lassus was trained as a landscape architect and the scientific contributions of horticulture faculty members yielded uneven results. Yet, Chemetoff maintains, the ENSP was a fertile ground for "learning to learn."[10] As a main protagonist of what would soon be known as the French Landscape School, Corajoud advocated for design as a "work of experimentation", drawing from the scalar lessons of Le Nôtre's gardens expanded into the urban-rural landscape continuum. Learning from Versailles – its pedagogy and its gardens – Desvigne was strongly marked by the French

5. Garrett Eckbo, "The Question of Theory", in *Landscape for Living* (New York: Duell, Sloan and Pearce, 1950), pp. 58, 60.
6. "Conversations with Michel Desvigne", p. 24.
7. Early ENSP faculty members included practitioners, designers and artists such as Jacques Simon, Jean-Bernard Perrin, Bernard Lassus and Bertrand Lavier, as well as professors drawn from the National Horticulture School (ENH) and the National Institute of Agricultural Research (INRA). See Pierre Donadieu, "La Saga des diplômes de paysagiste", https://topia.fr/2018/05/28/la-saga-des-diplomes-de-paysagiste/, 22 June 2018, accessed 29 January 2019.
8. For the ENSP statute, see article 15 of the decree dated 24 October 1976, signed by then Prime Minister Raymond Barre. Cited by Donadieu in "La Saga des diplômes de paysagiste".
9. Pierre Donadieu, "Les Débuts de la recherche à l'ENSP", https://topia.fr/2018/12/04/les-debuts-de-la-recherche/, accessed 1 December 2018. For a description of the pedagogy and goals of the Atelier Le Nôtre, see Michel Corajoud, *Le Paysage, c'est l'endroit où le ciel*

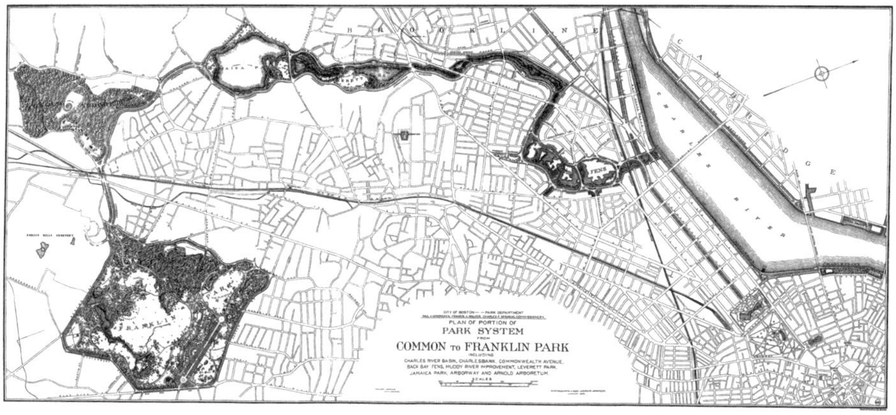

Landscape School. Crafting a method where observation and deduction drove design investigations, he acquired what he termed "territorial intelligence."[11]

Desvigne openly acknowledges an affinity for the professional ambiguity of the late nineteenth century, when landscape, urbanism and civil engineering contributed to the reform of the city. In Paris, the scenographic nature of the remodelled Bois de Boulogne and Parc des Buttes-Chaumont speaks not only of aesthetics and social practices, but also of advances in technology. Chief Gardener Jean-Pierre Barillet-Deschamps brought his expertise in nurseries and greenhouses, plant propagation and acclimatisation, and transplanting of mature trees to the production and management of Adolphe Alphand's landscape system.[12] Alphand's volume *Parcs et promenades de Paris* (1867) provided a roadmap for maintenance with a highly codified catalogue of plants, urban furniture and watering equipment. The remaking of Paris parks and promenades rested on the exchange between design, horticultural production and maintenance. The massive scale of planting and thinning taking place over forty years – 236 km of streets planted with 110,000 trees, 5 metres on centre, with one of every two trees to be removed over time – form a direct precedent to Desvigne's large-scale and *longue durée* projects for Bordeaux or the Plateau de Saclay, south of Paris.[13]

Although belonging to the French Landscape School, Desvigne has also expressed a particular fondness for the work of Frederick Law Olmsted's office, likewise concerned with urban development, stormwater management, circulation system and public amenity. Aesthetically, Olmsted's Boston Back Bay Fens (1878–1895) evoked the disappearing New England coastal landscape. Structurally, it offered an engineering solution to a drainage and sanitary problem. The Fens system of retention ponds, promenades and parkways later informed the studio Desvigne taught at Harvard University in the 1990s, and continue to feature prominently in his list of precedents. It is not, however, the aesthetics of the nineteenth-century landscape that attracts him, but the mastery of engineering and topography across scales. The subtly graded long meadow of Brooklyn's Prospect Park, by Olmsted and Calvert Vaux, offers a precedent for the network of vales and clearings in Desvigne's central park for the New Jersey campus of Novartis. Similarly, he calls attention to the handling of slope and woods, water and vistas in the road system of Washington, D.C.'s Rock Creek Park, by Frederick Law Olmsted Jr.

The nineteenth-century landscape architecture feedback loop between design and sitework also resonates with Desvigne's back-and-forth between studio work and pilot project. The analytical stage is informed by experience, challenged by a hypothesis and tested by manipulating rough models and precise photomontages. The models are usually simple: a foam core base supporting parallel bands of acetate printed with black-and-white or monochromatic tree silhouettes. When viewed from an oblique angle, the lines of trees offer a clear indication of mass, while the shadows cast by the acetate layers emphasise the voids between the banded vegetation. Such models present a synthetic view that is at once expansive and focused, their quick iterations facilitating the exchange between idea and verification.

The relation between design and sitework and between oblique view and mock-up, speak of Desvigne's

et la terre se touchent (Arles: Actes Sud; Versailles: ENSP, 2010), pp. 239–258.

10. Alexandre Chemetoff in conversation with Dorothée Imbert, 22 January 2019.

11. Corajoud, "Le Projet de paysage: lettre aux étudiants", in Jean-Luc Brisson (ed.), *Le Jardinier, l'artiste et l'ingénieur* (Paris: Éditions de l'Imprimeur, 2000), pp. 38, 47; Michel Corajoud, Jacques Coulon, Marie-Hélène Loze, "Versailles: Lecture d'un jardin", *Les Annales de la recherche urbaine*, no. 18 (1983), pp. 105–117. See also Michel Desvigne on École française du paysage: http://micheldesvignepaysagiste.com/fr/michel-desvigne-bio, accessed 6 February 2019.

12. On the horticultural advances and transplanting techniques of Jean-Pierre Barillet-Deschamps (1824–1873), *jardinier en chef* under Alphand and Haussmann, see Luisa Limido, *L'Art des jardins sous le Second Empire: Jean-Pierre Barillet-Deschamps 1824–1873* (Seyssel: Champ Vallon, 2002).

13. For a description of tree plantings in Paris, see Henri Pasquier, "Les Surfaces vertes dans la ville", *Urbanisme* volume 8, no. 68 (January-February 1939).

Oblique aerial view of Marrakech, showing olive and palm groves, gardens and irrigation ditches in different areas of the great plain of Haouz: the Sultan's residence, the Muslim city and the European city. In the distance, the Jebilet mountains.
Marcel Larnaude, *Découverte aérienne du monde*, Paul Chombart de Lauwe (ed.), 1948.

Michel Desvigne, excerpts from *Jardins flottants*, polaroid, 1984.

persistent interest in human geography. In Paul Chombart de Lauwe's *Découverte aérienne du monde* (1948), geographer Pierre Marthelot argued for the necessity of combining the aerial viewpoint with the patient discovery of nature. To him, the gathering of concrete information, forms and structural clues obtained by criss-crossing a region, "glued to the glebe like a peasant", was only half of understanding a landscape. The other half was acquired in the air, by making the landscape at once whole and less detailed. The "shock" of a higher viewpoint, Marthelot explained, triggers a synthetic reading of the landscape, gathering its multitude of signs.[14] The aerial view has long been a favourite of planners and landscape architects, from Ludwig Hilberseimer's urban settlements stretched over an endless landscape to Ian McHarg's "ecological inventories." James Corner himself measures and manipulates the earth's "interrelated ecology" through the orthographic view, whose flattened topography offers a vast diagram of human and natural systems on which to project designs.[15] Corner's early map-drawings, generated from photographic or satellite imagery and USGS maps, highlight associations and tensions across scales. They measure human determination against natural resistance. Unlike Corner, Desvigne tends to rely on the oblique view. It is a spatial, intensely visual, almost tactile perspective. The ecological, topographic, hydrologic and historical traces are read through a formal lens, as physical manifestations of natural and human factors. In a sense, Desvigne remembers the *pagus* in *paysage*. To Henri Pasquier, an advocate for large-scale landscape interventions in the 1940s, *pagus* described a natural region characterised by a dominant geographical feature (such as *bocage* or river valley) and *paysage*, a temporary human perception of a portion of *pagus*. Pasquier underscored the phenomenological aspect of *paysage* as an "atmosphere" determined by geographic, ethnic, economic and aesthetic components and argued for the *paysagiste* to take on the territorial scale of *paysage*.[16]

Desvigne's perceptual reading of the greater landscape and its "atmosphere" can be traced to his early conceptual explorations of gardens. In the early 1980s, while a student at the ENSP, Desvigne used a Polaroid camera to document the markings left by wind, rain, flooding and sunlight on various ground surfaces. The square Polaroid format was not a casual choice. The soft-focus pictures abstracted everyday details to form a field of patterns and textures, a catalogue of natural and artificial elements, scaleless and highly graphic. The format and effect referenced art and film, from the anonymous portraits of Christian Boltanski to the *repérages* of Wim Wenders. In this approach, Desvigne distinguished himself from his peers and built on the natural history tradition of the field guide. The field guide is extensive yet selective, organising a multitude of data in a specific register. It provides the groundwork for speculations. As such, Desvigne's Polaroid matrix was the field guide of his student thesis, *Jardins flottants*, or Floating Gardens. The gardens were metaphors for a wider environment shaped by human actions, geological and climatic forces. Imaginary gridded constructs interacted with natural phenomena to generate new landscape forms. Just as the Polaroid diffused the reading of scale and heightened the qualities of patterns, the grid of the floating gardens registered dimension. Desvigne continued this experiment on nature and artifice during a two-year fellowship at the French Academy in Rome. There he produced a series of *jardins élémentaires* or elementary gardens. Painstaking graphite reproductions of aerial photographs functioned as real-time observations of natural phenomena (wind, rain, freshet)

14. Pierre Marthelot, "La Terre et la vie", in *Découverte aérienne du monde*, sous la direction de Paul Chombart de Lauwe (Paris: Horizon de France, 1948), p. 98.
15. James Corner, "Aerial Representation and the Making of Landscape", in *Taking Measures across the American Landscape* (London, New Haven: Yale University Press, 1996).
16. Pasquier's argument was published in the early 1940s, a period marked by political uncertainty and professional opportunism. Henri Pasquier, "Les Avocats du paysage", *Urbanisme*, no. 86 (January 1943), pp. 16–17.

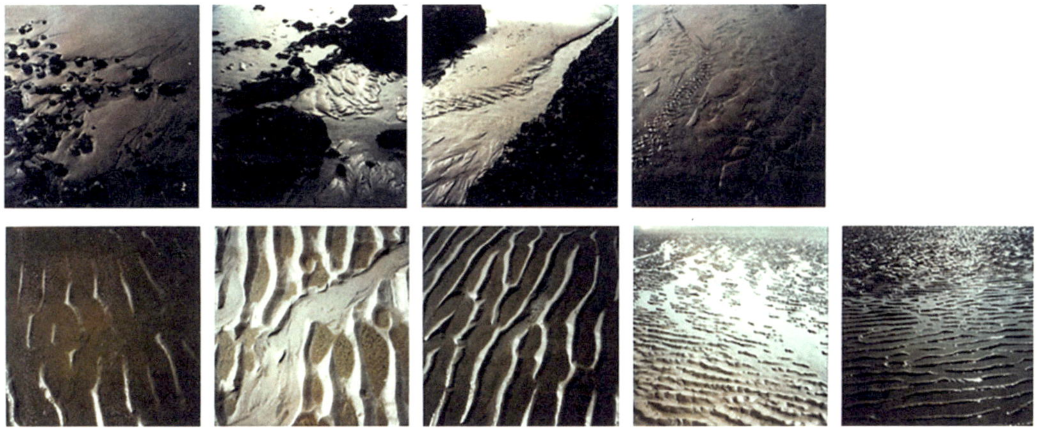

affecting, and reacting to, man-made constructions (dam, wall, ditch). Desvigne describes how this obsessive, slow translation of photographs into drawings freed him from the overwhelmingly historical context of Rome, while further developing his scientific eye. By reverse engineering the impact of an embankment or a cut on a slope, by retracing the mechanisms of erosion, flooding or landslide, he applied the lessons of his *jardins élémentaires* to the territory. With this project, the aerial view offered clues for shaping space across scales, and the garden, a mental map of the physical landscape.

Experiments and smaller-scale projects function as sketches, warm-up exercises or mock-ups for larger designs, states Desvigne. However, his practice has not evolved along a linear process of maturation. The 1980s exchange between garden and natural phenomena are played out again, in the Plateau de Saclay. There, the exchange occurs between the scale of amplified geography and the *jardin des essais*, where techniques and materials are tested before being deployed across the larger site. Ultimately, Desvigne is a true product of the Versailles school and a relentless advocate for the specificity of landscape architecture. He takes in the horizon, interprets signs to develop frameworks, demonstrating a fundamental understanding of scale. He also remembers the nineteenth-century overlap of landscape architecture and urbanism. It should come as no surprise that the pioneers of the French Landscape School – Corajoud, Chemetoff, Desvigne and, recently, his fellow student Henri Bava – are all recipients of the prestigious award for planning and urban design, the Grand Prix de l'Urbanisme.[17] It is a broader view of urbanism, in which landscape systems engage garden and geography to arbitrate between natural processes and human disruptions. It is a territorial attitude.

17. Alexandre Chemetoff was awarded the Grand Prix de l'Urbanisme in 2000, Michel Corajoud in 2003, Michel Desvigne in 2011 and Henri Bava (of Agence Ter) in 2018. Bava studied at the ENSP at the same time as Desvigne; they both graduated in 1984.

Alexander Cozens (1717–1786), plate 6 of *New Method of Assisting Invention in Drawing Original Compositions of Landscape*, aquatint on paper, 24.5 x 31.4 cm, c. 1785.

GILLES A. TIBERGHIEN
AN IDEA IN LANDSCAPE

Gilles Deleuze, when invited to speak about the creative act to an audience of students at the Fémis film school in Paris, began his lecture by asking: "What does it mean to have an idea in cinema?" In the first place, he stated, having an idea is not common, but in fact rather exceptional, so when you have one it's like "a kind of celebration". Above all, he continued, an idea is always dedicated to a special field, painting, the novel, science, literature, philosophy etc. This means, explained Deleuze, that ideas are potentials that are already engaged in such and such a mode of expression: we never have an "idea in general" but an idea *in something* – in painting, in cinema etc.[1] Each idea is an invention in its own field. Thus, having an idea in cinema would be, for example, to invent blocks of duration-movement, or in painting blocks of lines-colours, and so on. But what all these disciplines have in common, what in a sense allows them to communicate, is that they all lead to the same thing, the formation of space-times.

On the basis of these considerations, we could ask ourselves here what it means to have an idea "in landscape". This would require a reflection on the concept of project but with other expectations. The project could, in fact, be defined as the set of "intellectual and plastic lines of action, theoretical and practical, through which an intuition takes form whatever the complexity of those lines, the technical means and the physical conditions that restrain and promote at the same time its expression".[2] This notion of intuition can, in a sense, be assimilated with the "idea" described by Deleuze, with a material idea so to speak.

The theories developed by Luigi Pareyson strike me as particularly interesting in this respect, despite – but perhaps also because of – their idealistic origins, which go back to Benedetto Croce's philosophy. The latter's thinking dominated the whole first half of the twentieth century in Italy, but there was a moment when his reflection on artistic creation caused his entire system to falter. This was the starting point for Pareyson to further develop his theory of formativity. In a 1904 text, "A Theory of the Macchia", Croce takes up the conclusions of Vittorio Imbriani, a Neapolitan writer close to the Macchiaioli, the Italian painting school that could be situated between impressionism and tachism. Imbriani –at the time pursing a neo-Hegelian path he was to abandon not long after – argues that painting must represent the idea; but, he added, not an abstract idea, a *pictorial idea* – or an "idea in painting" as Deleuze would say. But what kind of idea is that? The stain. And what is the stain? "It is the *sine qua non* of the painting", says Imbriani, "the indispensable quintessence that can make you forget certain other qualities that are absent yet cannot be replaced by any other. The stain is the pictorial idea, just as the musical idea is a certain combination of sounds that the great musician calls a melody."[3] But beware: the stain is neither trace nor blot. It is the result of a process of elaboration for the artist who, when he discovers it on the wall, on paper or in nature, finds in it a motivating force and makes it the starting point of his creation.

A trace is nothing in itself: it only becomes the primary driving force of a work if it is noticed by a spirit that actualises it and brings into existence that which is still only a potential. For "the stain", comments Croce, "is not objectively in things but it is the creation of the artist who believes he can find it in the things he has put it into".[4] Croce's words bring to mind the eighteenth-century painter Alexander Cozens and his *New Method of Assisting Invention in Drawing Original Compositions of Landscape*, which consisted in starting from the observation of blots to draw and then paint landscapes.[5]

This is essentially what Luigi Pareyson, meditating on this same text, will call the *spunto* (cue, spark) in his *Theory of*

1. Gilles Deleuze, "Qu'est-ce que l'acte de création ?" lecture given at the Fémis foundation on 17 May 1987. A transcription (in French) was published online at http://www.lepeuplequimanque.org/en/acte-de-creation-gilles-deleuze.html, accessed 25 October 2019. An English translation is available here: https://www.kit.ntnu.no/sites/www.kit.ntnu.no/files/what_is_the_creative_act.pdf.
2. Gilles A. Tiberghien, "Form and project", *Studies in the History of Gardens & Designed Landscapes*, Volume 24:4, 2004, p. 304. I had proposed this definition in the inaugural lecture at the symposium "French Contemporary Landscape Architecture" organised by John Dixon Hunt at the University of Pennsylvania in 2003. A French version was published in *Les Carnets du paysage*, no. 12, "Ça & là", Spring 2005, p. 90.
3. Benedetto Croce, "Une théorie de la tache", *Essais esthétiques*, translated and prefaced by Gilles A. Tiberghien (Paris: Gallimard, 1991).
4. Ibid.
5. Alexander Cozens, *New Method of Assisting Invention in Drawing Original Compositions of Landscape* (London: Paddington, 1977).

Michel Desvigne and Christine Dalnoky, the birch square for the Rue de Meaux housing project (architect: Renzo Piano) photographed in 2008 by the MDP agency.

Formativity.[6] In the creative process, the form is at the same time *formed* and *forming*, or rather it is at each moment of its formation anticipating the form it will be, without the latter being *necessary*. Therefore, to form is to invent a form, which, in the process of its formation, is its own law unto itself. In consequence "there is no distinction between project, operation and result, since the form itself is growing and maturing". Thus, the form is "the maturation of an organic process of which it is itself the seed, the individual law of organisation and the internal purpose: it exists only once it has been made in the only way it could be made".[7] Even if it was not Pareyson's intention to follow the pre-ordained development of living matter, by transposing this theory one can see all the benefits it offers the landscape gardener. Michel Desvigne knows this well when he accompanies this development while intervening to compose the landscape with it.

This question of the project brings us back to the question of the status of works of art. Étienne Souriau, a largely forgotten philosopher who had ruled over aesthetics in post-war France up to the 1960s, and whose theories have recently been revived by Bruno Latour and Isabelle Stengers, devoted a large part of his energy to reflecting on the different "modes of existence" of beings. Pondering the question of whether existence could be considered as a good, he posited: "Is it not rather an aspiration and a hope?" Undoubtedly but not only, he pointed out, for it must also be conceived as a *potential* that, as such, requires "an initiating action".[8] This inquiry led Souriau to conclude that the work of art was "a work-to-be-made".

This complex and somewhat outdated thinking – mired in archaic categories and yet impossible to be completely reduced to these categories – can be useful to us here as a kind of platform or launching pad for reflection. It clearly shows that while something can have an indisputable physical existence, its mode of existence cannot be completely reduced to this. Thus, for example, a table made by a carpenter remains to-be-made for the artist or philosopher. An apple in a fruit dish placed among other fruits is not the same as the one represented by Cézanne, even if it served as a model for him. Similarly, a site is never just a site to anyone who visits it – a walker, a geographer, a painter or a landscape gardener.[9]

The "works-to-be-made" are indeed physical beings, yet they are rich in different possibilities. Each of these beings is perceived on a plane of existence but "is accompanied by its own presences or absences on other planes [and] intensifies itself by seeking itself on them". Consequently, a being – such as "a mountain, a wave, a plant, a stone – is as if doubled above itself by increasingly sublime images of itself".[10] The use of the term "sublime" may sound a little strange today, but we can understand why, in the field of landscape, this observation is apt. What the landscape gardener sees in front of him is a possible landscape *in* a real landscape, what one could call a potential. A little like when Olivier Cadiot says that he "turns out" the poem in language: it was there in potential, but it still needed to be extracted. Many other poets proceed in this manner unawares or formulate the process differently, but in any case, they never see the same poem.

Existences that are still virtual will thus be actualised in the free choice made by the artist among all the possible contingencies that present themselves to him or her, according to their degree of feasibility. But Étienne Souriau refuses to reduce this process to a project, defined by him as "that which, within us, sketches out the work in a kind of surge and so to speak casts it ahead of us so that we may find it again at the

6. Luigi Pareyson, *Esthétique. Théorie de la formativité*, translated by Gilles A. Tiberghien with Rita di Lorenzo (Paris: Éditions rue d'Ulm, 2006). Title of the Italian original published in 1954: *Estetica. Teoria della formatività*.
7. Luigi Pareyson, *Théorie de la formativité*, vol. II, chap. 12, p. 77.
8. Étienne Souriau, *Les Différents Modes d'existence*, followed by *De l'œuvre à faire*, presentation by Isabelle Stengers and Bruno Latour (Paris : PUF, 2009), p. 196.
9. This is also what John Dewey says when he writes that "the fundamental mistake is the confusion of the physical product with the esthetic object, which is that which is perceived. Physically, a statue is a block of marble, nothing more. It is stationary, and, as far as the ravages of time permit, permanent. But to identify the physical lump with the statue that is a work of art and to identify pigments on a canvas with a picture is absurd." *Art as Experience* (New York: Perigee, 2005), p. 228. Similarly, identifying a landscape with its natural elements alone is not enough to *qualify* it as a landscape.
10. Op. cit., p. 199.

moment of completion". Such a conception of the project has the disadvantage, in his opinion, of viewing the creative act as something that is preformed, needing only to "unfold its states", as Leibniz would say, in concrete experience. It would imply, continues Étienne Souriau, a creative act in which "we eliminate discovery, exploration and everything contributed by experience",[11] in other words, the errors and the process of trial and error by which the work develops.

He prefers the term *journey* to that of project, the work being the result of "all the encounters" made during the process of its initiation, which supposes following and exploring a path. But this path is not a royal one: in Étienne Souriau's work there is always the idea of possible failure and creation as a form of experimentation in which the result is not guaranteed. Ultimately, in his view, the concept of the project derives from an overly idealistic interpretation of creation.

There are in fact quite a few echoes of Pareyson in Étienne Souriau's work: the insistence on the fact that success is never guaranteed in advance, the importance of the attempt but also the way in which the work guides the person who is supposed to determine its form. For "the emerging being", he says, "demands its own existence. In all of this, the agent has to bow to the will of the work itself, to foretell what this will is, and renounce himself for the sake of this autonomous being which he seeks to foster according to its own right to exist".[12]

This approach could be compared with a conception of the landscape project in which the site is seen as "the starting point and horizon".[13] It is indeed impossible to separate the two, as the site is ultimately only a potential landscape whose idea is actualised by the landscape architect. But, as pointed out, each landscape architect manifests something that another will not reveal and that is also there. As if the site contained an infinite number of possible landscapes or gardens in the making. Are all landscape ideas equal then? And if not, which is the right one?

But what is right? It is not "that which is already there" and at the same time gives itself only to the person who invents it, precisely in the sense that the treasure hunter invents the treasure he or she seeks? But what is the *treasure* of the site? Without a doubt, it lies in the encounter that occurs with the landscape architect, in the way that the latter reveals the former by testing it in a way. "Every time a distribution or a form insists on appearing and closing," writes Michel Corajoud, "you must examine its contours, test its resistance and slip into its porosities."[14]

A project is first of all land, water, plants, living matter, a soil – this soil that in Paris, for example, is no longer allowed to breathe and live as Michel Desvigne regrets. A few rare agricultural engineers highlight the importance of soil, such as Claude and Lydia Bourguignon, founders of the Laboratoire d'analyse microbiologique des sols (LAM, Laboratory for the Microbiological Analysis of Soils). But despite some media coverage in recent years, they are still in the minority. But how can we act on the surface of soils if we do not think of them in terms of depth? The widespread ignorance of these issues is responsible for the alarming state of some contemporary public spaces. Where vegetation is concerned, Michel Desvigne has a clear predilection for trees over other plants, flowers for example. His first realised project, an important one at that, was a small birch wood in the courtyard of a Renzo Piano building on the Rue de Meaux in Paris.

11. Ibid., p. 207.
12. Ibid., p. 208.

13. Sébastien Marot, "L'alternative du paysage", *Le Visiteur*, no. 1, autumn 1995, p. 68.
14. Michel Corajoud, "Le projet de paysage: lettre aux étudiants", in Jean-Luc Brisson (ed.), *Le jardinier, l'artiste et l'ingénieur* (Paris: Les éditions de l'Imprimeur, 2000), p. 41.

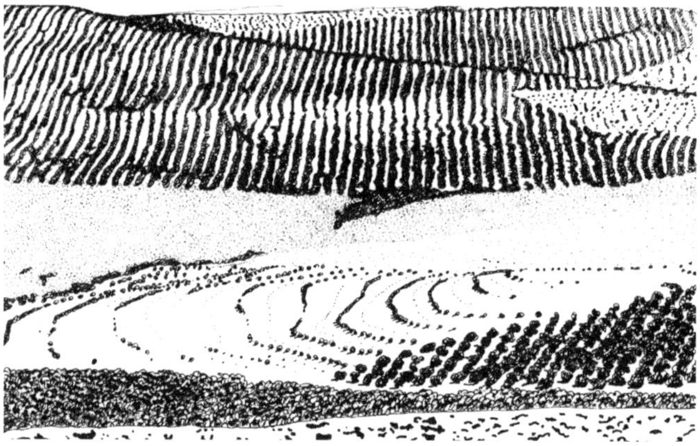

Michel Corajoud, drawing featured in the article "Le paysage : une expérience pour construire la ville", Atelier Michel Corajoud, July 2003.

To speak of plants is to speak of growth and temporality, yet the time of architects is not the time of landscape architects. It is an enemy to the former, but an ally to the latter – provided, however, that nature is supervised and supported in its growth process. Michel Desvigne notes the concern of the technical services of the City of Bordeaux regarding the density of his plantings, which he plans to trim further, in the manner of a sculptor.[15] Whereas a politician thinks in terms of space, the landscape architect thinks in terms of time. For the former, it is the image that counts; for the other, it is matter, its depth and its evolution. But also the way in which the inhabitants of the city will take possession of the landscape created, how they will live there by passing through it, stopping to spend time there and taking it into consideration, in such a way that after a certain number of years their lives will no longer be really dissociable from it. This interweaving of existences and environments is the most delicate of operations, and Michel Desvigne is well aware that a project is only successful when what was once a source of doubts, even worries for the public, seems, as is the case now in Bordeaux, to have become almost self-evident. This is the landscape architect's responsibility because, as he says, "if the site were misunderstood or maltreated, the project would have to be modified".[16]

The landscape architect does not draw a form, a garden or a landscape, to physically translate it with diggers and bulldozers and then enrich it with plantings. He conceives the form in matter and in relation to it. If we return to Tim Ingold's analyses, as inspired by Gilles Deleuze, Félix Guattari and Gilbert Simondon, we clearly understand that what these philosophers refer to as the hylemorphic model, the extrinsic application of a form on matter, is an abstract conception used to reflect on *making* and a fortiori on any activity in the field of landscape. These are not discrete operations distributed among the various actors of the project, however numerous they may be, but a continuous flow that proceeds from the same idea. An "idea in landscape" is, as Gilles Deleuze and Félix Guattari say, "an intuition in action", or "matter in movement, in flux, in variation".[17] This is a far cry from a mere *application*. On the contrary, we find ourselves in a relationship of entanglement and follow-up or, if one prefers, continuous transformation. We can cite Tim Ingold here, substituting the term artisan, which he uses, with that of landscape architect: "It is the landscape architect's desire to see what the material can *do*, by contrast to the scientist's desire to know what it *is*."[18]

But Michel Desvigne knows very well that working with the landscape and its inherent temporality is like writing on sand. For the Skolkovo project, a 500 hectare site in Russia on which a research campus is to be built by several teams of architects,[19] he acknowledges that the fixed image of the moving phenomena he is chasing cannot yield their reality because he must "constantly update plans that are constantly outdated".[20] The forms of time are primarily mental and their sedimentation in the landscape ephemeral. The landscape architect's lucidity is cruel for he knows that he will disappear in this process. Already his *authority* is blurred, practically invisible. In architecture, we are often vaguely familiar with the author of a particular building – in some countries better than others. But the work of a landscape architect, except for within the profession, for his peers as one says, has almost no reality for the public except for the use they make of it, the care they take of it, and the pleasure they find in it. Thus the landscape architect is absorbed by the garden or landscape he has created, into which he will gradually disappear like the painter Wang-Fô into his painting, as recounted in the wonderful Chinese tale by Marguerite Yourcenar.[21]

15. Something he also did for the "prefiguration garden" on the Île Seguin, in Boulogne-Billancourt, in 2010.
16. Michel Desvigne, "Time and coherence", pp. 58–59 of this volume. Concerning these woodland structures designed to evolve and thereby create "an intermediate nature" between two states of the project, Michel Desvigne comments: "The process is an accompaniment of time, but the matter itself testifies to this time and evolves with it." Michel Desvigne, "Mutations urbaines et paysages à contretemps", interview with Gilles A. Tiberghien, *Les Carnets du paysage*, no. 13–14, "Comme une danse", January 2007, p. 244.
17. Gilles Deleuze and Félix Guattari, *A Thousand Plateaus: Capitalism and Schizophrenia* (London/New York: Continuum, 1987 [1980]), pp. 451, 452.
18. Tim Ingold, *Making. Anthropology, Archaeology, Art and Architecture* (London: Routledge, 2013), p. 31.
19. Herzog & de Meuron, Valode et Pistre, Sanaa (Kazuyo Seijima), OMA.
20. Michel Desvigne, "Representing over time", pp. 120–121 of this volume. Further on in the same text he comments: "We purport to give a stable image of an unstable multitude and in doing so fuel the illusion that updating a plan is the same thing as having a project."
21. Marguerite Yourcenar, "How Wang-Fô was saved", in *Oriental Tales*, transl. Alberto Manguel (New York: Farrar, Strauss & Giroux, 1985 [1938]).

MICHEL DESVIGNE BIOGRAPHY

Michel Desvigne was born in 1958 in Montbéliard, France. After studying natural sciences at the Faculty of Sciences in Lyon, he enrolled at the École nationale supérieure de paysage (ENSP) in Versailles in 1979. Shortly after graduating (1983), he won the Académie de France competition in Rome and spent a two-year residency (1986–1988) at the Villa Medici. Upon his return to Paris, he founded a practice with Christine Dalnoky; their association ended in 1996 but they continued to develop some studies jointly.

In 1989, Renzo Piano entrusted them with the garden of his housing complex on the rue de Meaux, in the 19th arrondissement of Paris. This acclaimed "birch square" (1990) launched their careers. A number of projects followed, including public spaces in Lyon, the areas surrounding the stations on the TGV Méditerranée line (1992–2002), the Port-Marianne district and approach road to the city of Montpellier (1993). From the outset, the office (Desvigne & Dalnoky, then MDP/Michel Desvigne Paysagiste after 1996) adhered to a conception of landscape design that focused on the production of large territories and public spaces. Major projects such as Lyon-Confluence (1999) and, in Bordeaux, the landscape charter (2002), the Garonne plan (2003) and the development of the right bank (2005) were implemented in the early 2000s.

Alongside these projects, the office continued to work on a smaller scale, creating numerous gardens – the Caille garden (Lyon, 1992), the patios of the European Parliament (Strasbourg, 1996), the garden of the French Ministry of Culture (Paris, 2004–2011), a garden for Vacheron Constantin (Geneva, 2003), the garden of the Maison de la Radio (Paris, 2006), the prefiguration garden on the Île Seguin (Boulogne-Billancourt, 2009) and the Jussieu campus garden (Paris, 2013). The office also participated in ideas competitions, such as the consultations for the future Grand Paris (2008–2009), Lille Métropole 2030 (2011), and the Water and Landscapes project for Métropole Nantes Saint-Nazaire (2014).

Michel Desvigne has always maintained collaborations abroad while working on his French projects. He designed the Greenwich Peninsula Park in London (with Richard Rogers, 1997–2000), the Dräi Eechelen Park in Luxembourg (with Ieoh Ming Pei, 1999–2008), the central square of Almere in the Netherlands (with Rem Koolhaas, 2000–2005), the outdoor spaces and gardens of the Dallas Center for the Performing Arts (with Foster + Partners and OMA, 2004–2009), the reinterpretation of a Noguchi garden for Keio University in Tokyo (2004–2005), the Burgos railway boulevard (with Herzog & de Meuron, 2006–2012), and multiple projects in Doha (with Ieoh Ming Pei, Ateliers Jean Nouvel and OMA).

In addition to these partnerships with both world-renowned and emerging architects and urban designers, Michel Desvigne sometimes acts as their representative for large-scale projects such as the Paris-Saclay cluster (2009–), Euralens and the chain of parks in the surrounding mining basin (2010–), or the Old Port of Marseille (2012–).

His work has been the subject of several monographs: *Jardins élémentaires* (Carta Segrete, 1988); *Desvigne & Dalnoky. Il ritorno del paesaggio* (Motta Architettura, 1988); *Intermediate Natures. The Landscapes of Michel Desvigne* (Birkhäuser, 2009); *Le Paysage en préalable* (Parenthèses/DGALN, 2011); *A Landscape Inventory. Michel Desvigne Paysagiste* (ORO Editions, 2018).

Michel Desvigne has taught since the early 1990s: first at the ENSP in Versailles and subsequently at the EPFL in Lausanne, the UCL in Louvain, the AA School in London, and the Accademia Svizzera in Mendrisio. As a visiting professor at the Harvard Graduate School of Design and having worked on numerous projects in the United States, he has been able to play a novel role as a "smuggler" of ideas and practices between European and North American urban cultures.

His research and landscaping projects have been recognised by several important national and international awards. In 2011, France's Grand prix de l'urbanisme rewarded his contribution to and reflection on the city and wider territory. The renovation of the Old Port of Marseille was awarded the European Prize for Urban Public Space in 2014. More recently, the project developed for the Detroit East Riverfront Framework Plan (with SOM) was awarded the National Honor Award for Urban Design (2019) by the American Institute of Architects (AIA).

AUTHOR BIOGRAPHIES

Patrick Faigenbaum is a photographer. He teaches at the École nationale supérieure des beaux-arts in Paris. A painter by training, he first came to attention for his black-and-white photographic portraits of the great families of the Italian aristocracy whose names marked the Renaissance. Other portraits followed, in which his both intimate and documentary gaze focused on the identity of landscapes, cities and objects. His work has been shown in numerous exhibitions accompanied by catalogue-books, including *Tulle* (Le Point du jour, 2007), *Santulussurgiu* (Éditions Xavier Barral / Musée de Grenoble, 2008), *Paris, proche et lointain* (Paris-Musées, 2011), and *Kolkata/Calcutta*, alongside texts by Jean-François Chevrier (Lars Müller Publishers, 2015). The latter project won the Henri Cartier-Bresson prize in 2013.

Françoise Fromonot, an architect by training, is an architecture critic and a professor at the École nationale supérieure d'architecture de Paris-Belleville. She has devoted numerous articles and books to the contemporary production of the built environment, including two monographs on Australian architect Glenn Murcutt (Electa-Gallimard, 1995 and 2003), a history of an iconic building (*Jørn Utzon: The Sydney Opera House,* Electa/Gingko, 1998), a portrait of a city (*Sydney: The History of a Landscape,* with Christopher Thompson, Vilo, 2001) and a diptych that analyses the troubled history of the latest renovation project for the centre of Paris: *La Campagne des Halles. Les nouveaux malheurs de Paris*, in 2005, and *La Comédie des Halles. Intrigue et mise en scène*, in 2019, both published by La Fabrique. She co-founded the journal *criticat* in Paris in 2008, serving on its editorial team for ten years.

Dorothée Imbert is an architect and landscape architect by training, a garden historian, and head of the landscape architecture department at Ohio State University, where she holds the Hubert C. Schmidt '38 Chair. She is the author of numerous works on the modern and contemporary landscape, including *The Modernist Garden in France* (Yale University Press, 1993), *Garrett Eckbo: Modern Landscapes for Living*, with Marc Treib (University of California Press, 1996, 2005), and *Between Garden and City: Jean Canneel-Claes and Landscape Modernism* (University of Pittsburgh Press, 2009). She is the editor of *Food and the City: Histories of Culture and Cultivation* (Dumbarton Oaks, 2015) and, more recently, of *A Landscape Inventory: Michel Desvigne Paysagiste* (ar+d, 2018). Along with Andrew Cruse she designed the Square on the Novartis campus in Basel.

Gilles A. Tiberghien is a philosopher. His work straddles art history and aesthetics, in which he lectures at the University of Paris I-Sorbonne. He is the author of many books (*Nature, art, paysage*, Actes Sud/École nationale supérieure de paysage de Versailles, 2001; *Notes sur la nature, la cabane et quelques autres choses,* Le Félin, 2005 and 2014; *Land Art*, Princeton Architectural Press, 1996), and, along with Jean-Marc Besse, is joint editor-in-chief of the journal *Les Carnets du paysage*. He recently published *Le Paysage est une traversée* (Parenthèses, 2019).

All texts from pages 30 to 173 are drawn from interviews with Michel Desvigne conducted by Françoise Fromonot.

Michel Desvigne would like to thank the architect and critic Jean-Paul Robert, who initiated this book for MDP following their joint participation in the Nouvel team's project for "Le Grand Pari(s)" in 2008–2009, as well as all MDP co-workers, for their valuable contribution to the office's research and production over the years.

ILLUSTRATION CREDITS

All illustrations:
Agence MDP Michel Desvigne Paysagiste

Except for the following pages:

P. 1-16
Patrick Faigenbaum

P. 22
Courtesy of the United States Department of the Interior, National Park Service, Frederick Law Olmsted
National Historic Site

P. 30
Gilles Martin-Raget Photographe

P. 35
Florent Joliot Photographe

P. 36 (bottom)
Tangram

P. 37 (col. 2, no. 1), 40 (top)
Florent Joliot Photographe

P. 45 (2 and 4)
Florian Delon

P. 48 (top), 52 (bottom), 54 (col. 1; col. 2 ; col. 3, no. 1 and 3), 55, 56, 57 (bottom)
Guillaume Leuregans

P. 57 (middle)
Christian de Portzamparc, architecte

P. 60 (top)
SPL Lyon-Confluence

P. 70
Desvigne Conseil

P. 77 (col. 1, no. 2)
Google Earth

P. 77 (col. 2, no. 2)
Dorothée Imbert

P. 78 (top)
Guillaume Leuregans

P. 79
Florian Delon

P. 80 (top)
Alex MacLean + MDP Michel Desvigne Paysagiste

P. 81 (col. 1, no. 1; col. 2, no. 1)
Paysages Possibles, Jean-Pierre Grunfeld

P. 81 (col. 1, no. 3 and 4; col. 2, no. 3 and 4)
Guillaume Leuregans

P. 84 (col. 2, no. 3 and 4)
Florian Delon

P. 88
AltiClic

P. 93, 95
Établissement public d'aménagement
Paris-Saclay

P. 97 (bottom)
XDGA-FAA

P. 98 (col. 2, no. 2)
Établissement public d'aménagement
Paris-Saclay

P. 99 (bottom)
Florian Delon

P. 100, 101
Françoise Fromonot

P. 105 (col. 2, no. 3)
Carlos Ayesta Photographe

P. 110 (top)
Future Documentation EO

P. 110 (bottom), 117
Herzog & de Meuron

P. 118 (col. 1, no. 2; col. 2, no. 2), 119 (col. 1, no. 1 and 3; col. 2, no. 1 and 3)
Future Documentation EO

P. 122 (top)
Guillaume Leuregans

P. 122 (bottom)
G. Huchette, Euralens 2013

P. 126
Guillaume Leuregans

P. 130 (top; col. 2, no. 1), 131
Christian de Portzamparc, architecte

P. 132 (bottom), 134 (col. 1, no. 1; col. 2, no. 1; col. 3, no. 1), 135 (col. 1, no. 1; col. 2, no. 1; col. 3, no. 1)
G. Huchette, Euralens 2013

P. 135 (col. 1, no. 2)
Guillaume Leuregans

P. 136 (col. 2, no. 1, 2 and 3), 137 (col. 2, no. 1, 2 and 3), 142, 143 (bottom), 144
Florian Delon

P. 148
Novartis

P. 152, 153
Florian Delon

P. 155
IHA Inessa Hansch Architecte

P. 156
Google Earth

P. 164, 165
Taro Ernst

P. 166 (bottom), 168 (col. 1, no. 1, 2 and 3; col. 2, no. 1), 173 (col. 1, no. 3; col. 2, no. 2 and 3)
Florian Delon

P. 176
University of California, Berkeley, Environmental Design Archives

P. 178
The New York Historical Society, Getty Images

P. 179
Courtesy of the United States Department of the Interior, National Park Service,
Frederick Law Olmsted National Historic Site

P. 180
Chombart de Lauwe

P. 182
Tate, London, 2019

P. 186
Atelier Michel Corajoud

P. 188, 193-198
Patrick Faigenbaum